Songs of Slavery and Emancipation

SONGS OF SLAVERY AND EMANCIPATION

MAT CALLAHAN

INTRODUCTION BY *Robin D. G. Kelley*

AFTERWORD BY *Kali Akuno*

UNIVERSITY PRESS OF MISSISSIPPI / JACKSON

Margaret Walker Alexander Series in African American Studies

The University Press of Mississippi is the scholarly publishing agency of
the Mississippi Institutions of Higher Learning: Alcorn State University,
Delta State University, Jackson State University, Mississippi State University,
Mississippi University for Women, Mississippi Valley State University,
University of Mississippi, and University of Southern Mississippi.

www.upress.state.ms.us

The University Press of Mississippi is a member
of the Association of University Presses.

Any discriminatory or derogatory language or hate speech regarding race, ethnicity,
religion, sex, gender, class, national origin, age, or disability that has been retained or
appears in elided form is in no way an endorsement of the use of such language outside a
scholarly context.

Copyright © 2022 by Mat Callahan
Introduction © Robin D. G. Kelley
Afterword © Kali Akuno

Negro Slave Revolts in the United States, 1526–1860 (1939) by Herbert Aptheker
reprinted by permission of International Publishers.

All rights reserved

First printing 2022
∞

Library of Congress Cataloging-in-Publication Data

Names: Callahan, Mathew, 1951– author.
Title: Songs of slavery and emancipation / Mat Callahan ; introduction by
Robin D. G. Kelley ; afterword by Kali Akuno.
Other titles: Margaret Walker Alexander series in African American studies.
Description: Jackson : University Press of Mississippi, [2022] | Series:
Margaret Walker Alexander series in African American studies | Includes
bibliographical references and index.
Identifiers: LCCN 2022004673 (print) | LCCN 2022004674 (ebook) | ISBN
9781496840172 (hardback) | ISBN 9781496840189 (trade paperback) | ISBN
9781496840196 (epub) | ISBN 9781496840226 (epub) | ISBN 9781496840219
(pdf) | ISBN 9781496840202 (pdf)
Subjects: LCSH: Spirituals (Songs)—United States—History and criticism. |
Slavery—United States—Songs and music—History and criticism. |
Slaves—United States—Songs and music—History and criticism. | African
Americans—Music—History and criticism.
Classification: LCC ML3556 .C35 2022 (print) | LCC ML3556 (ebook) | DDC
782.42089/96073—dc23/eng/20220331
LC record available at https://lccn.loc.gov/2022004673
LC ebook record available at https://lccn.loc.gov/2022004674

British Library Cataloging-in-Publication Data available

Publication of this book was supported in part by
the Rosa Luxemburg Stiftung New York Office with funds from
the German Foreign Office (AA) and by
the Förderbeitrag 2017 von Kanton und Stadt Schaffhausen.

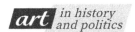

HEAR THE MUSIC

The companion to *Songs of Slavery and Emancipation* is available as a double album on CD and digital download from Jalopy Records.

The album includes thirty-one new recordings of the songs in the book, produced by Mat Callahan. It features numerous musicians performing the songs in a traditional style, plus a seventy-two-page liner notes booklet with complete lyrics, historic images, and more information about the recordings.

Listen and order at JalopyRecords.org.

CONTENTS

Preface. ix

PART I: DISCOVERY AND AUTHENTICATION

Introduction by Robin D. G. Kelley 3
Chapter 1. Finding the Songs 25
Chapter 2. History, Geography, Language, and Music 42
Chapter 3. Slave Songs: Sources and Documentation 56
Chapter 4. Abolitionist Songs: Sources and Documentation 68
Afterword: The Contemporary Relevance of Songs of Slavery
    and Emancipation by Kali Akuno 72

PART II: LYRICS

Slave Songs

The Dirge of St. Malo 82
Rebeldia na Bandabou. 84
Uncle Gabriel, the Negro General 86
Hymn of Freedom. 88
The Negro's Complaint 90
Recognition March of the Independance of Hayti 91
The African Hymn. 92
Nat Turner 93
We'll Soon Be Free/My Father, How Long? 94
March On. 95
Children, We All Shall Be Free 97
The Enlisted Soldiers, or The Negro Battle Hymn 98
Old Massa, He Come Dancin' Out 100
The Year of Jubalo, Year of Jubilo, and Kingdom Coming 101
Agonizing, Cruel Slavery Days 106

Abolitionist Songs

We're Coming! We're Coming! 110
A Song for Freedom 111
Flight of the Bondman. 112
Right On 113
The Underground Railroad 114
To the White People of America 116
Song of the "Aliened American". 118
The Voice of Six Hundred Thousand Nominally Free 119
The Band of Thieves 121
The True Spirit 122
Come Join the Abolitionists. 123
Woman's Rights. 125
Liberty. 126
What Mean Ye? 127
Stole and Sold from Africa 128

Acknowledgments 129
Appendix: *Negro Slave Revolts in the United States, 1526–1860* (1939)
   by Herbert Aptheker 135
Notes 188
Selected Bibliography 196
Index 201

PREFACE

SONGS OF SLAVERY AND EMANCIPATION IS, FIRST, A COLLECTION OF SONGS composed and sung by slaves either preparing for or commemorating revolt and resistance. To this collection is added songs of the abolitionist movement dedicated to eradication of the slave system. Many of the abolitionist songs were composed by fugitives escaping slavery or free Black people and were widely disseminated in the northern states between the American Revolution and the Civil War. To bring these songs to life, I have chosen a representative sample, arranged musical accompaniment, and made recordings. The result is a musical and historical document available for the first time to the general public. What began in 2015 with my discovery of a song composed by slaves planning an insurrection in 1813 has come to fruition with two hours of recorded music, a film documentary, and publication of this book. In the pages that follow, the story of that discovery and the journey that led to finding all thirty songs in this collection will be recounted. The contributions of Robin D. G. Kelley and Kali Akuno provide historical background and contemporary relevance.

As is well known, the Atlantic trade in African slaves lasted four hundred years. From beginning to end and throughout the Americas, enslaved people organized resistance, escape, and open rebellion. Sustaining them in this long struggle was their music, some examples of which are sung to this day. Historically and musically, this took particular form in the United States. Yet, while the existence of slave songs, especially "Negro spirituals," is widely heralded, their character is often obscured by misunderstanding. Slave songs were not only lamentations of suffering or a beseeching of God for deliverance. Nor, conversely, were the jovial banjo and fiddle tunes for which the slaves were so admired and imitated only distractions from a life of misery. The evidence presented here shows that, at least as early as the American Revolution, there were slave songs openly calling for liberty and revolution. Furthermore, there are songs celebrating heroes such as Gabriel Prosser and Nat Turner, as well as, and above all, songs celebrating the Haitian Revolution.

While the foundation and driving force were always the struggle of enslaved people themselves, the fight for freedom included free Black people and their white counterparts. This broad effort brought forth a second group of songs that were widely disseminated at the time but are now largely forgotten. These are the songs of the abolitionists, the first of which appeared in the eighteenth century and continued to be written and sung until the Civil War. Following the American Revolution, the abolitionist movement expanded rapidly, publishing songbooks to be used at public meetings. These songs not only express outrage at the condition of slavery, but call for militant resistance and the ultimate destruction of the slave system. Many such songs had musical accompaniment presented in tablature and can thus be reconstructed and performed as originally intended. There can be no doubt as to their purpose: the abolition of slavery, the emancipation of African American people, and a clear and undeniable demand for equality and justice for all humanity.

Part I

DISCOVERY AND AUTHENTICATION

INTRODUCTION
ROBIN D. G. KELLEY

> To those songs I trace my first glimmering conception of the dehumanizing character of slavery. I can never get rid of that conception. Those songs still follow me, to deepen my hatred of slavery, and quicken my sympathies for my brethren in bonds.
> —FREDERICK DOUGLASS, *NARRATIVE OF THE LIFE OF FREDERICK DOUGLASS*

> The only thing they had that couldn't be taken from them was their music. Their song, it was coming right up from the fields, settling itself in their feet and working right up, right up into their stomachs, their spirit, into their fear, into their longing. It was bewildered, this part in them. It was like it had no end, nowhere even to wait for an end, nowhere to hope for a change in things. But it had a beginning, and that much they understood. . . . it was a feeling in them, a memory that came from a long way back.
> —SIDNEY BECHET, *TREAT IT GENTLE*

WHAT ARE WE TO MAKE OF THE FACT THAT HUMAN BEINGS HELD AS PROPerty are responsible for the Americas' greatest cultural and artistic gift to the world? That America's modern freedom songs can be traced directly to enslaved Africans and the men and women dedicated to destroying human bondage? Given the sheer volume of music created by Africans held in captivity, fugitives, and their abolitionist allies throughout the Atlantic World, it is not an exaggeration to claim that "American" folk music was forged in the crucible of slavery. And what has been recovered and documented represents just a fraction of the music created by the enslaved. Lost are the many thousands of songs improvised in slave coffles, in the holds of ships, by work gangs on plantations and waterfronts—songs sung in Hausa, Ki-Kongo, Bambara, Yoruba, Ibo, Fante, Wolof, Twi, Mende, Krio, or creolized versions of these languages synthesized and mixed with French, Dutch, Portuguese, Spanish, and English.

On the other hand, we've all been taught that the slaves sang, and sang well, courtesy of racist stereotypes of Africans as naturally musical people. From antebellum minstrel shows to technicolor movies, American popular culture peddled images of Black bodies dancing and singing in cotton fields, in the master's house, at makeshift prayer meetings. Ironically, the hypervisibility of the singing and dancing slave contributed to the erasure of the African's repertoire, reducing the full breadth of music to select tunes—mostly spirituals: "Steal Away," "Go Down, Moses," "Roll, Jordan, Roll," "Brothers, Don't Get Weary," and the like. Scholars and educated folk singers know better; thanks to their efforts there is a fairly small body of recordings and book-length studies of these original freedom songs.[1]

Enter Mat Callahan. An extraordinary musician, social critic, activist, Mat came of age in the San Francisco Bay area during the tumultuous 1960s and 1970s, shaped by antiwar, anti-imperialist, and antiracist struggles for a more just world. Through a variety of bands and collectives, including Red Rock, Prairie Fire, the Looters, and Komotion International, Mat sought to roll back the right-wing ascendance of neoliberalism with music and protest. He watched in horror as popular music increasingly became the expression of this new order, dulling minds and promoting unbridled consumption as the new religion. And he responded with a powerful manifesto, *The Trouble with Music* (AK Press, 2005), and a deep dive into the radical legacy of American antislavery music.

Without repeating the story he tells below, I will note that this book and the accompanying film and recording project were inspired by a 1939 pamphlet by the late historian Herbert Aptheker titled *Negro Slave Revolts in the United States, 1526–1860*.[2] In its pages Mat encountered "A Hymn of Freedom," sometimes known as "The Negro Hymn of Freedom," most likely the earliest known example in North America of a song by enslaved people openly calling for rebellion. Aptheker himself discovered the song while perusing Benson J. Lossing's massive *The Pictorial Field Book of the War of 1812* (1869).[3] The call for revolution by means of armed struggle is precisely what caught Mat's attention, propelling him on this journey to discover the clandestine repertoire that was never intended to be discovered, collected, and catalogued until freedom came, alongside the abolitionist songbook whose clarion call deliberately set out to break slavery's hold in the presumptive land of liberty.

You won't find your standard work ditties or classic spirituals in *Songs of Slavery and Emancipation*. Rather, Callahan has selected songs that make demands, expose truths, tell stories of rebellion from Virginia to Louisiana, from Haiti to Curaçao. We owe their preservation to the free Black community, the children of the Civil War who lived long enough to share their memories of slavery with interviewers in the 1930s, the white allies who encountered freedom songs in the heat of abolitionist meetings or on the Civil War battlefield, and those inveterate collectors who looked to Black music for the best traditions of American resistance to injustice.

And yet, to claim that these songs were exceptional, distinct from the larger body of music produced by African people in the New World, would be a grave mistake. We have to understand the power of song as expressions of pain *and* joy, memory *and* morality, fear *and* faith, hope *and* humor, love, loss, and longing. Their lyrical swords were aimed not only at the Goliath of modern capitalist slavery, but the daily acts of dehumanization it wrought. Enslaved Africans forged America's first abolitionist political culture—a culture grounded in the realm of everyday life of work, family, religion, art, and a memory of the African past. In other words, they did not need an abolitionist movement to teach them about freedom. They were the first abolitionists, and they emerged out of bondage with a clear vision of what freedom should look, feel, and sound like. Historian Manisha Sinha said it best: "the story of abolition must begin with the struggles of the enslaved."[4]

ROOTS

Although we tend to associate Africans with the drum, the peoples kidnapped from West and Central Africa came from cultures with a rich tradition of stringed instruments—lutes, koras, bowed fiddles, and what on this side of the Atlantic came to be known as the banjo. Tonal instruments were commonplace and were re-created in some form or another in the Western Hemisphere. These include the balafon (wooden xylophone), fife, panpipe with single and double reeds, mbira ("thumb piano"), and a variety of mouth bows (called the "Jew's harp" by blues musicians). Drums were certainly important in many African cultures, but their absence did not mean the disappearance of rhythm. Performers kept time on the body by hand clapping, body slapping, foot patting, and dancing.[5]

All music begins with the body. The supreme instrument in every culture is also the oldest: the voice. The voice embodies tone, timbre, sonority, rhythm, messages, ideas, prayers, collective aspirations, and the call and response. Through the voice, Africans heard each other in languages familiar and foreign, in deep tones and pitch-bending falsetto. Because secular songs were generally sung beyond earshot of the master or overseer, their messages were often more explicit: "Run nigger run / the patter-roller get you..." and

> Yes, my ole Masser promise me;
> But "his papers" didn't leave me free.
> A dose of poison helped him along
> May de Devil preach his funeral song...

Not every song was a call to arms, nor did every song carry a hidden message for runaways. Song as expression of a vision of freedom meant that the everyday challenges of living life, loving, raising children, burying the dead, honoring ancestors, and obeying God took precedence over the routinized oppression of slavery. Enslaved Africans were not always obsessed with slave power when they had other powers to contend with—spiritual and magical powers. Christianity did not become the dominant religion among enslaved Africans until the nineteenth century. Nearly half of the Africans transported to North America during the slave trade came from areas where Islam was practiced, particularly in the Senegambia region. By one estimate, almost a quarter of a million Africans brought to the US were Muslim. Ancestor divination and the ritualized use of certain substances, spells, and incantations were also fairly common well into the nineteenth century.[6]

By 1830, most Black people—enslaved and free—embraced Christianity but not the gospel according to the master. The official plantation preachers' admonitions on slavery as God's will, submission as a virtue, "theft" as sin, and the desire for liberty as the devil's work fell upon deaf ears. Black people turned Christianity into a prophetic theology of liberation. Masters were the sinners; the enslaved God's children and the true believers. The Bible consistently sided with the oppressed and the poor, and the God of the Old Testament had no qualms about employing redemptive violence to purge the land of sin. The enslaved anchored their beliefs in Matthew 20:16: "the last shall be first and the first shall be last." In the story of Exodus, where Black people identified with the flight of Jews out of Egypt. In Psalm 68, verse 31: "Princes come out of Egypt. Ethiopia stretches forth her hands unto God." In the idea of "Jubilee" outlined in Leviticus chapter 25, which not only promises the periodic return of land to divine authority ("the land is mine, and you are coming into it as aliens and settlers") and the cancellation of all debt, but the freeing of slaves. Rebels such as Denmark Vesey, the free Black carpenter executed in 1822 for planning a massive slave uprising in Charleston, South Carolina, found the clearest expression of Jubilee in Isaiah 61:

> The spirit of the Lord God is upon me
> Because the Lord has anointed me;
> He has sent me to bring good news to the humble,
> To bind up the broken-hearted,
> To proclaim liberty to the captives and release to those in prison;
> To proclaim a year of the Lord's favor and a day of vengeance of our God.

Black people expressed this radical prophetic Christian vision in song, most famously in "Go Down, Moses," in which Moses threatened to kill the first-born child of the Egyptian pharaoh if he did not free the Israelites. But themes of violence and vengeance appeared less frequently than prophecy and deliverance—which is to say, visions of a post-slavery world or "next world." Songs such as "No More Auction Block for Me," "Children, We Shall Be Free," "This World Almost Done," "O Brothers, Don't Get Weary," "We'll Soon Be Free/My Father, How Long?," and "I Want to Go Home" employed metaphors of heaven or judgment day to speak of emancipation or escape, as in this example:

> There's no rain to wet you
> O, yes I want to go home
> There's no sun to burn you
> O yes, I want to go home....
> There's no hard trials....
> There's no whips-a-crackin....

However, "I Want to Go Home" and "We'll Soon Be Free/My Father, How Long?" were collected by the abolitionist Thomas Wentworth Higginson during his command of an all-Black regiment during the Civil War.[7] Higginson was already a legend in abolitionist circles, having participated in militant efforts to protect fugitives from re-enslavement and helping fund John Brown's raid on Harpers Ferry. On the battlefield and in the contraband camps, the people he encountered were no longer slaves, and their songs reflected this new reality as well as their determination to remain free. These were the people who had waged what the eminent scholar W. E. B. Du Bois called the "General Strike" that brought down the Confederacy—the escapees who saw war as the opportunity to seize their freedom and confront their masters on the field of battle. These were the Black men who donned the Union blue to bring an end to human bondage. "The Enlisted Soldiers, or

The Negro Battle Hymn," "The Year of Jubalo (Kingdom Comin')," and "Old Massa, He Come Dancin' Out," all included here, are examples of these new Civil War-era freedom songs. The future they imagined, the next world, had arrived, and what they sang in these military camps marked a decisive break from the plantation. The great jazz musician Sidney Bechet captures this change in his memoir, *Treat It Gentle*:

> It was years they'd been singing ["Go Down, Moses"]. And suddenly there was a different way of singing it. You could feel a new way of happiness in the lines. All that waiting, all that time when that song was far-off music, waiting music, suffering music; and all at once it was there, it had arrived. It was joy music now. It was Free Day . . . Emancipation.[8]

SONGS OF ABOLITION

Songs of Slavery and Emancipation is unique for bringing together the music of the enslaved with what has come to be known as the abolitionist songbook. These repertoires are usually treated as discrete bodies of music—the former the veiled expression of the enslaved, the latter popular ditties and hymns composed for the purposes of mobilizing antislavery sentiment. But Manisha Sinha's keen observation suggests the line demarcating slave songs from abolitionist songs may not be so sharp.[9] Abolition begins with the slave rebellion, and as Mat Callahan demonstrates, some of the earliest examples of antislavery songs were accounts celebrating insurrections or conspiracies. Included in this collection are rare songs bearing titles such as "Rebeldia na Bandabou," "Uncle Gabriel, the Negro General," "The Dirge of St. Malo," "Recognition March of the Independance of Hayti," "The African Hymn," "Nat Turner," and "March On."

Slave rebellions and conspiracies birthed the modern abolitionist movement, not the other way around. The period between the 1780s and 1830s—also known as the era of democratic revolutions throughout the Atlantic world—represented a kind of highwater mark for slave uprisings. The chief inspiration for this wave of rebellions and conspiracies was not the Boston Massacre or the storming of the Bastille, but the Haitian Revolution. That revolution began with a slave insurrection on the island of San Domingue in August 1791 and ended thirteen years later, after all-Black armies led by Jean-Jacques Dessalines, Henri Christophe, and Toussaint L'Ouverture defeated France, Spain, and Britain on the battlefield. When Haiti declared its independence in 1804, it was the first nation in the Western Hemisphere to abolish slavery.[10]

Events in Haiti shocked the world, leaving whites who believed their own myths about Negro docility in a state of denial.[11] It was the stuff of legend and the subject of poetry and song. News about the uprising spread like wildfire to Caribbean and US ports and across the ocean, often carried by Black sailors who embraced an antislavery, antinomian, leveling vision of Republicanism—a vision of the future world far more radical than anything being pursued in Paris or Philadelphia.[12] Virginia, the home of slaveholder and author of the Declaration of Independence Thomas Jefferson, felt the reverberations of Haiti almost immediately. Between May 1792 and October 1793, at least half a dozen conspiracies and insurrections broke out in Northampton County, Powhatan County, Richmond, and Norfolk, all of which referenced the slaves of San Domingue. In April 1795, word that the Jacobins had abolished slavery throughout the French empire and that rebels had taken over San Domingue inspired slaves, a few sympathetic whites, and Indigenous people to plan an armed uprising in Pointe Coupée Parish, Louisiana. However, they were betrayed by an informant, resulting in the execution of twenty-three alleged conspirators.[13]

Arguably, elements of the story of the Pointe Coupée conspiracy appear in the song "The Dirge of St. Malo," included in this book. Based on a poem originally in Creole ("Ouarra St. Malo"), the song has been dated by some scholars back to 1785, making it possibly the earliest known song about a slave conspiracy in North America. The song presumably tells the story of Juan San Malo, also known as Jean St. Malo, a fugitive from slavery and principal leader of a maroon colony in the marshes and swamps outside of New Orleans—present-day St. Bernard Parish. The colony's ability to remain free and survive through forms of social banditry (mainly raiding neighboring plantations) posed a constant threat to the slavery regime. Spanish colonial authorities sent expeditions to capture runaways and destroy the maroon settlements beginning around 1781–1782, but on one of those expeditions they encountered resistance from San Malo and his compatriots. San Malo and a few of his lieutenants initially escaped arrest and then attacked a boat in a failed effort to free the captured fugitives on board, inadvertently killing one of the slaves. He now had a bounty on his head for murder. In 1784 colonial authorities finally captured San Malo and his band, during which he was shot and seriously injured. The state sidestepped a trial and declared him guilty of murder; he was hanged on June 19, 1784.[14]

In truth, there was no insurrection or conspiracy. "The Dirge of St. Malo" does not celebrate San Malo as an insurrectionist but indicts an unjust system. While the lyrics avoid the question of his guilt or innocence, they attribute to him the charges levelled at the Pointe Coupée conspirators. His heroism rests on his refusal to speak, though historian Gilbert C. Din found evidence that he and his lieutenants confessed to authorities about their activities. In fact, Din concludes that the "The Dirge of San Malo" is truer as a representation of the events surrounding the Pointe Coupée conspiracy. Din writes:

> Dogs were not used to hunt down San Malo, as the poem asserts; they were useless in the marshes of the St. Bernard district.... He was not dragged into town behind a horse but was brought by pirogue.... The poem asserts that San Malo was hanged on the levee; but in reality, the execution took place in the Plaza de Armas (today Jackson Square), as contemporary documents attest. The New Orleans levee served as the site for the execution of two slaves who participated in the 1795 Pointe Coupée conspiracy. The poem's allegation that San Malo plotted to cut the throats of all whites in Louisiana fits the Pointe Coupée conspiracy better than it does the *cimarron* leader's activities in 1784; there is no proof that San Malo planned a slave uprising.[15]

Sylviane A. Diouf, the leading historian of maroonage in the United States, concurs: "In the original Creole version, it is a beautiful ode to St. Malo. But despite its seemingly documentary tone, it strays, significantly, from reality."[16]

None of these criticisms render the song any less authentic. On the contrary, precisely because of its presumed post-1795 provenance, "The Dirge of St. Malo" reveals how histories deemed inconceivable to the racial regime of slavery are passed down, linked through memory and storytelling, and refashioned as a river of struggle. Diouf writes:

> That a folk song is not an infallible historical source and aggrandizes its hero is a given, but what is significant is the fact that St. Malo was eulogized, that a song to his memory was composed at least a decade after his death, and that he was still remembered a hundred years later. What he represented as a maroon—freedom, defiance, courage, and resistance—struck a chord. As did the ignominious manner in which he and others were treated. No other maroon has been so honored.[17]

The rebels who have been so honored, at least in North America, have come to symbolize slave insurrection in story and song. We know their names: Gabriel, Denmark Vesey, and Nat Turner. Gabriel was born into slavery on a Virginia plantation in 1776. As a skilled blacksmith allowed to hire himself out to other masters in and around Richmond, Gabriel was relatively mobile, literate, and friendly with other skilled workers across the color line. In 1799, he got into a fight with a white overseer who claimed Gabriel and two of his friends were in the act of stealing a pig. Gabriel fought back, biting off part of the overseer's ear, for which he was convicted of maiming a white man. He was sentenced to public branding and a month in jail. Soon after his release, he deployed his skills to forge weapons and planned a massive slave insurrection that involved taking Virginia governor James Monroe hostage as a bargaining chip to negotiate the complete abolition of slavery. Inspired by the Haitian Revolution, he mobilized about a thousand enslaved people, as well as a couple of white men, and issued a directive to spare the lives of Methodists, Quakers, and Frenchmen since he believed they opposed slavery. The plan was to rise up on August 30, 1800, under the banner "Death of Liberty," take Governor Monroe hostage, and negotiate the end to slavery. But torrential rains forced Gabriel and his lieutenants to postpone the uprising, and by then other slaves had informed authorities. Gabriel fled but was eventually captured and hanged, along with twenty-five others.

Born Telemaque on the Danish Caribbean colony of St. Thomas around 1767, the man later known as Denmark Vesey was, at age fourteen, purchased by Joseph Vesey, a ship captain and slave trader from Bermuda. Telemaque learned to read and write and worked as Captain Vesey's interpreter and personal assistant. The captain eventually retired from the business of human trafficking and, with Telemaque still his property, settled in Charleston, South Carolina. In 1799, the thirty-two-year-old Telemaque won $1,500 in a city lottery, which he used to buy his freedom. He began the new century with a new status, a new vocation, and a new name. Working as a free, independent carpenter, he took his former master's surname and renamed himself "Denmark" in honor of his birthplace in the Danish West Indies.

Denmark Vesey quickly learned that there was no such thing as a free Black person. He married an enslaved woman named Beck but was rebuffed by her master every time he tried to buy her freedom and that of their children. He was required to pay a registration fee to obtain "freedom papers," and he knew fully well that those papers were insufficient to protect him from possible re-enslavement. He had to navigate a world where "free" Black people could not carry guns without a special license, were denied access to many public accommodations or restricted to certain sections, and were barred from certain skilled jobs and sometimes denied the right to work. He joined the white-controlled Second Presbyterian Church only to endure segregation and daily degradation. In 1817 he helped found the African Methodist

Episcopal Church in Charleston, but a year later white authorities temporarily shut down the church and arrested 140 congregants for violating laws prohibiting Black literacy and night services for Black congregants and requiring that all churches must have majority white membership. Black congregants were variously jailed, whipped, and fined. The authorities declared the church a hotbed of sedition, and they were not wrong. Vesey had begun to deliver sermons against slavery, insisting that Africans, like all of God's children, were born free and were entitled to use whatever means at their disposal to gain their liberty. Like Gabriel before him, Haiti was his inspiration. His inner circle included a couple of comrades born in San Domingue whose masters had fled to Charleston. He planned what would have been the largest slave insurrection in US history to begin on July 14, 1822—Bastille Day. When a slave working in his master's house informed his master about the plot, Vesey moved up the date by a month, but by then it was too late. State authorities arrested 130 Black people (primarily slaves) and four white men. Thirty-six were hanged, including Vesey. The church he helped found was torn down, brick by brick.[18]

The mere threat of insurrection led southern legislators to tighten the machinery of repression. They passed laws limiting movement of free Black people and their right of assembly, restricting manumission, prohibiting the enslaved from hiring out their free time, and requiring every free Black person over fifteen to have a registered white guardian who could vouch for their character. In fact, the city of Charleston built the Citadel precisely as a bulwark against potential slave insurrections.[19] Authorities grew particularly wary of the growing free Black population. Even the defenders of gradual abolition believed that the United States could only survive as a white man's country and therefore free Black people had to be deported. In 1816, with financial support from the US Congress, a prominent group of philanthropists, clergy, politicians, and slaveholders founded the American Colonization Society (ACS) for the purpose of resettling African Americans in the West African colony of Liberia. Its members included James Madison, James Monroe, Andrew Jackson, Sir Francis Scott Key, Henry Clay, and Daniel Webster. The ACS enjoyed limited support from a small segment of the Black community who believed they had no future in a nation where racism and slavery appeared to be a permanent condition. But by the 1830s, the majority of Black leaders vigorously opposed the ACS's masterplan, not because they loved America but because they saw it as a scheme to eliminate the free Black population and considered fleeing to Africa a dereliction of their obligation to free all of their people. Rather than abandon their sistren and brethren in bondage, they chose to fight, organizing local vigilance committees in northern cities to defend fugitives from recapture, printing and distributing broadsides against slavery, and creating institutions and businesses enabling free Black communities to thrive. Such sentiments are poignantly captured in "Colonization Song: To the Free Colored People," a satirical commentary—possibly composed by Black abolitionist William Wells Brown—on the intolerable conditions for Black people in the land of the free and the ironies of African colonization as a solution:

> Will you, will you be colonized?
> Will you, will you be colonized?
>
> 'Tis a land that with honey
> And milk doth abound,
> Where the lash is not heard,
> And the scourge is not found.
>   Chorus, Will you, etc.
>
> If you stay in this land
> Where the white man has rule,
> You will starve by his hand,
> In both body and soul.
>   Chorus.
>
> For a nuisance you are,
> In this land of your birth,
> Held down by his hand,
> And crushed to earth
>   Chorus . . .
>
> But only consent,
> Though extorted by force,
> What a blessing you'll prove,
> On the African coast.
>   Chorus.[20]

In 1829, a Boston-based radical Black abolitionist named David Walker published a small booklet titled *Appeal to the Colored Citizens of the World*, which made a biblical argument for the immorality and injustice of slavery, called out the hypocrisy of the United States as a Christian nation holding human beings in bondage, excoriated colonization schemes, and predicted a violent end to the system. Walker, who was born in Wilmington, North Carolina, and lived in Charleston during Vesey's formative years as a Black leader, was clearly inspired by his example. In 1826, he cofounded Boston's General Colored Association (GCA), arguably the nation's first abolitionist organization, and urged free Black people everywhere to build an antislavery movement. Walker's *Appeal* incited resistance and sent the slaveholding class and its allies into a panic. Despite a blanket ban on the text throughout the South, Black seamen surreptitiously distributed it in port cities throughout the region. Southern mayors and governors blamed Walker's *Appeal* for an outbreak of fires and Black insubordination in cities and on plantations. Anyone possessing the document or caught printing copies was jailed. By 1831, Georgia, North Carolina, and Mississippi had imposed severe penalties for possession of antislavery literature, which for Black people could mean execution. And while it was customary to deny enslaved people education, between 1829 and 1831, several southern states passed strict laws prohibiting literacy instruction to all Black people—enslaved or free.[21]

Northern cities were not much safer. In 1829, Cincinnati reinstated a law requiring new Black residents to post a $500 bond in an effort to deter Black migration to the city. White workers regarded the rapidly growing African American community as an imminent threat to their own job security. When Black leaders attempted to protest the law, white mobs stormed Black neighborhoods, torching homes, schools, and churches and driving some two-thousand Black residents from the city. Hundreds joined a growing exodus to Canada, laying the foundation for what would become a Black abolitionist movement in exile. The Cincinnati riots were also a catalyst for launching the national Black Convention Movement in 1830, in which Black leaders agreed to meet in order to develop a coordinated strategy to end slavery, oppose colonization, and protect the rights of African Americans.[22]

This was the context for the bloody Southampton Rebellion led by Nat Turner, the most feared and exalted slave rebel in US history. Turner was born in Southampton County, Virginia, just one week before Gabriel was hanged. A devout Christian encouraged by his master to preach the gospel to fellow slaves, he eventually came to see himself as a prophet and interpreted signs and visions as directives from God. In May 1828 he experienced what would prove to be his most consequential vision: to wage war on the sin of enslavement. Once God gave the sign, "I should arise and prepare myself and slay my enemies with their own weapons."[23] Following a series of signs and aborted plans beginning in February 1831, Turner succeeded in mobilizing a force of some forty enslaved men and women. Launched on August 22, exactly forty years to the day after the beginning of the Haitian Revolution, the Southampton rebels moved from house to house, killing whites they confronted and marching toward the town of Jerusalem. Ultimately, white militias as well as state and federal troops overwhelmed Turner's army and captured some of the rebels, but not before they had killed at least fifty-five whites and a few Blacks loyal to their masters. Turner evaded capture for over two months, during which white mobs massacred some two hundred Black people in southeastern Virginia, most of whom had no connection to the rebellion. Turner was finally captured on October 30 and was tried and executed along with fifty-five other Black people implicated in the uprising.[24]

For Virginia slaveholders, Nat Turner was their worst nightmare. The Southampton Rebellion frightened some masters to back proposals for compensated emancipation coupled with forced repatriation of all Africans back to the continent as their only hope for survival. They turned to the ACS to make America white and to save their skins. The majority of southern slaveholders, however, were not ready to lose their source of wealth. Instead, they proposed more repressive measures and expanded the state's military capacity. If anyone had to go, they reasoned, it was the free Black population. Rebellious slaves could simply be traded away. For Black people, Nat Turner became a martyr, a folk hero, a symbol of resistance that persists to this very day. One of the songs included here, "Nat Turner," slyly memorializes Turner and lampoons the master class by using an ingenious pun to say his name:

> You mought be rich as cream
> And drive your coach and four horse team.
> But you can't keep de world from moverin' round
> And *not turn her* [Nat Turner] from the gaining ground....
>
> And your name it mought be Caesar sure
> And got you cannon can shoot a mile or more,
> But you can't keep de world from moverin' round
> And *not turn her* [Nat Turner] from the gaining ground.[25]

While David Walker's *Appeal*, the formation of the Black Convention Movement, and the Southampton Insurrection sent the slaveholding class into a panic, they also sparked a resurgent interracial abolitionist movement. Historians usually refer to this as "second wave" abolitionism to distinguish it from an earlier period of abolitionist sentiment during the eighteenth century, inspired by the Quakers, the Great Awakening, the Declaration of Independence, and the rebellions of enslaved people themselves.[26] The best-known white figure of the second wave was the fiery William Lloyd Garrison, who despite his commitment to pacifism praised Walker's *Appeal*, hailed the Haitian Revolution, and admired Nat Turner. In 1831, the twenty-five-year-old Garrison founded an antislavery newspaper called *The Liberator*. The paper could not have survived without Black patronage; during its first year in circulation, 400 of the 450 subscribers were Black. Nor could the paper or the antislavery movement have survived without women. Black and white women formed female antislavery societies throughout the North. They flagrantly violated gender conventions by speaking publicly, participating in vigilance committees, and taking the lead in the campaign to abolish slavery. Black women such as Maria Stewart, Sarah Forten, Sarah Mapps Douglass, Mary Ann Shadd Cary, and Sojourner Truth joined with white women Angelina and Frances Grimké, Lydia Maria Child, Susan Paul, Prudence Crandall, Elizabeth Cady Stanton, Lucretia Mott, and others to not only build a powerful antislavery movement but lay the foundations for first wave feminism in the United States. In 1833, Garrison, Frederick Douglass, and Arthur Tappan launched the American Anti-Slavery Society (AASS), a national organization calling for the immediate abolition of slavery.[27]

Garrisonians remained skeptical of electoral politics because they regarded the US as a de facto slaveholders' republic backed by a proslavery Constitution. They weren't entirely wrong. Articles I, II, and IV all had clauses that protected slavery and slave-produced commerce, even as it included a sunset provision on the international slave trade. The Constitution was designed to protect private property and defined liberty in terms of one's ability to control and dispose of property. The Fifth Amendment declaring that no person can be deprived of "life, liberty, or property without due process of law," in conception and practice, protected slaveholders, not slaves. Enslaved Africans were property, and government-imposed abolition violated property rights. Moreover, the Constitution enacted mechanisms that artificially expanded the South's legislative power. The so-called three-fifths compromise apportioned congressional representation in the slave states by counting the white population along with 60 percent of enslaved people. Whether we call it a proslavery document or not, it is clear that the Constitution put slavery in the states beyond the reach of federal power. For these reasons, the Garrisonians did not believe abolition could be achieved through Congress and argued instead for dissolving the Union in order to isolate and economically weaken the slave regime.[28]

Garrison's ideas did not always sit well with his comrades, especially Black abolitionists who knew fully well that slaveholders also promoted dissolution. The injunction to boycott electoral politics was hard to swallow when the vast majority of Black people could not vote at all, and northern states were beginning to disenfranchise property-owning free Black men while extending the vote to propertyless white men.[29] And very few African Americans were prepared to disavow violence or believed that moral suasion could have any significant effect on whites given the depths of American racism. In fact, Black abolitionists were already organizing self-defense groups to resist kidnappers.[30]

For the hardcore Garrisonians, however, moral suasion was more than a tactic; it was a way of life, an ethical stance that profoundly shaped the movement's culture. Faced with the constant threat of mob violence and arrest in every state of the union, radical abolitionists relied on solidarity, dedication, and sheer fearlessness for their very survival. Similar to civil rights activists a century later, singing was an essential part of movement culture. Singing reinforced solidarity and instilled activists with courage, and abolitionist songs were an effective form of agitprop in an era when abolitionist literature was considered seditious contraband, even by the US postal service. The all-Black Garrison Juvenile Choir, for example, was seen by some AASS members as their most powerful weapon in the abolitionist movement. One correspondent to the *Liberator* believed the choir "will do more towards curing people of prejudice... than the best sermon which the most able orator could give."[31] Indeed, abolitionists, like the New England transcendentalists and Christian reformers, saw music and poetry as the highest form of communication as well as an effective means for promoting moral and social development.

But just as abolitionists were split over the questions of violent resistance versus nonviolent civil disobedience, pro-union vs. anti-union, and pro-Constitution vs. anti-Constitution, aesthetic tensions over music also divided the movement. Abolitionists generally recognized spirituals as authentic Black expression and evidence that enslaved persons possessed a soul and a human desire for freedom. However, some abolitionists distinguished spirituals from antislavery songs, insisting that the latter necessarily held a higher aesthetic and moral standard. In his preface to *The Liberty Minstrel* (1844), George W. Clark—singer, songwriter, musician, and poet—envisioned "music of a chaste, refined and elevated style, shall go forth with its angel voice, like a spirit of love upon the wind, exerting upon all classes of society a rich and healthful moral influence."[32] So while the archetypal abolitionist song might be described as slave testimony set to music, the composers were often white abolitionists—figures such as James Russell Lowell, Jesse Hutchinson Jr., William Lloyd Garrison, and John Greenleaf Whittier. Most of the songs in Clark's collection played on white sentimentality through representations of Black people as victims of brutality, vivid descriptions of the auction block, and lamentations in the voice of an enslaved mother, father, or child bearing witness to the splitting of families or violence meted out to loved ones. Such appeals were succinctly captured in the wildly popular image of the "supplicating Negro"—the image of the kneeling slave, chained at the wrist, an inscription reading "Am I Not a Man and a Brother?" The emblem was first designed in London in 1787 as a seal for the Quaker-led Society for Effecting the Abolition of the Slave Trade, though the original artist is unknown. Later that year, the society commissioned one of its members, the eminent industrialist Josiah Wedgwood, to render the emblem as a jasperware cameo at his pottery factory. The cameos were mass-produced and within a year became the hottest fashion accessory among the abolitionist and anti-slave trade elite.[33] The "supplicating Negro" was everywhere in the Atlantic world, in print, on plates and snuff boxes, and in song. Among the many "refined" songs included in *The Liberty Minstrel* was "Am I Not a Man and a Brother," set to the melody of "Bride's Farewell."[34]

William Wells Brown's *The Anti-Slavery Harp: A Collection of Songs for Anti-Slavery Meetings* (1848), the first abolitionist songbook published by a fugitive from slavery, not only opens with "Am I Not a Man and a Brother," but includes many lamentations penned by the same white abolitionist composers as in Clark's collection. But Brown also included at least one song said to be written by "a slave," "Song of the Coffle Gang," as well as his own compositions "Fling Out the Anti-Slavery Flag" and "A Song for Freedom." His inclusion of songs such as "Right On" and "We're Coming" displayed a fundamental break with moral suasion in favor of militant action and outright revolt. Brown also embraced humor and irony, recasting popular minstrel songs and doggerel to expose the contradictions of slavery in the land of liberty. A startling example is "Jefferson's Daughter," whose lyrics were inspired by a newspaper story:

> The daughter of Jefferson sold for a slave!
> The child of a freeman for dollars and francs!
> The roar of applause, when your orators rave,
> Is lost in the sound of her chain, as it clanks.[35]

Brown set his "A Song for Freedom" to the popular 1844 minstrel tune "Dandy Jim from Caroline." In doing so, he turned a vile, racist attack on Black people into a powerful weapon against slavery and anti-Black racism. The imagined protagonist humorously reflects on the irony of slaves listening to their master boast that America is a land of liberty, the result of a revolution "To save a three-pence tax on tea"—a cause presumably nobler and more consequential than ending human bondage. Brown didn't simply borrow the melody and the structure. He parodied the original chorus:

> For my ole massa tole me so
> I was de best looking nigga in de country, O
> I look in de glass an found t'was so
> Just what massa tole me, O.[36]

And transformed it into a stinging rebuke of American hypocrisy:

> My old massa tells me O
> This is a land of freedom O
> Let's look about and see if't is so,
> Just as massa tells me O.

The singer and the imagined gathering of enslaved men and women to whom the lyrics are addressed conclude that their best option would be to leave this "Christian" slave country for Canada, where they can secure freedom under the British empire.[37]

Antislavery songs also reflected key *political* splits within the movement. In 1840, abolitionists who disagreed with Garrison's position on electoral politics formed the Liberty Party and ran former-slaveholder-turned-abolitionist James Birney for president. Founding members of the Liberty Party argued that the Constitution did not necessarily sanction slavery since it defined "slaves" as persons held in service rather than property. While conceding that the federal government cannot supersede the rights of states to permit slavery, they argued that the Constitution prohibited slavery everywhere under *federal* jurisdiction—that is, territories that were not yet states and the high seas. The Liberty Party's platform, therefore, called for immediate abolition in the territories and the District of Columbia, ending the interstate slave trade, and the ultimate goal of a slavery-free nation. Clark's *The Liberty Minstrel* was peppered with songs promoting the Liberty Party and the vote as the chief weapon in the antislavery movement. "Strike for Liberty," "Liberty Battle Song," "The Ballot," "Ode to James Birney," and "The Liberty Voters Song," among others, appealed directly to free men to "strike" at the ballot box.[38] Despite increased popular support for abolition and growing tension over whether newly acquired western territories would be slave or free, the Liberty Party failed miserably at the ballot box. Its uncompromising opposition to slavery and mild support for Black civil rights were considered too radical. In 1848, a group of moderates left to form the Free Soil Party, whose platform focused entirely on limiting slavery where it existed and ensuring that all new states and territories remained free.[39]

The other major split in the movement centered on the question of violence. In 1843, at a meeting of Black abolitionists in Troy, New York, a young minister named Henry Highland Garnet stunned his fellow delegates by delivering a speech calling for mass slave insurrections throughout the South. He urged his comrades, "Rather die freemen than live to be slaves. Remember that you are FOUR MILLIONS! Let your motto be resistance! resistance! resistance!"[40] The speech was met with both vigorous applause and consternation from those who believed his words were incendiary and dangerous. By a margin of one vote, the delegates elected to suppress Garnet's speech and remove any reference to it from the official minutes. But it opened up a discussion of the limits of moral suasion and the potential of armed rebellion, especially waged by the enslaved themselves. The successful mutinies by captive Africans on the slave ships *Amistad* (1839) and *The Creole* (1841) not only demonstrated the effectiveness of slave rebellions but gave legal and moral justification for Africans to use violence in defense of their liberty. These two mutinies, which ultimately resulted in the freedom and repatriation of the rebels, most likely inspired Garnet's words. His speech underscored what the African mutineers always knew: that they were the real *victims* of a crime. They did not need a constitution or the so-called blessings of Western civilization to explain what is right, just, and humane.[41]

With the passage of the Fugitive Slave Law of 1850, proponents of armed self-defense and resistance were no longer outliers. The new federal law amended the 1793 Fugitive Slave Law, allowing slaveholders or their agents to arrest runaways without due process and without warrants, doubling the reward for capture, and placing enforcement in the hands of US commissioners and marshals. It essentially extended slave patrols to the North since federal marshals were empowered to form a posse comitatus of armed (white) citizens to capture fugitives. But anyone caught helping a suspected fugitive faced up to six years in prison and a fine of $1,000. Lacking legal protections and the right to testify, every Black person risked kidnapping and re-enslavement. The law was the result of a political crisis that had been brewing since the Missouri Compromise of 1820, which theoretically was meant to contain slavery below the Mason-Dixon line as the country expanded west. The idea was to maintain a balance of power between "slave" and "free" states. But all it did was postpone an inevitable war among slaveholders, who believed that no state or territory should have the right to ban slavery; "free soilers," who believed slavery degraded free labor and undermined farm economies; and abolitionists, who believed slavery should not exist. The abolition of slavery in the French and British empires, the admission of more free states, and the dramatic growth of the abolitionist movement clearly threatened slave power. So, to avoid dissolving the republic, Congress gave slaveholders the Fugitive Slave Law in exchange for admitting California as a free state and allowing New Mexico and Utah to vote on the slavery question.[42]

The free Black community responded with protests, meetings, more vigilance committees, and an open assertion of their right to armed self-defense. "Death to kidnappers!" became a common slogan, even among the more moderate abolitionists. In August 1850, the New York Vigilance Committee organized a convention attended by nearly two thousand to condemn the imminent passage of the Fugitive Slave Law. The delegates endorsed a statement committing "the great mass of the colored men of the North" to support slave insurrections "with deep-stored and long-accumulated revenge in their hearts, and with death-dealing weapons in their hands."[43] Abolitionists built the Underground Railroad, participated in raids to liberate fugitives held by kidnappers, federal agents, and the courts, and dramatically increased Black emigration to Canada.[44]

The state of emergency that sparked abolitionism's militant, revolutionary turn also shaped antislavery songs of the era. The leading figure of the era was the Black abolitionist songwriter and poet Joshua McCarter Simpson. A conductor on the Underground Railroad, Simpson composed original antislavery music that was often irreverent and satirical, exposing the hypocrisy of a Christian nation holding human beings in bondage. He often said, "You can sing what it would be death to speak," though many of his lyrics were probably considered seditious by authorities opposed to abolition. His portraits of the enslaved were a departure from the kneeling, "supplicating Negro." Like the fugitives he helped shepherd to freedom, the slaves in Simpson's songs had grit and were determined to free themselves rather than beg whites for their liberty. Two years after passage of the Fugitive Slave Law, the thirty-two-year-old Simpson published *Original Anti-Slavery Songs*, which included titles such as "No Master, Never." Set to "Pop Goes the Weasel," "No Master, Never" is the tale of a runaway who confronts his master on his way to Canada, promising never to return. Simpson's songs circulated widely in the 1850s and were popular among abolitionists, but many of them were not published until the appearance of his 1874 collection, *The Emancipation Car: Being an Original Composition of Anti-Slavery Ballads Composed Exclusively for the Underground Railroad* (Sullivan and Brown, 1874). Callahan features several Simpson titles here, including "The Underground Railroad," "To the White People of America," "The Voice of Six Hundred Thousand Nominally

Free" (set to "The Marseillaise"), and his irreverent take on "America (My Country, 'Tis of Thee)" titled "Song of the 'Aliened American'":

> My country 'tis of thee
> Dark land of Slavery
> In thee we groan. . . .
> The white man rules the day
> He holds despotic sway
> O'er all the land. . . .

And the final verse offers a transformed America through Black collective struggles for justice:

> We now "Eight Millions Strong"
> Must strike sweet freedom's song
> And please ourselves, our wrong—
> Our chains must break.[45]

Simpson's music comprised the soundtrack for abolition's most militant generation, the men and women of the 1850s who actually started the Civil War a decade before the slaveholders declared independence from the Union and fired on Fort Sumter. I'm speaking of Sojourner Truth, Harriet Tubman, Jermaine W. Loguen, William Parker, Frederick Douglass, Henry Bibb, James McCune Smith, Thomas Wentworth Higginson, and, of course, John Brown, to name but a few. Stirred by a wave of slave resistance (incidents of arson, flight, strikes, and mysterious deaths of masters and overseers) and a federal government that appeared to be moving with lightning speed toward protecting slavery everywhere, the 1850s generation understood that justice in America was impossible without war. This fact became crystal clear when Congress passed the Kansas-Nebraska Act in 1854—essentially obliterating the Mason-Dixon wall against slavery's expansion and opening up all new territories to human bondage by allowing settlers to vote on the matter—and after the Supreme Court ruled against Dred Scott in 1857.

The case of Dred and Harriet Scott was arguably the most consequential Supreme Court decision of the antebellum period. In 1846, with help from abolitionists in St. Louis, the couple sued for their freedom, arguing that during the 1830s their master relocated to free territory—first Illinois and then Wisconsin Territory (present-day Minnesota). They eventually settled in St. Louis and were hired out while their master, John Emerson, collected their wages. After his death in 1843, his widow, Irene Emerson, convinced the St. Louis county sheriff to take custody of the Scotts while she continued to hold them as property and collect their wages. In 1850, the St. Louis Circuit Court ruled in their favor, but two years later the Missouri Supreme Court reversed the decision, arguing that, despite having spent at least three years in free territory, the moves were temporary. When the case came before the US Supreme Court, it ruled 7–2 against Scott. The outcome should not have been that surprising since five justices, including Chief Justice Roger Taney, came from slaveholding families, and seven justices were affiliated with the proslavery Democratic Party. But the consequences were far-reaching, even beyond Chief Justice Taney's infamous line in his majority opinion that Black people "had no rights which the white man was bound to respect." The court was less concerned with the fate of Dred and Harriet Scott than with rendering the Missouri Compromise unconstitutional and opening the door to make slavery legal *everywhere in the US*. The court ruled that Congress never had the power to govern territories and therefore had no power to prohibit slavery, adding that slaves were property and to strip slaveowners of their property without due process was a violation of the Fifth Amendment. Taney's declaration that Black people were not citizens was bad enough, but the court violated the Constitution and basic principles of jurisprudence by ruling on the Missouri Compromise *after* declaring that Black people did not have the right to sue in courts. The case should have been dismissed at this point, but the majority ruled anyway because their real agenda was to overturn prohibitions on slavery.

Enter John Brown, the antislavery icon for whom the most enduring abolitionist song ("John Brown's Body") was titled. The Dred Scott decision was the reason John Brown decided to wage an armed attack on the federal arsenal at Harpers Ferry, West Virginia, instead of launching guerrilla raids on plantations as he had originally planned. Why? Because the Dred Scott decision proved to Brown that while slaveholders were morally accountable for holding human beings in bondage, it was the federal government that *sanctioned and sustained the institution of slavery*. Slavery, in other words, was not a sectional issue but a national crime, and the federal government was slavery's prime source of authority and protection. In 1858, in preparation for the raid on Harpers Ferry, Brown spent several weeks at Frederick Douglass's home where he drafted "A Declaration of Liberty by the Representatives of the Slave Population of the United States of America" and a "Provisional Constitution and Ordinance for the People of the United States." This new constitution was not only the antithesis of Chief Justice Taney's opinion on Dred Scott; it recognized enslavement itself as "*none other than a most barbarous, unprovoked, and unjustifiable war of one portion of its citizens upon another portion.*"[46]

Arguably both the most venerated and the most despised abolitionist in US history, John Brown was born in 1800 to a deeply religious antislavery family in Connecticut. He became completely immersed in Black abolitionist circles after meeting Frederick Douglass in 1847. He participated in the Underground Railroad by hiding and transporting fugitives, helped defend the Black community of North Elba, and organized armed self-defense groups in Springfield, Massachusetts, to protect fugitives from capture. In 1848, he published a pamphlet at his own expense combining David Walker's *Appeal* with Henry Highland Garnet's suppressed speech in Troy, New York. Brown and his sons waged war against slaveholders on the bloody fields of Kansas in 1854 in a vain effort to secure liberty for all. And on October 16, 1859, Brown and a ragtag army made up of sixteen white men and five Black men—Osborne Perry Anderson, John Copeland Jr., Shields Green, Dangerfield Newby, and Lewis Sheridan Leary—took on the federal government and the southern planter class in what seemed like a foolhardy attempt to free four million Black people held in bondage. They were defeated, and Brown was hanged; but within two years the entire system of chattel slavery began to collapse.[47]

We can debate the raid's accomplishments, but what Brown did, in effect, was what the songs collected here were intended to do: force antislavery sympathizers to come off the fence, for there was no moderation or compromise on the question of slavery. For Brown, what was in question was not Black humanity but white humanity—or more precisely whether or not white people could break the shackles of racism and become fully human. Silence and inaction in the face of human bondage meant complicity, and complicity was dehumanizing because slavery was barbarism. To become human required risking life and limb to end slavery. For whites willing to follow Brown, freedom was an unearned privilege in a land of slavery; the act of insurrection was a symbolic repudiation of that privilege.[48]

So when Black people and antiracist organizers continued to sing "John Brown's Body" over the course of the next century and a half, declaring that his "truth goes marching on," they recognized that the struggle is not over. Far from it. Mat Callahan and his band of rebels understand this all too well, knowing that these songs are not for posterity, not to be archived or displayed on museum walls or the subject of NPR stories. They are to be circulated, sung, and passed on and, above all, to be the fire that inspires us to act.

Chapter 1

FINDING THE SONGS

I WAS POKING AROUND IN AN ANTIQUARIAN BOOKSTORE, BOLERIUM BOOKS in San Francisco, when I stumbled upon an old, dog-eared pamphlet with the title "Negro Slave Revolts in the United States, 1526–1860." Both the subject and the dates caught my eye, and I recognized immediately that they challenged notions prevalent among scholars and the general public alike. It is commonly believed that slave revolts were rare, notable more for their absence than for their occurrence. Furthermore, 1619 is the year most often referred to as the starting point for slavery in North America, for that is when a cargo of captive Africans was brought to the British colony at Jamestown, Virginia, by a Dutch slaver. Placing not only slavery but slave revolts almost a century earlier was thought-provoking, to say the least.

Closer inspection told me the pamphlet had been published in 1939. Its author, Herbert Aptheker, was known to me since I'd grown up in a household where W. E. B. Du Bois, Paul Robeson, Benjamin Banneker, Harriet Tubman, and Frederick Douglass were among a pantheon of heroes to be studied and emulated. Aptheker, I recalled, was a close associate of Du Bois and had written extensively on African American history. Yet Aptheker was also a controversial figure—as a historian, a communist, and even, allegedly, as a father.[1] Not only had McCarthyism and the "Red Scare" targeted his politics, but his politics were reputed to have made his scholarship of dubious quality. One thing was for sure, though: I had never heard of this pamphlet, much less read it, nor was I prepared for what I discovered in its pages.

In the pamphlet, Aptheker documented the frequency and consistency of rebellions beginning with one in a doomed Spanish colony in what is now South Carolina in 1526. Enslaved Africans brought there that very year staged a revolt, killing many of the Spanish before running off to join Indians in the neighborhood. Judging by the more than two hundred reported revolts from 1526 through the Civil War, I saw a pattern emerge, raising serious questions about how history has been constructed. That this pamphlet was publicly available eighty years ago raises more questions about how history continues to be constructed in the present day.

To avoid any ambiguity, Aptheker defined revolts or rebellions as qualitatively different from spontaneous outbursts or individual acts of resistance. To qualify as a revolt or rebellion in his definition, an event must have been planned or carried out by at least ten slaves with the intention of forcibly removing any obstacle to their freedom. While most rebellions ended in failure, there were nonetheless numerous instances in which groups of slaves managed to flee to remote locations such as the Great Dismal Swamp in southeastern Virginia or to join Native peoples hostile to, first, colonial administrations, then to the US government. These revolts erupted within a broad field of individual or smaller group acts of insubordination, sabotage, and escape. It is estimated that between 1830 and the onset of the Civil War a minimum of 100,000 slaves ran away, many to Canada and others to Mexico and various Caribbean islands. This total does not include countless others who ran away prior to 1830, a fact attested to by the first Fugitive Slave Law passed in 1793. Had there been no fugitive "problem," there would have been no such legislation. Furthermore, such land-based activity was mirrored by its equivalent on the high seas or coastal trade. The *Amistad* and *Creole* cases are only the most famous of many mutinies and seizures of vessels by enslaved persons either being transported or working on ships' crews.

Such assertions were stunning to me, having about them the "ring of truth" that resounds when missing pieces of a historical puzzle fit into place. One item, however, leapt off the pages to grab my attention and ultimately launch this project.

Amidst all the dates and names, the numbers and incidents, were the lyrics to a song. These lyrics, according to Aptheker, had been composed and sung by enslaved persons at a clandestine meeting to plan an insurrection in 1813. Aptheker presented the last stanza of this song:

> Arise! Arise! shake off your chains!
> Your cause is just, so Heaven ordains;
> To you shall freedom be proclaimed!
> Raise your arms and bare your breasts,
> Almighty God will do the rest,
> Blow the clarion's warlike blast;
> Call every Negro from his task;
> Wrest the scourge from Buckra's hand,
> And drive each tyrant from the land!

Chorus: Firm, united let us be,
    Resolved on death or liberty!
    As a band of patriots joined,
    Peace and plenty we shall find.

Anyone familiar with that great body of music known as the "Negro spirituals" will share my surprise at reading this text. This is not coded speech. Nor is it religious. Indeed, it is explicitly revolutionary and in a literary form that can only be described as sophisticated. I grew up singing "Go Down, Moses," "Deep River," "Many Thousands Gone," and numerous other songs whose beauty is unrivalled in melodic and poetic power. But I had never before heard a song, composed by a slave in 1813 no less, that read like this one.

My first reaction was to question the song's veracity. Could this be an example of the exaggerations Aptheker has been accused of? Could this be wishful thinking on the part of a well-intentioned scholar who nonetheless was reinterpreting or even manipulating the facts to give a false impression? Because, if this song was indeed what Aptheker claimed it to be, then a major gap in our knowledge, of music as well as history, was revealed. This text, from this period, immediately posed questions that demanded answers. Might there be more such songs? And if there were, why had they not been found and brought to public attention by now? If, moreover, there were more such songs and they had not been hitherto brought to light, then by whom and for what reasons had they been overlooked if not deliberately buried?

I started out assuming my own ignorance, expecting to find the answers neatly arranged by historians, musicologists, or song collectors. I figured this little pamphlet from 1939 had long ago been superseded by generations of diligent scholarship, and I was simply unaware that such scholarship existed.

What I discovered came as a surprise. Indeed, what unfolded was a series of surprises eventually leading to a conclusion greater than I originally imagined.

THE SEARCH BEGINS

For the first two years of my search, I kept expecting to discover that someone, somewhere had already found what I was looking for. I kept expecting some historian of music or ethnomusicologist to have made the connection between slave revolts and their musical expression. After all, the subject of African American music is so widely studied and of such interest to so many people that it seemed impossible no one had asked the questions I had. Eventually, I did find others who preceded me, contributing mightily to my effort. But their fate helps explain why and how these songs remained obscure. We'll return to that subject later on.

At first, all I wanted to do was either to quickly solve the mystery or to justify further inquiry. I began calling friends and acquaintances in folklore studies and musicology. None had even heard of Aptheker's pamphlet, let alone the song presented in it. More significantly, the question itself seemed baffling. If this song is authentic, it's an anomaly. If an anomaly, then it suggests that other songs of this type were never written. When I pressed the question "But if there were slave revolts, isn't it more likely there were songs related to them than that there were not?," the answers became more ambivalent. Such a hypothesis might bear further scrutiny, but it seemed to never before have arisen.

Next, I consulted the record assembled by those scholars devoted to the legacy of African American song, dance, and story—in particular, the outstanding work of musicologist Eileen Southern. I located the authoritative *African-American Tradition in Song, Sermon, Tale, and Dance, 1600s–1920: An Annotated Bibliography of Literature, Collections, and Artworks* compiled by Southern and Josephine Wright. A dear friend purchased a copy of this expensive book, and I began to search its detailed registry for songs like the one in Aptheker's pamphlet and where they might be found. I soon realized that I would have to search through many song collections and other reference books since the Southern-Wright bibliography lists only title and first lyrical lines. To view the complete texts would mean finding the sources listed. The songs were scattered throughout hundreds of songbooks, histories, articles, and essays by diverse authors over several centuries. The Library of Congress might be the only place I could see them all.

This daunting task might have stopped me but for the fact that in this comprehensive bibliography there was a strange omission: the song in Aptheker's pamphlet. It was nowhere to be found. I was intrigued and pondered why such conscientious scholars as Southern and Wright might have missed this important text. Shortly thereafter, other discoveries came to my attention suggesting possible explanations.

First, I happened upon a story about a young graduate student who, in 2013, uncovered a poem, published in 1786 and written by an enslaved man named Jupiter Hammon, called "Essay on Slavery."[2] Hammon, the first published African American poet (beginning in 1761), was long considered an apologist for slavery. But this hitherto unknown poem raised two questions, the first being that Hammon was far more critical of slavery than had previously been thought. The second was less the content of the poem than the fact that it lay hidden until very recently. Perhaps there were more such texts to be unearthed. Taken together, these two points raised yet another: the literacy of slaves, the poetry they wrote (whether it was to be sung or not), and the possibility that perhaps the reason songs such as the one Aptheker presented were not well known was that they were only available in printed form. Might the fact that folklorists and song collectors focused on oral traditions—what people sang as opposed to what was written down—explain why our existing song collections were incomplete?

No sooner had I learned of the discovery of Hammon's poem than I read of a similar discovery that had even greater significance. Another graduate student had, in 2007, uncovered a record kept by Sydney Howard Gay, an operative on the Underground Railroad.[3] Gay's meticulous accounts show the real workings and full extent of an institution that was more legendary than established by historical fact. Historian Eric Foner immediately grasped that this new evidence called for a reappraisal, and his *Gateway to Freedom: The Hidden History of the Underground Railroad* (2015) was the result. I wrote to Foner, who graciously answered my questions and confirmed that there were very likely more such documents and that it might never occur to a folklorist or musicologist to look for them. Generally speaking, historians rely on written records, while folklorists and ethnomusicologists focus more on oral accounts, whether spoken or sung. With this distinction in mind, I decided to examine what had been collected to date.

Using the Southern-Wright bibliography as a guide, I began consulting those collections that were best known, starting with *Slave Songs of the United States*, edited by William Francis Allen, Charles Pickard Ware, and Lucy McKim Garrison and published in 1867, the same year as Thomas Wentworth Higginson's collection. Higginson's was among the first efforts to record what slaves composed and sang themselves, for each other and not for their masters' entertainment. His *Army Life in a Black Regiment* included a chapter entitled "Negro Spirituals" with thirty-six complete songs and a couple of fragments. Higginson also wrote down commentary provided by the soldiers about the songs and how they were composed. There were several crucial pieces of evidence and one particular song that provided support for what was becoming my working hypothesis: there were more songs such as the one Aptheker had presented, but they were not going to be easy to find.

Slave Songs of the United States presented 136 songs, among which were variations of those Higginson had compiled. The great majority fit the mold to which we are accustomed. Many have long since become famous either as "Negro spirituals" or spirituals sung in various Protestant churches (regardless of ethnicity). One, however, stood out. It was a variation of a song in

Higginson's collection; indeed, we ended up recording a composite of the two versions set to the music in *Slave Songs of the United States*. The song is "My Father, How Long?" Beneath the tablature and lyric is a note from Higginson: "For singing this the negroes had been put in jail at Georgetown, S.C., at the outbreak of the Rebellion [as the Civil War was called at the time]. 'We'll soon be free' was too dangerous an assertion, and though the chant was an old one, it was no doubt sung with redoubled emphasis during the new events."[4] (See the song notes later in this volume for more about this illuminating example.)

I next consulted other famous collections including those by John Wesley Work Jr., John W. Work III, Miles Mark Fisher, James Weldon Johnson, and J. Rosamond Johnson, as well as the collections of Howard Odum, Dorothy Scarborough, and John Lomax. I consulted the major studies done by Henry Krehbiel and Dena J. Epstein. All told, I read several hundred distinct songs, some of which are famous and often quoted. Those frequently referred to in movies, plays, novels, and histories include "Roll, Jordan, Roll," "Steal Away," "Follow the Drinkin' Gourd," "Jacob's Ladder," "Eyes on the Prize (Hand on the Plow)," "Wade in the Water," and "Mary, Don't You Weep." While a significant number have lyrics unmistakably encouraging flight or fortitude in the struggle, none were overt expressions of revolutionary intent. In fact, I still hadn't found any mention of the song Aptheker quoted, let alone that it was authentic!

At this point, it became imperative to go to the Library of Congress for a closer look. With the invaluable assistance of Todd Harvey, folklife specialist at the American Folklife Center, I began combing through the vast archives. What I found fell into two distinct categories: songbooks or collections made during and after the Civil War, and sound recordings made in the first three decades of the twentieth century, the largest body of which were made under the auspices of the Federal Writers Project between 1936 and 1939. In addition, there were miscellaneous articles published in *American Music Quarterly* in the 1960s and 1970s that provided important historical details and an overview of scholarly disputes in the field.

The overall impression all this provided was that, on the one hand, there was great and enduring interest in the subject of slaves and their music, while, on the other hand, there was an unquestioned assumption guiding the collection of data—namely, that the slaves did not rebel. While some researchers and song collectors acknowledged that enslaved and formerly enslaved persons may have been unwilling to take a white researcher into their confidence and that it was undoubtedly the case that there was danger in expressing rebellious thoughts in any form, this challenge did not prevent these researchers from jumping to the conclusion that the evidence they were presenting was the full extent of what existed.

I suddenly faced the realization that the very questions I was posing challenged this conclusion. I had started out naively unaware that what I had stumbled upon was so strikingly at odds with conventional wisdom, but there was now no escaping the implications. In short, what we have come to view as the music of African Americans in the United States is woefully incomplete and inadequately, indeed inappropriately, organized into categories that do not reflect the musical or lyrical breadth of the African American experience. More specifically, songs containing explicit reference to freedom, militant resistance, and organized opposition to the slave system were summarily dismissed as anomalous or nonexistent. Yet, that conclusion was refuted by two examples I uncovered at the Library of Congress itself demonstrating that such songs did exist. They furthermore supported the hypothesis that I was now determined to prove or disprove as the evidence mounted.

RECOGNITION MARCH AND SLAVERY DAYS

The first example is a piece of sheet music written by Francis Johnson. Its title attracted my attention when I saw it listed in a catalogue: "Recognition March of the Independance [sic] of Hayti." The piece was written for piano forte and flute. It was dedicated to the president of Haiti, J. P. Boyer, which means it could not have been written before 1820 but probably was written precisely then, when Boyer became president of Haiti. I photocopied the music and began to study it.

Several features of the piece and its author were revelatory. First, it was clearly a march typical of the period using classical European instruments. Second, it provided for a Kent bugle solo, an instrument Francis Johnson was widely renowned for playing. Third, Johnson was a free Black man and one of the most popular band leaders of his era. His fame was so great that he had been invited to lead his band at the ceremony welcoming Marquis de Lafayette, legendary Revolutionary War hero, on his triumphal return to Washington, DC, in 1824.

The second example I uncovered at the Library of Congress was a song recorded by the Federal Writers Project called "Agonizing, Cruel Slavery Days." The man performing the song was ninety-three years old at the time. I would find out more about him later. But there was enough in the notes about the song and its lyrics to indicate that it was composed by former slaves, was popular among them, and expressed their abhorrence of a system of bondage that they'd managed to outlive. Musically, it bore no resemblance to blues, work songs, or spirituals. If anything, it resembled show tunes popularized by traveling theater troupes in the post-Civil War era.

These two pieces of music puncture several deep-seated myths about slavery, music made in the United States, and, ultimately, the role that slave resistance, up to and through the Civil War, played in abolishing that system. The mere fact that a popular band leader and free man of color would use a European-derived musical form to celebrate the independence of Haiti does not fit prevalent images, even those purporting to be sympathetic with the cause of the enslaved. Yet here is music inspired by the first successful slave revolt in history, presented at a time when the United States still refused Haiti recognition.

And when, after the Civil War, a song is composed by former slaves unequivocally denouncing that condition as agonizing and cruel, it is irrefutable evidence that such feeling was common among them and therefore likely to have been expressed in more than one song.

PREDECESSORS

At this juncture I came upon two more books that contained not only supporting argument but more songs of the type I was looking for. First was a book published in 1953 called *American Folksongs of Protest*. Its author, John Greenway, had obviously done the kind of digging I was now doing and had discovered two songs collected by Lawrence Gellert in the late 1920s or early 1930s. One was called "Uncle Gabriel," which was about Gabriel Prosser, leader of an aborted slave revolt in 1800. The other was "Nat Turner," celebrating the leader of perhaps the most famous slave revolt in U.S. history, which took place in 1831. In addition, Greenway presented two other songs, "The Year of Jubalo" and "Ol' Massa, He Come Dancin' Out," that were clearly composed during the Civil War. Greenway had found these songs in the archives of the Federal Writers Project, manuscripts I would later consult myself.

The second book was a short one entitled *The Social Implications of Early Negro Music in the United States*, edited by Bernard Katz and published in 1969. As stated in its introduction, "The pages that follow contain pioneering writings on the early history of Afro-American music. Never before have they been gathered together for the easy access of the general reader or the research of the musicologist and the historian."[5] In this book were many slave songs, most of which fit the familiar mold. But one stood out from all the rest. "The Dirge of St. Malo" was a fragment of a ballad composed in Louisiana Creole and collected by George Washington Cable. Cable had published this song along with its English translation in *The Century Magazine* in 1886. Jean St. Malo was the leader of a band of maroons (runaway slaves) in then Spanish-ruled Louisiana. St. Malo was not only an effective leader; he was a symbol inspiring slave resistance, which required an expeditionary force to suppress. St. Malo was ultimately captured and was hanged in New Orleans in 1784.

Also in *The Social Implications of Early Negro Music in the United States* was an essay by John Lovell Jr. titled "The Social Implications of the Negro Spiritual." This essay, first published in 1939, challenged ruling dogma concerning interpretation of the spirituals and did so while quoting from the very Aptheker pamphlet, published the same year, that had started me on my quest. If nothing else, Lovell's essay showed that Aptheker's original thesis was in circulation at the time and was not unknown to his contemporaries.

Perhaps more significant was Lovell's contention that three characteristics of the spirituals identified them as revolutionary: "first, the Negro's obsession with freedom"; "Second was the slave's desire for justice"; and finally, "the slave song was an awesome prophecy," fulfilled in slave revolts and ultimately the Civil War.[6] That such an assertion would challenge notions held by a white-supremacist establishment is no surprise. But Lovell's criticism extended even to those great champions of emancipation and social justice W. E. B. Du Bois, Alain Locke, and James Weldon Johnson, whose interpretation of spirituals as "impassioned and beautiful" was, to Lovell, "sentimentalism, still."[7] We have only to recall Du Bois's famous characterization of the "Negro spirituals" as "sorrow songs"[8] to grasp the import of Lovell's claim.

It was on the strength of this essay that I sought out Lovell's book-length treatment of the theme: *Black Song: The Forge and the Flame*. This magisterial study, published in 1972, is clearly the culmination of work Lovell had undertaken back in 1939. One point was especially compelling. Lovell claimed there are six thousand spirituals that to one degree or another express exactly those thoughts and feelings that fit my criteria—that is, songs composed by slaves explicitly calling for freedom and collective resistance to slavery. This large number is not as surprising as it may first appear given the almost four-century duration of slavery in North America. More puzzling is the fact that Lovell's argument had not been followed to its logical conclusion and the record set straight simply by presenting the evidence.

Lovell's work was certainly encouraging, but more than that, I found in his book the text to "The Negro's Complaint" composed in 1820 by fugitive slave-turned-Methodist minister Thomas Cooper and set to the tune of "Old

Hundred," among the best known of all Christian hymns. I now had nine slave songs and the certainty that there were more. The questions raised by these discoveries were becoming more urgent as well.

THE ABOLITIONIST MOVEMENT

I returned to Eric Foner and posed these questions in light of what I'd found. He directed me to *The Slave's Cause: A History of Abolition* by Manisha Sinha and *Amazing Grace* by James Basker. These two books were published in 2016 and 2002, respectively, and indicate how historiography has advanced since the tumultuous 1960s and 1970s. In brief, *The Slave's Cause* is a monumental study of the long struggle to abolish slavery, while *Amazing Grace* is a compendium of poetry about slavery spanning the years 1660 to 1810. The authors of both books were kind enough to answer my questions and provide valuable leads to more songs. While confirming that distinctions between academic disciplines were a factor contributing to songs' being lost or unaccounted for, both said there was more to it than that.

Basker's excavation of more than four hundred poems by more than 250 poets published between the time England became fully involved in the slave trade and its eventual prohibition is a landmark study in more ways than one. Included within his book are poems by people from England, North America, and the Caribbean, slave and free, men and women. The poets range from anonymous to world-renowned. Virtually all are united in their determination to abolish slavery. They push back the date of antislavery writing to well before what most Americans are familiar with: the antebellum period between 1807 and the Civil War. They furthermore demonstrate that enslaved people themselves were writing and being published—in the case of former slave Olaudah Equiano, a bestselling autobiography.[9]

Yet Basker's volume was the first such compilation of its kind. In it, Basker notes that it "documents in massive detail the degree to which poets were the most outspoken and persistent critics of slavery, and fostered massive changes in public perception and attitude." He goes on to describe how in the intervening centuries various theories have been advanced claiming "English literature was 'complicitous in Empire' that the majority of writers supported and condoned the goals and practices of the 'imperial project' including its worst features such as the slave trade and plantation slavery." Today, however, "The question for us is, how could theories that are so far at odds with the historical evidence have flourished in the first place?"[10]

Sinha's work documents the vast scale and complexity of the international movement to abolish slavery, providing a much-needed antidote to certain falsehoods that stubbornly cling to the popular imagination. To this day, many people think that abolitionists were bourgeois do-gooders whose objection to slavery was that it disturbed their delicate sensibilities. These privileged northerners were responsible for a needless conflict, the Civil War, without which slavery would have eventually disappeared of its own accord. Sinha demonstrates not only the falsehood of such notions but what such notions were concocted to conceal.

Abolitionism as a movement began in the mid-eighteenth century and developed over the course of two great waves: the revolutionary period (1760–1820), and in 1830–1865. It was, furthermore, an international movement on four continents—Africa, Europe, and North and South America—involving hundreds of thousands of active participants and, necessarily, producing a great deal of literature, much of which still exists. It was Sinha's great achievement that convinced me how important it was to have, along with the slave songs, a representative sampling of abolitionist songs. Besides, Sinha informed me of the work of Joshua McCarter Simpson, which would become a crucial source in this collection.

Both these scholars pointed out patterns of historical revision and theoretical obfuscation that helped me understand the difficulties I'd encountered in my search. Naturally, this applied not only to texts but to music as well. The terrain shifts when you move from English literature to popular music. This was evident in the process of gathering representative abolitionist songs.

A MUSICAL BATTLEGROUND

Two songbooks became cornerstones of my presentation of abolitionist songs in this book. The first, published in 1848 by a fugitive slave named William Wells Brown, is entitled *The Anti-Slavery Harp*. I found it on my visit to the Library of Congress. The second, *The Emancipation Car*, was first published in 1854 and was the composition of Joshua McCarter Simpson, a free Black man who became an abolitionist after attending Oberlin College. This book was preceded by Simpson's *Original Anti-Slavery Songs* in 1852.[11] Together, these books convey the militancy and intelligence guiding a multi-faceted and multi-ethnic movement. While a few abolitionist songs survive in the canon of American music, they are not remembered as such, nor is their connection to the more than five hundred songs of this type still available.

"Amazing Grace" and "Darling Nelly Gray" are two famous examples still performed today, but who knows they were written by abolitionists?

In addition to the rich textual material contained in these songs, the music to which they were set sheds light on what was popular in the United States prior to the Civil War, and this, too, challenges many common misconceptions. There were stirring revolutionary anthems such as the French Revolution's "The Marseillaise" and the Scottish rebel ballad "Scots Wha Hae," as well as parodies of patriotic songs such as "America (My Country, 'Tis of Thee)." But there were also numerous minstrel songs, well known at the time to be mockeries of African American speech, dance, and music. The history of blackface and the minstrel show is too big a subject to be addressed in this chapter, but suffice it to say that Joshua McCarter Simpson commented on his own use of such songs in the introduction to his *Original Anti-Slavery Songs* (1852), writing:

> In offering my first little production to the public, I am well aware that many superstitious, prejudiced, and perhaps many good, conscientious, well-meaning christians [sic] will have serious objections to the "Airs" to which my poetry is set. My object in my selection of tunes, is to kill the degrading influence of these comic Negro Songs, which are too common among our people, and change the flow of these sweet melodies into more appropriate and useful channels.[12]

Simpson's statement is of greater import than it might first appear to be. How he selected music for his lyrics and the controversy that selection aroused shed light on the forces at work, then and ever since, to suppress or erase, first, the overtly revolutionary slave songs and, secondly, the large number of abolitionist songs.

"Comic Negro songs," as they were called, were indeed widely popular, and many recent studies have been devoted to the blackface minstrel phenomenon. With a few notable exceptions, these studies overlook a great many other forms popular music took at the time, and few discuss the work of abolitionists such as Simpson.[13] Moreover, most ignore the fact that there were musicians of international renown who were dedicated abolitionists— the outstanding example being the Hutchinson Family Singers. This group was, in fact, the most popular group in America between 1845 and the Civil War. Many years later, Frederick Douglass wrote of the Hutchinsons:

> their fine talent for music could have secured for them wealth and fame; but, like Moses, they preferred to suffer affliction in the cause of

justice and liberty than to enjoy the fruits of a concession to slavery. ... I saw this family in all the vicissitudes of its career. ... I saw it in times that tried men's souls. I saw it in peace and I saw it in war; but I never saw any one of its members falter or flinch before any duty, whether social or patriotic; and it is a source of more satisfaction than I can express, to have lived, as I have now done, to bear this high testimony to the character of the Hutchinsons.[14]

Also missing in past accounts, whether written by historians or folklorists, is the role of the music industry, which was formed during the very period Sinha defined as abolition's second wave. Recall that "Jump Jim Crow" was first performed in 1828. The commercial success of this performance was quickly grasped by publishers of sheet music and promoters of traveling shows, becoming within a few years a highly profitable business. Indeed, blackface minstrelsy was a cornerstone upon which the music industry in the United States was built. The culpability of that industry in the propagation of racism and exploitation of Black musicians is beyond doubt. From "Jump Jim Crow" to the film *The Jazz Singer* (1927) one hundred years later, great wealth was generated for corporations that have yet to be held accountable. Is it surprising then that there would be little interest in discovering songs that attacked their premises from the outset?

In a blistering rejoinder to an editorial condemning the Hutchinsons as "poor performers" whose "popularity was on the wane" because their "abolitionism had ruined them," Frederick Douglass took its author to task:

> We believe he does not object to the "Virginia Minstrels," "Christy's Minstrels," the "Ethiopian Serenaders," or any of the filthy scum of white society, who have stolen from us a complexion denied to them by nature, in which to make money, and pander to the corrupt taste of their white fellow-citizens. Those performers are undoubtedly in harmony with his refined and elegant taste! Then those beautiful and highly sentimental songs which they sing, such as "Ole Zip Coon," "Jim Crow," "Ole Dan Tucker," "Jim along Josey," and a few other of such specimens of American musical genius, must spread over his spirit a charm, and awaken in his bosom a rapture only equalled by that celestial transport which thrills his noble heart on witnessing a TREMENDOUS SQUASH![15]

With the songs from Brown's *Anti-Slavery Harp* and Simpson's *Emancipation Car*, I had only to add selections brought to my attention by musician and historian Tim Eriksen, who leads a community singing group in Amherst, Massachusetts. This group sings from *The Sacred Harp*, a songbook written in shape-notes (as opposed to conventional musical notation), in a tradition with links to the abolitionist movement. Several of the songs I'd selected from *The Anti-Slavery Harp* were already in the group's repertoire. This community-based singing and its expression of abolitionist themes present another challenge, musically and historically, to a prevailing image of what popular secular music in the United States consisted prior to the Civil War—that is, Stephen Foster, Dan Emmet, Christy's Minstrels, on the one hand, and European stars like Jenny Lind, on the other.

The repertoire I'd assembled at this point was nearly complete. The goal I'd set was not to dig up every song that exists. Rather it was to present a representative sample big enough to make the case. Somewhat arbitrarily I set the number at fifteen slave and fifteen abolitionist songs. This total conforms to the conventional length of an album (CD or LP) and could be presented to the public as a concert or recording for the pleasure of listening and not only for the archivist or scholar.

THE LAWRENCE GELLERT STORY

One final piece of the puzzle remained to be found. Through all the twists and turns of my research, I had not been able to locate the song with which I began. The mystery was only solved through verifying and authenticating other songs.

Two songs presented in John Greenway's *American Folksongs of Protest* were attributed to Lawrence Gellert. I had found Gellert referenced in other books about folk music. In fact, I recalled once having a record in my personal collection called *Negro Songs of Protest*, which comprised songs Gellert had recorded in the 1930s. But I knew very little about him, much less where these two songs, "Uncle Gabriel" and "Nat Turner," had come from. I began scouring libraries and my own books and came across a few references. But none clearly and definitively corroborated the songs' authenticity or their origins. I then stumbled upon the work of Steven Garabedian, especially his essay "Reds, Whites, and the Blues."[16]

Garabedian's essay gave detailed information about Gellert and the controversy surrounding his song collecting. According to Garabedian, Gellert had set out to find a type of song many authorities claimed did not exist. Gellert openly declared that he was not a folklorist, had no interest in folklore, and was only concerned with, and sympathetic to, the struggles Black people were waging at the time. Apparently, his search had begun in the early 1920s, but his work came to public attention in 1936 when *Negro Songs of Protest* was celebrated in publications as varied as the *New York Times* and the Marxist *New Masses*. For a few years, Gellert was lauded as having made an important contribution.

Yet despite this momentary acclaim, *Negro Songs of Protest* never attained the stature that one might expect. Unlike the work of other song collectors, especially Alan Lomax, Gellert's collecting was consigned to oblivion. Selections from the original record were released as an LP in 1973, but by this time Gellert's reputation had been damaged by accusations of fraud. It was asserted that Gellert had coached his informants, whom he refused to identify, eliciting from them lyrics they would never have otherwise sung, perhaps even writing them himself. Gellert, it was claimed, imposed his radical politics on unsophisticated people to make it appear the Black masses were revolutionary in outlook.

Since two songs Gellert had presented were among those I planned to use, it was imperative that I authenticate them or risk undermining the credibility of the entire project. I contacted Steven Garabedian, who told me that his own research not only confirmed the authenticity of Gellert's findings; it revealed a great deal about the forces at work in the two distinct periods—the 1930s and 1960s—when folk music revivals focused attention on vernacular music in the United States, especially the music of African Americans. Similar to the obfuscation and dismissal that I found prevalent in the song collecting done mainly by white southerners after Reconstruction, later folklorists and aficionados of blues seemed unable to hear what Black people were singing.[17] Why would anger and militancy directed at white supremacy and capitalist exploitation be surprising?

Nevertheless, Garabedian had laboriously studied all five hundred of Gellert's recordings and could find no evidence of coaching or coaxing. Furthermore, a careful comparison of the lyrics Gellert collected with other Black songs revealed no discrepancies in dialect, vocabulary, or style. There was, in fact, no reason to doubt the authenticity of the "protest" songs in the first place. Instead, the bias of the critics—that is, the assumption that Black people had passively accepted their fate—was exposed.

In addition, Garabedian was able to furnish me with more details regarding the song "Nat Turner," sharing with me interviews he'd conducted with Pete Seeger and others who were in no doubt about Gellert's reliability (see song notes). It was at this point I posed my dilemma concerning the song I'd found in Aptheker's pamphlet. Garabedian generously offered to use his academic access to archives to do a bit of digging.

THE HYMN OF FREEDOM

Within a few days I received an email containing Garabedian's findings. He'd found not only all three verses of the song, but the music the lyrics were set to. Furthermore, the full story of the song's composition, the circumstances in which it was performed and how it came to be written down were now available. They fully confirmed Aptheker's claims and more (see song notes).

This fascinating story deserves a book-length treatment, but it is briefly told in the following entry from *Harper's Encyclopedia of United States History* (1905):

> When [British] Admiral Cockburn began his marauding expedition on the American coast in the spring of 1813, he held out a promise of freedom to all slaves who should join his standard. Many were seduced on board his vessels, but found themselves wretchedly deceived. Intelligence of these movements reached the plantations farther south, and, in the summer of 1813, secret organizations were formed among the slaves to receive and co-operate with Cockburn's army of liberation, as they supposed it to be. One of these secret organizations met regularly on St. Johns Island, near Charleston. Their leader was a man of great sagacity and influence, and their meetings were opened and closed by singing a hymn composed by that leader—a sort of parody of Hail Columbia.[18]

This account was itself based on the record kept by the slaveowner who'd witnessed the meeting. His story was recounted in correspondence between clergyman John Forsyth and a writer named Benson John Lossing. Forsyth named the song the "Negro Hymn of Freedom" and followed the complete text with the words: "I think you will agree with me that the above is no mean addition to Negro Literature."[19] John Hammond Moore of Winthrop College in South Carolina gathered this correspondence together, mentioning as well that the story bore a striking resemblance to one told by abolitionist Lydia Maria Child in her *Freedmen's Book* (1865). Moore's article was published in the *Journal of Negro History* in 1965.

The discrepancy between Aptheker's publication in 1939 and Moore's publication in 1965 is explained by the fact that Aptheker used Lossing's recounting of the tale (including lyrics) in Lossing's 1868 book, *A Pictorial Field-Book of the War of 1812*. Evidently, this is where Aptheker originally discovered the story and the song.

My last step was comparing "Hail Columbia" to the "Hymn of Freedom." It turns out that "Hail Columbia" was the national anthem of the United States at the time of the War of 1812. Obviously, such an anthem would, in time of war, have been performed widely and often. This explains why slaves would have heard the song, and it would form the basis for a parody of sorts. And, indeed, the words to "Hymn of Freedom" fit the music perfectly.

With this accomplished, I was ready to gather all the materials, musical and lyrical, and proceed to recording them for presentation to the world at large. The evidence presented by the fifteen slave songs I'd uncovered augmented by the fifteen abolitionist songs I'd chosen was conclusive.

From the beginning of the Atlantic slave trade to the Civil War, enslaved people resisted in diverse ways including armed rebellion. Resistance was furthermore expressed in poetic and musical form, not only to strengthen resolve and prepare for battle but to win support for the abolition of slavery. Attempts to rewrite this history began immediately after Reconstruction. They included burying the evidence and replacing it with a fictitious narrative that justified the renewed subjugation of people who'd been nominally emancipated. This effort greatly expanded in the early years of the twentieth century with films such as *Birth of a Nation*, novels such as *Gone with the Wind*, and the promulgation of the "Lost Cause" narrative of a glorious southern civilization destroyed by northern invaders. This blatant distortion was accompanied by a more nuanced and apparently sympathetic portrayal of Black people and their music. An edifice was erected that did include the "Negro spiritual" along with blues and jazz. Yet even the most laudatory exaltation of Black musical achievement was simultaneously erasing an entire category of expression.

It is my hope that the evidence presented by these songs will convince readers that a great wrong has been done and can now be put right. It is furthermore necessary to expand this field of research to include all the countries affected, including especially the Caribbean, Brazil, and other Latin American countries. What young people can learn about music and history is of incalculable importance. Their future will be better for reclaiming the past.

Chapter 2

HISTORY, GEOGRAPHY, LANGUAGE, AND MUSIC

FINDING SONGS AND VERIFYING THEIR AUTHENTICITY RAISED QUESTIONS that required I look beyond the formal boundaries of folklore or cultural studies into other fields. These other fields can be roughly categorized as history, geography, and linguistics. In addition, the work of certain individuals had to be more fully explored not only to give credit where it's due but to aid further exploration of what they pioneered.

Historically, slavery is a vast subject, international in scope and predating the Atlantic slave trade with which this book is concerned. Even within the confines of the Atlantic slave trade, the evolution of a system took different forms in different regions within the Western Hemisphere, conquered at one time or another by various European powers. In North America, the evolution of the slave system was not one straight line but followed a torturous course (literally and figuratively). Different means at different times were employed to ensure the security of the slave system. At one point, for example, it was thought necessary and beneficial to educate slaves in order that they become good Christians. At least, they should be taught the Bible and Christian hymns.

This is among the reasons that well before the American Revolution there were literate and highly articulate people who, though enslaved, were able to write poetry and essays, some of which clearly denounced the system of slavery. It also explains the use of music popularized by Protestant denominations to accompany texts written to combat the lies and slanders used to justify that system. Only when it became apparent that slaves and free Black people were using the story of Exodus and the biblical prohibition of man-stealing to rally support for their cause did the slaveowners change tack. The event that signifies and to a large extent caused this change was, of course, Nat Turner's rebellion in 1831.

Subsequently, two contradictory trends emerged. The first was brutal suppression of literacy, public gatherings, and even Christian education of enslaved people in most of the South. The second was the rapid growth of the abolitionist movement, the Underground Railroad, and international opposition to slavery. On August 1, 1833, slavery was abolished in the British Commonwealth, a date celebrated to this day in Jamaica. It took thirty more years of intense struggle for the Emancipation Proclamation to be issued in the United States.

LANGUAGE

Another dimension of this history is linguistic. Almost all the songs I found are in English. "The Dirge of St. Malo" and "Rebeldia na Bandabou" are the exceptions. "The Dirge of St. Malo" was sung in Louisiana Creole. "Rebeldia na Bandabou" was sung in Papiamentu, the language enslaved people spoke in Curaçao (Papiamentu remains an official language in Curaçao). I devoted considerable effort to locating songs from the Caribbean and Louisiana, especially in French or Creole. I consulted several experts on the Haitian Revolution and Louisiana including Gwendolyn Midlo Hall and David Geggus. I read Hall's *Africans in Colonial Louisiana: The Development of Afro-Creole Culture in the Eighteenth Century* and Geggus's *The Haitian Revolution*, both of which make reference to slave singing and link that singing directly to resistance; but, with the exception of the "Dirge of St. Malo," they do not present actual songs. When I wrote to Hall and Geggus, both kindly responded and said there is plenty of evidence that such songs existed but, alas, they were not written down.[1]

Nonetheless, the two songs I found are indicative of a type of song that we should expect and not be surprised to find. Why? Throughout the world, in many cultures, ballads, dances, stories, and graphic imagery conveying battles, uprisings, heroes, and visions of freedom abound. There is no reason to expect enslaved Africans or their descendants born in the Western Hemisphere to be any different, especially given the central role music played in the lives of the enslaved. The two songs I did locate are representative and not anomalous. They are characteristic of balladry and commemoration common to a type of song through which the history of oppressed people is preserved and passed down. The reasons we have so few examples at present are therefore important to explore.

One reason is obvious: suppression. That at certain times and places, drumming was forbidden is a well-established fact. Should it be surprising that songs celebrating rebellion would be suppressed as well? It was nonetheless commonly reported that slaves gathering in insurrections or caught planning one were also observed singing. Here, it is not so much suppression as incomprehension that explains the apparent lack.

A perfect example is the Stono Rebellion, which took place in South Carolina in 1739.[2] Eyewitnesses described the slaves marching down the road, beating drums, and carrying a banner that read "Libertad." They were reported to have been singing at many points along the march route, which was in the direction of Florida where the Spanish had promised freedom to those escaping slavery. Evidently, the leaders were recent captives from the Kingdom of the Congo and were likely to be speaking and perhaps singing in Portuguese. In any case, the witnesses recording the events could not understand them; hence, we don't know what words the rebels sang.

On the other side of the linguistic question is why there are so many songs in English. It is beyond the scope of this book to go into the many peculiar features of slavery in North America, but a few points can be made. By 1660, the slave system was on a firm enough basis there to make the English, latecomers to the slave trade, more than interested. Indeed, at this point the English sought to overtake their competitors—the Dutch, French, Spanish and Portuguese—in what was an increasingly profitable venture. As James Basker explains:

> Between 1672 and 1713 the Royal African Company sent five hundred ships to Africa which, in addition to other trade, carried away 125,000 slaves for transatlantic sale. By 1730, Britain (as it was called after the Union with Scotland in 1707) had become the world's leading slave-trading nation, and would occupy that position until the abolition of the slave trade in 1807. And it wasn't just as cargo that slaves were entering British consciousness. Beginning in the 1730s, articles about slave insurrections appeared regularly in London periodicals: a total of 52 articles about 43 different insurrections, for example, were published in the *Gentleman's Magazine* between the late 1730s and the eve of the American Revolution.[3]

Such reports were followed almost immediately by the first denunciations of the evils of man-stealing. From this point forward, growth in the English slave trade was mirrored by opposition to it that had no equal in size or influence in the other imperial powers (an exception being the French revolutionary period when a great proliferation of abolitionist texts appeared in France such as those of Fr. Henri Gregoire). There were, moreover, relatively large numbers of religious dissenters who migrated to North America and who, to one degree or another, consciously opposed slavery. Quakers, Methodists, and Baptists were especially vocal. In the early period, the Methodists and Baptists were among the most active in the education of slaves, and there are numerous examples not only of their proselytizing but of their training Black people as ministers.

Three outstanding examples are Richard Allen of Philadelphia; Thomas Cooper, who preached not only in the United States but in London and Africa as well; and Shadrack Bassett of Maryland. Allen was the founder of the African Methodist Episcopal Church (AME) in Philadelphia in 1794 and produced a hymnal, *A Collection of Spiritual Songs and Hymns Selected from Various Authors by Richard Allen, African Minister* in 1801. In 1816, the AME became the first independent Black denomination in the United States with congregations in Pennsylvania, New Jersey, Delaware, and Maryland. Allen's example and leadership soon inspired others.

The Reverend Thomas Cooper was a fugitive slave who, in 1820, produced *The African Pilgrim's Hymns*, comprised of 372 hymns he either composed or collected. According to John Lovell, Cooper's hymns are "reminiscent of the most radical of the spirituals."[4] He made the collection for the use of congregations in London and Africa where he also preached. It was Cooper who wrote the text "The Negro's Complaint" to the tune of "The Old Hundred," included in this book.

The Reverend Shadrack Bassett was sent by his Maryland congregation of the AME Church to preach in Virginia. There is evidence that his preaching is what inspired Nat Turner. Apparently due to his emancipatory interpretation of the biblical narrative, Bassett was barred from preaching by the authorities. But not before he'd composed "The African Hymn," which, records show, was sung in the region of Turner's activities and is also included here (see song notes in chapter 3).

Another contributing factor was the revolutionary agitation that led up to the American, French, and Haitian Revolutions. To a great extent, this agitation was directed at a populace capable of reading or at least understanding what was written down, as reflected in the tenor and tone of many extant poems and essays written by enslaved, fugitive, and free Black people in both England and America. Moreover, the revolutionary period is marked by a shift in emphasis from moral argument based on Christian teachings to political argument based on concepts of liberty and justice.

Eileen Southern notes that, in 1775, "The Dunmore Proclamation, promising freedom to all slaves who joined the British Army, caused liberalizing of colonial laws that prohibited the enlistment of Negroes as servicemen."[5] This was followed in 1778, according to Southern, by the "first enactment of laws offering freedom to slaves who should serve in the [Continental] army for a number of years." By the time the first census was taken in the United States in 1790, "the black population was more than three quarters of a million, including 59,000 free blacks."[6] By 1860, there were approximately four million slaves and half a million free Black people,[7] a great many of whom were active in the abolitionist movement and the Underground Railroad.

The basic fact that slave revolts erupted from the beginning to the end of slavery led to a number of consequences. Had slaves not rebelled, there would have been no abolitionist movement. Without an abolitionist movement, there would have been no Civil War. This war might not have been won without the almost two hundred thousand slaves who joined the Union Army and Navy in fighting the Confederacy.[8] Certain songs included in this collection bear witness to this often-overlooked aspect of history. The triumph of the enslaved and their supporters was the abolition of slavery.

The betrayal of the promise of post-Civil War Reconstruction is most responsible for the burial of this history and this music. Until the civil rights movement of the 1960s and 1970s began to undo the damage, the old planters and their capitalist brethren in the North were successful enough in propagating their self-serving version of history that, even as resistance continued, they would leave a pile of debris through which subsequent generations have had to dig.

OVERCOMING THE OBSTACLES

The diversity of sources and their diffusion through many libraries and archives are no doubt key elements in the difficulties of recovering material. But as several of my colleagues pointed out, much of what I discovered was, as the saying goes, hiding in plain sight. All my sources were previously published. All were available in one library or another and in most cases had been for some time. This raises a final point that should be considered in evaluating the results of this inquiry.

My criteria, established at the beginning, were based largely on the first song I found, "Hymn of Freedom." I was looking for songs composed by slaves containing lyrics explicitly invoking liberty and justice, advocating collective resistance, and unequivocally demanding, not beseeching. The celebration of heroes such as Nat Turner is another form of the same advocacy. So, too, are those songs that are only slightly coded, such as "Children, We All Shall Be Free," wherein "the Lord" is a veiled reference to the Yankees, as attested to by a young drummer interviewed by Thomas Wentworth Higginson, as reported in his *Army Life in a Black Regiment*. Furthermore, other versions of certain songs, such as "March On," even dispense with the code and are more explicit than the version I recorded (see song notes in chapter 3).

To a certain extent, the boundary between slave and abolitionist songs is blurred since some abolitionist songs were composed by slaves and one of the slave songs ("Recognition March of the Independance of Hayti") was composed by a free Black man. Yet the latter is a clear reference to the greatest slave revolt of all—and the only one to succeed, leading to an independent state. The categories are not hard and fast in any case, but they serve the purpose of establishing their common foundation among the enslaved population itself while at the same time bringing to light the breadth of support for the cause of emancipation. Taken as a whole, the repertoire covers a range, musically and lyrically, that at the very least enhances understanding of slave songs, Black music more generally, and the complex interplay over centuries between diverse influences originating in Europe, Africa, and the Western Hemisphere.

Hopefully, this book will lead to a reappraisal of this music and how it is commonly transmitted and used. Many of the disputes I learned of concerned the origins of the music slaves used to express themselves. To a large extent, such disputes involved efforts to reinforce racist stereotypes and had no basis in the facts, musical or otherwise. Two extremes were proposed: everything Black people sang they learned from the white man; or, conversely, everything they sang came from Africa or from some inbred talent. Examples of the former are found in the works of George Pullen Jackson, Newman I. White, and Guy B. Johnson, all of whom were taken to task by John Lovell in his *Black Song: The Forge and the Flame*. Lovell exposed the flawed methods and erroneous conclusions of studies these authors conducted, which purported to prove that the "Negro spiritual" is essentially a copy of the white spiritual. The implication was obvious: Black people were only capable of imitation, not creativity. At the other pole of misapprehension lay the image of the "happy slave," singing and dancing as natural and carefree as a child. This image was promoted widely by defenders of the slave system and decried by abolitionists, most famously Frederick Douglass, who in his autobiography specifically targeted this view of slaves and their music. Debunking this image was further complicated, however, by blackface minstrelsy, as Dena Epstein explains, "Adding to their [the abolitionists'] dilemma was the emergence of the minstrel theater, with its increasingly offensive portrayal of plantation slaves as mindless buffoons who spent their time singing and dancing on the old plantation."[9]

This dichotomy, moreover, ostensibly concerned with music, in fact expressed an attitude toward the enslaved and their descendants designed to keep Black people "in their place." Such attitudes were succinctly summarized by W. E. B. Du Bois in *Black Reconstruction*: "Everything Negroes did was wrong. If they fought for freedom, they were beasts; if they did not fight, they were born slaves. If they cowered on the plantation, they loved slavery; if they ran away, they were lazy loafers. If they sang, they were silly; if they scowled, they were impudent.... And they were funny, funny—ridiculous baboons, aping men."[10]

Many defenders of the humanity of Black people necessarily reacted to these slanders and distortions by asserting the opposite—that is, the opposite of whichever skewed perspective was being advanced by defenders of the status quo. But this duality has often led to further confusion.

The truth is both more obvious and more interesting. Over centuries, enslaved people preserved certain practices handed down from their African ancestry while incorporating music derived from various European and Native American sources. They also created utterly novel forms that appeared nowhere else but in the United States. Furthermore, interchange among Black, white, Native, and Hispanic musicians was continuous and fluid, defying racial or ethnic characterization of any kind.

A NOTE ON SOURCES

Certain sources were of such significance to this project that they require further comment. In some cases, sources can be described as seminal or so widely referred to that they are indispensable: for example, Allen, Ware, and Garrison's *Slave Songs of the United States*. Others are less widely known but are nonetheless indispensable. Three notable examples are *The Story of the Jubilee Singers with Their Songs* by J. B. T. Marsh (1880), *Cabin and Plantation Songs as Sung by the Hampton Students* (1901), and *Folk Song of the American Negro* (1915) by John Wesley Work Jr. Not only did these three books provide songs in my collection, but they are of considerable historical interest as well. All three are products of Reconstruction and the struggle that ensued following its tragic end in 1877. All three are based on or include the work of African American scholars connected with institutions (Fisk University and Hampton Institute) originally established to educate newly freed people. All three predate the much better-known studies that followed, but which were produced by scholars credentialed or recognized as authorities by elite, predominantly white institutions. On the one hand, *Slave Songs of the United States*, made in the heat of victory in the Civil War and popularized widely soon after, could be considered the authoritative text to be ignored by no one. But the other books were published in the wake of the defeat of Reconstruction, by Black institutions struggling to survive as the story of the Fisk Jubilee Singers attests. (Briefly, it was to raise desperately needed funds that the Fisk singers went on tour. This tour was not only successful financially and musically, bringing world renown to the group, but it was responsible for the popularization of the "Negro spiritual" as a musical form, distinct from secular songs or even "folk songs." The training and refinement displayed by the singers clearly distinguished them from rural, uneducated plantation laborers. This image helped combat the degrading image conveyed by blackface minstrelsy, but it inadvertently aided the erecting of an artificial boundary, of which the music business is so fond, between ostensibly religious or "serious" music fit for urban bourgeois audiences and other types of songs. Designating genres suits marketing, but it obscures the complex interplay of influences present in most music, especially music originating among the common people. See song notes in chapters 3 and 4 for more.)

Another noteworthy source is *Music and Some Highly Musical People*. Written by James M. Trotter and published in 1878, this book, according to Eileen Southern and Josephine Wright, is a "landmark publication" and "the first survey of American music to be published in the United States."[11] Trotter was born in slavery, escaped via the Underground Railway, and eventually fought in the Civil War, becoming the first African American to achieve the rank of Second Lieutenant in the Union Army. Though it provided no songs for my collection, Trotter's book is nonetheless indispensable as it broadens the view of African American music from the early nineteenth century through Reconstruction. Francis Johnson, discussed by Trotter and in chapter 1 of this book, is only one example of the sophistication, musical skill, and wide acclaim attained by Black people, both free and enslaved, long before emancipation. Indeed, Trotter's work complicates the whole conception that guided so many song collectors that Black music was limited to what field hands sang. Indeed, Trotter's aim, according to Southern and Wright, was "to trace the footsteps of the remarkable colored musician wherever they might lead."

In other cases, sources are lesser known or known only within a particular discipline. Manisha Sinha's *The Slave's Cause: A History of Abolition*, for example, is a vitally important work, well known among historians but not likely to be referred to by folklorists, musicologists, or the general public. In chapter 1, I described Sinha's pathbreaking study charting the centuries-long struggle to abolish slavery, but I might never have found it had I confined my search to the fields of folklore or musicology. In still other cases, sources are marginal, viewed with skepticism or even discredited. In this latter category might fall, for example, the Aptheker pamphlet that inspired my project or the song collecting of Lawrence Gellert, both of which supplied songs I have endeavored to authenticate beyond reasonable doubt. In any case, certain sources bear closer scrutiny than that given up to this point.

To begin with the Aptheker pamphlet, *Negro Slave Revolts in the United States, 1526–1860* (1939), I was aware of the controversy surrounding Aptheker's scholarship. I knew Aptheker was a communist and had long been marginalized by the academy. While this clouded his reputation, it did not prove he was wrong about slave revolts or that the song he presented was inauthentic. It did, however, require that I remove any doubt by verifying Aptheker's evidence and appraising the current status of his work. I started by asking a number of historians for their views.

Those most familiar with Aptheker were, as one might expect, those concerned with US history, slavery and its abolition, the Civil War, and the work of W. E. B. Du Bois. Among those I consulted were Eric Foner, author of many books on related themes; Manisha Sinha, author of *The Slave's Cause*; and Robin D. G. Kelley, who wrote the outstanding *Hammer and Hoe* as well as the introduction to this volume. I furthermore consulted *African American History and Radical Historiography: Essays in Honor of Herbert Aptheker* (1998), edited by Herbert Shapiro.[12] The general consensus was that Aptheker had indeed pioneered the study of slave revolts in the United States. None before him had systematically pursued the evidence because that evidence ran counter to prevailing opinion, which held that the slaves did not rebel. Or, if they occasionally had rebelled, it was neither often enough nor effective enough to be a factor in shaping government policy, the Civil War, or slavery's abolition. The popular saying "Lincoln freed the slaves" so dominated public discourse that to consider enslaved people as conscious, active participants in their own emancipation was practically unthinkable.

Aptheker's master's thesis (1931) was on Nat Turner's rebellion, followed in 1939 by the *Negro Slave Revolts* pamphlet, and then by his doctoral thesis, which was published as *American Negro Slave Revolts* in 1943. That book qualifies as both seminal and a classic. It remains in print and is widely read today. While it has certainly been augmented and built upon, it has not become outmoded. It furthermore amply demonstrates the depth of Aptheker's research and data-gathering, the rigor of which none of his critics could dispute.[13] This, again, was the consensus view of the historians I consulted.

I learned further that, in the ensuing decades, Aptheker's conclusions, initially far outside the mainstream, are now generally accepted, various caveats and reservations notwithstanding. Though Aptheker himself remains a controversial figure, his scholarship is nonetheless reliable. It took me more than two years to find and verify the full text of the song he presented in his pamphlet, but when I finally did find the complete song and the story of its transcription, his claims were validated in their entirety (see song notes in chapter 3).

THE AMERICAN SLAVE: A COMPOSITE AUTOBIOGRAPHY

At the Library of Congress, I encountered the Federal Writers Project, which was conducted under the auspices of the Works Progress Administration from 1935 to 1939.[14] This project produced the Slave Narrative Collection comprised of 2,300 first-person interviews with people who had been enslaved in every southern state as well as a few outside the South (Indiana and Ohio, in particular). It was in this collection that I found the song "Agonizing, Cruel Slavery Days."

As I was seeking to verify the songs presented by John Greenway in his *American Folksongs of Protest*, I realized I would have to consult the collection. Greenway had attributed the "Year of Jubalo" to "Informant: Merton Knowles, WPA Project Worker: 'Heard it from my mother, it was brought back by returning Union soldiers, and became a part of our folklore.' (Indiana) In Library of Congress, Archive of American Song." Greenway attributed "Old Massa, He Come Dancin' Out" similarly, noting it as "Library of Congress Archive of American Folk Song, WPA Collection. Collected by Merton Knowles of Indiana from his mother, who learned and sang the song after the Civil War."

What happened when I attempted to locate these attributions in the online archive provided by the Library of Congress was unexpected. First, I couldn't find the attributions where they were supposed to be. Second, I discovered that what was available online from the Library of Congress was incomplete. Further inquiry led me to a different collection based on the Federal Writers Project but enhanced by more extensive use of the original materials, which were in some cases never sent to Washington, DC, from the states where the interviews had taken place. Much material had been left collecting dust in state archives (Mississippi and Alabama, for example). The tedious work of sifting through this material was undertaken by George Rawick. His herculean effort resulted in the forty-one volume *The American Slave: A Composite Autobiography*. The first nineteen volumes were published in 1972, the next twelve in 1977, and the final ten in 1979. In 1997, a name index was created by

Howard Potts, and in 2004 the entire collection was made available online by Greenwood Publishing. Unfortunately, the online edition was no longer available when I went to consult it, so I had to locate an institution that had the printed books.

Public access was available at the open stacks of Tufts University in Somerville, MA. I spent three days going through all forty-one volumes seeking both verification for Greenway's attributions and more evidence to, hopefully, complete my research.

First, I was able to locate the attributions Greenway made and verify their accuracy. I was even able to solve the mystery of Merton Knowles. Greenway's attribution did not make clear if Knowles was the interviewer or interviewee. I discovered that Knowles was both. He was a former slave and had contributed his own recollections as well as those of his mother.

Second, I was able to discover a great deal more about one song in particular, "The Year of Jubalo." (See song notes in chapter 3 for details.)

Third, I was excited to discover in Rawick's *The American Slave* the complete text of "Agonizing, Cruel Slavery Days" and the story of the man who brought it to the collection. The entry read: "Elijah Cox (Uncle Cox) was free-born in Michigan in 1843 and consequently was not a slave. Association with the ex-slaves, however, after he came to Fort Concho in 1871, furnished him with a broad knowledge of slavery days and he wished to contribute the following song which he learned at Fort Concho, having heard the ex-slaves sing it many times, as it was one of their favorite songs."[15]

The Rawick collection provided more than these particular data, however. Certain songs appeared often, over a wide geographical range. Among these were "Amazing Grace" and "Run, Nigger, Run." I did not have the time to do a proper accounting, but it was my impression that "Run, Nigger, Run" was the most often mentioned song. Others frequently mentioned were Christian hymns or "Negro spirituals," but surprisingly few were those most famous such as "Deep River," "Roll, Jordan, Roll," or "Go Down, Moses."

Let me again emphasize that *The American Slave: A Composite Autobiography* is of incalculable importance. The treasures it contains will inspire historians and artists for decades to come.

SINFUL TUNES AND SPIRITUALS

I first encountered the work of Dena J. Epstein during my visit to the Library of Congress. The library contains a two-part essay published in sequential editions, spring and summer 1963, of *Music Library Association Notes*.

The essay's title, "Slave Music in the United States before 1860: A Survey of Sources," drew me to it for obvious reasons. Epstein's essay was more than informative; it was inspiring. Its existence made it clear to me that others had had similar questions to my own and that a great deal of work had been done to answer them. This essay led me, in turn, to Epstein's great book, *Sinful Tunes and Spirituals: Black Folk Music to the Civil War* (1977).

There are two reasons to call attention to this book among the many sources I relied upon. The first is the sheer quantity and quality of information regarding music and music-making it offers that other historical accounts do not provide. Epstein, for example, is largely responsible for proving beyond doubt that the banjo originated in Africa and not the United States. But this is only one among many popular myths she dispelled. Epstein went to great lengths to answer questions that had puzzled musicologists and folklorists for decades following the Civil War—indeed, down to the 1960s when Epstein assembled her data. For example, she explored how to account for not only African or European elements but also their hybrid or creolized offspring in North America, and why these differed from the music slaves made in the Caribbean and elsewhere in the Americas.

Epstein was well aware that racist ideology and defense of the slave system had warped previous research, not only burying important evidence but obscuring obvious facts. The slave system itself changed over time and affected musical practices accordingly. This helps explain the instruments slaves learned to play (e.g., the fiddle) and the interpenetration of diverse influences (e.g., European, African, and Native American) in composition and performance. Instead of mystification regarding Africans' "natural" musical proclivity, we now understand the role music played in slaves' survival aboard ship, their building of community in the Americas, and their being used as musicians by masters.

The information, however unequivocal it might appear to us today, is conditioned by controversies prevalent at various stages. It is difficult to imagine that, in the first decades of the twentieth century, it was still necessary to "prove" the humanity of Black people; that there were folklorists, song collectors, and musicologists still claiming that Black music derived exclusively from European sources (Africa having been long forgotten); or that Black scholars would have to defend Black composers' intellectual achievement as opposed to the "instinctual" or "natural" one assigned to them by racist ideologies. Different periods are marked by different writers fighting on multiple fronts, including Frederick Douglass before the Civil War, James Weldon Johnson in 1925, John Lovell in 1939, Amiri Baraka aka LeRoi Jones in 1963. The battles these and other writers waged were in large part defined by their opponents' changing positions, which, in turn, corresponded to the advances of the struggle for Black liberation.

Epstein's work, overall, complements that of Eileen Southern, whose invaluable contributions were discussed in chapter 1 of this book.

AMERICAN ANTI-SLAVERY SONGS

This collection of almost five hundred songs was meticulously assembled by Vicki Lynn Eaklor and published in 1988. Eaklor's work helped immeasurably in the selections I made for my project. Even though I had previously located William Wells Brown's *Anti-Slavery Harp* and James McCarter Simpson's *Emancipation Car*, which are collections of songs, I knew there were many other songs that lay scattered about in myriad newspapers (*The Liberator*, for example), hymnals, books of poetry, and so on. The range of sources expanded further when Tim Eriksen informed me of the connection between shape-note singing and abolitionism. Songs in *The Sacred Harp* and other songbooks used in the shape-note tradition also had to be included. I was overwhelmed with the amount of cross-referencing I would have to do to provide a selection that accurately reflected the musical and lyrical variety I knew existed. When I came upon Eaklor's *American Anti-Slavery Songs*, it made accomplishing this task possible. Having all the lyrics and the musical accompaniment in one well-arranged and documented source made all the difference. I could, for example, compare the introductions Joshua McCarter Simpson wrote to the various editions of his collections (there were three) as well as compare the lyrics that were put to the same tune by different authors. "The Marseillaise" and "Scots Wha Hae," for example, were frequently used as the musical basis for diverse texts, and Eaklor listed these tunes and how often they were employed. I could also go to Eaklor's sources both to verify accuracy and to view the songs in their published setting (e.g., *The Liberator* newspaper). Eaklor's research proved to be impeccable, while her analysis of the continued relevance of songs in the abolitionist movement is useful to this day.

OF SPECIAL NOTE

One more book needs mention since it provided early encouragement for my effort. This is *The Freedmen's Book* by Lydia Maria Child, published in 1865. This compilation of writings includes the work of three African American poets, Frances E. W. Harper, Phillis Wheatley, and George Horton, who are among those whose texts first convinced me there were songs of the kind I was looking for. Harper (1825–1911) was born free and was an abolitionist. Her poem "Bury Me in a Free Land" gained wide renown in her lifetime. Wheatley and Horton, though enslaved, became famous through their poetry, including Horton's book *The Hope of Liberty* (1829).

Child's *The Freedmen's Book* contains the writings of leading abolitionists Frederick Douglass, Charlotte L. Forten, and John G. Whittier, as well as many pieces by Child herself. Among these are brief biographies of Benjamin Banneker, John Brown, and Toussaint L'Ouverture. The book was dedicated to "the loyal and brave Captain Robert Small, Hero of the Steamboat Planter," and its purpose was clearly stated in the introduction: "To The Freedmen, I have prepared this book expressly for you, with the hope that those of you who can read will read it aloud to others, and that all of you will derive fresh strength and courage from this true record of what colored men have accomplished under great disadvantages." Robert Small (actually Smalls, with a final "s") was an enslaved man trained as a naval pilot. He managed to free himself and his crew by commandeering the *Planter*, a Confederate ship loaded with munitions, and skillfully navigating an escape to the Union Navy waiting outside Charleston harbor. This episode took place in 1862, and Smalls not only became a hero, but he played a role in convincing Lincoln to accept Black men into the Union Army.

Child's book is representative of a much larger body of literature born of the abolitionist movement, much of which is still readily available and continues to provide a useful antidote to mischaracterizations plaguing our understanding of history. With such resources, it is possible to more accurately follow the course of a centuries-long struggle and its poetical-musical expression.

Chapter 3

SLAVE SONGS
SOURCES AND DOCUMENTATION

THE SONGS DISCUSSED IN THIS CHAPTER ARE ARRANGED IN APPROXIMATELY chronological order, oldest first, except for two special cases at the end of the list. In titles of songs, small adjustments have been made to modernize capitalization, spelling, and punctuation. Lyrics of the songs, here and in Part II, are shown as they appeared in the most authoritative source, with a few obvious typos corrected.

1. "Uncle Gabriel, the Negro General" (ca. 1800)

I found three versions of this song. The first was in *Poor Jack*, a novel by Frederick Marryat published in 1840, in which the title was written as "Gin'ral Gabriel-sea chanty." The second version was collected by Lawrence Gellert and published in the February 1963 issue of *Mainstream*; and the third was in the Christy Minstrels' *Ethiopian Glee Book* (1849).[1]

I made a composite of the Gellert and *Ethiopian Glee Book* versions since they were quite similar. The sea chanty was substantively similar but formally different. The texts are obviously derived from the same source: the story is told in a similar way, but the music must have been different. The rhythm of Gellert's and the *Ethiopian Glee Book* versions is clearly the same, while the chanty doesn't fit.

2. "Hymn of Freedom" (1813)

I first discovered this song in 2015 in Herbert Aptheker's *Negro Slave Revolts in the United States, 1526–1860* (1939), where it had the following description: "Sung by the Negroes on the island opposite Charleston, during the late War with Britain composed by one of themselves."

Two years later, historian Steven Garabedian located the rest of the song by the following means. He located the lyrics in Vincent Harding's *There*

Is a River: The Black Struggle for Freedom in America (1993). On page 349 of his book, Harding cites his source as follows: "The words of the song and an account of its transmission are in John H. Moore, 'A Hymn of Freedom—South Carolina, 1813,' *JNH*, 50 (Jan. 1965), 50–53." The Moore article was published in the Association for the Study of African American Life and History's *Journal of Negro History*, vol. 50, no. 1.

The Moore article features excerpts from two primary sources. The first is Lydia Maria Child's *The Freedmen's Book* (1865). In what Child calls "The Meeting in the Swamp" (pp. 104–10), she provides a slaveowner's eyewitness account of the clandestine meeting where the insurrection was being planned and the "Hymn" performed.

The second primary source Moore cites is John Forsyth's letter to Benson John Lossing, lead editor of *Harper's Encyclopedia of United States History* (1905), in which there is another account of the same incident with further elaboration. Added to the original account is a report of the related movements of British Admiral Cockburn directly off the coast of South Carolina. This report deserves quoting in full:

> When Admiral Cockburn began his marauding expedition on the American coast in the spring of 1813, he held out a promise of freedom to all slaves who should join his standard. Many were seduced on board his vessels, but found themselves wretchedly deceived. Intelligence of these movements reached the plantations farther south, and, in the summer of 1813, secret organizations were formed among the slaves to receive and co-operate with Cockburn's army of liberation, as they supposed it to be. One of these secret organizations met regularly on St. Johns Island, near Charleston. Their leader was a man of great sagacity and influence, and their meetings were opened and closed by singing a hymn composed by that leader—a sort of parody of *Hail Columbia*. The following is the last of the three stanzas of the hymn alluded to:
>
> > Arise ! arise ! shake off your chains !
> > Your cause is just, so Heaven ordains ;
> > To you shall freedom be proclaimed !
> > Raise your arms and bare your breasts,
> > Almighty God will do the rest.
> > Blow the clarion's warlike blast ;
> > Call every negro from his task ;
> > Wrest the scourge from Buckra's hand,
> > And drive each tyrant from the land !

(Chorus.)
Firm, united let us be.
Resolved on death or liberty!
As a band of patriots joined,
Peace and plenty we shall find.

They held meetings every night, and had arranged a plan for the rising of all the slaves in Charleston when the British should appear. At one of the meetings the question, "What shall be done with the white people?" was warmly discussed. Some advocated their indiscriminate slaughter as the only security for liberty, and this seemed to be the prevailing opinion, when the leader and the author of the hymn came in and said: "Brethren, you know me. You know that I am ready to gain your liberty and mine. But not one needless drop of blood must be shed. I have a master whom I love, and the man who takes his life must pass over my dead body." Had Cockburn been faithful to his promises to the negroes, and landed and declared freedom to the slaves of South Carolina, no doubt many thousands of colored people would have flocked to his standard. But he was content to fill his pockets by plundering and carrying on a petty slave-trade for his private gain. (pp. 211–12)

I subsequently located Aptheker's original source in the bibliography of *American Negro Slave Revolts* (1943) as "Lossing, Benson J., *A Pictorial Field-Book of the War of 1812* (1868)." In a footnote, Lossing recounts the tale, records the lyrics, and says it was sung to the tune of "Hail, Columbia."

Finally, I found a recording of "Hail Columbia" and checked for a correspondence with the words of "Hymn of Freedom." Not only did the text accord with the structure of the original song, but the text of the original had clearly been used as a basis for a transformation—that is, a parody with a twist. It was not sarcastic parody poking fun, but rather a rejoinder to the pompous claims of the original.

3. "The Negro's Complaint" (ca. 1820)

This song was sung to the tune of "Old Hundred" by Rev. Thomas Cooper (ca. 1775–ca. 1823) as published in his *The African Pilgrim's Hymns* (1820), which contained 372 hymns used by congregations in London and Africa. My source for this information is John Lovell's *Black Song: The Forge and the Flame* (1972), in which he writes, "His [Cooper's] book . . . , partly composed and partly collected, contained 372 hymns; many of them are reminiscent of the most radical of the spirituals" (pp. 106–7).

4. "Recognition March of the Independance of Hayti" (published in 1820)

I discovered this composition in the Library of Congress. The march, written for piano and flute, was composed by Francis Johnson, a free Black man who was an abolitionist and one of the most famous band leaders of the early nineteenth century. Johnson also composed "The Grave of the Slave" to a poem published in *The Liberator* that was written by Sarah Forten, a leading abolitionist author using the penname "Ada."

5. "The African Hymn" (ca. 1830)

My source for this song is Stephen B. Oates's *The Fires of Jubilee: Nat Turner's Fierce Rebellion* (1975). Oates writes: "And in Prince William, Stafford, and King George counties along the Potomac River, in the sweltering stone quarries there, the slaves sang a spiritual called 'The African Hymn,' composed by the Reverend Shadrack Bassett. The lyrics were more prophetic than the slaves in northern Virginia could have known" (pp. 133–34).

Oates cites these sources for the lyrics: "Copy of 'African Hymn' in Floyd's Free Negro and Slave Letterbook, Archives of the Virginia State Library; George Cooke to Floyd, September 13, 1831, Virginia Governors' Papers, ibid.; N. Sutton to Floyd, September 21, 1831, ibid.; 'A Friend to the City' to Floyd [November, 1831], ibid.; and Richmond Enquirer, September 17, 1831."

According to *Scraps of African Methodist Episcopal History* by Rt. Rev. James A. Handy, "Rev. Shadrack Bassett was appointed to the Eastern Shore. ... He organized churches at Easton, Denton and Ivory town, and extended the church to French Town, and the Rev. Jeremiah Miller organized churches at Cecilton, Port Deposit and Octorara. These pioneers of our church in Maryland spread the work from the Choptank, on the Eastern Shore, to the Susquehanna River."

One additional piece of verification comes from Dena J. Epstein's summer 1963 article in *Music Library Association Notes* titled "Slave Music in the United States before 1860: A Survey of Sources (Part 2)."

Epstein quotes an interview conducted by the abolitionist Lydia Maria Child with an old formerly enslaved woman named Charity Bowery, "who was born," Epstein writes, "at Pembroke, North Carolina, about 1774." Epstein continues:

Child asked Bowery about the reaction following the Nat Turner insurrection of 1831 and Bowery said:

"The brightest and best men were killed in Nat's time. Such ones are always suspected. All the colored folks were afraid to pray in the time of the old Prophet Nat. There was no law about it; but the whites reported it round among themselves that, if a note was heard, we should have some dreadful punishment; and after that, the low whites would fall upon any slaves they heard praying, or singing a hymn, and often killed them before their masters or mistresses could get to them."

I asked Charity to give me a specimen of their hymns. In a voice cracked with age . . . she sang:

> A few more beatings of the wind and rain,
> Ere the winter will be over—
>   Glory, Hallelujah!
> Some friends has gone before me,—
> I must try to go and meet them—
>   Glory, Hallelujah!
> A few more risings and settings of the sun,
> Ere the winter will be over—
>   Glory, Hallelujah!
> There's a better day a coming—
> There's a better day a coming—
>   Oh, Glory, Hallelujah!

With a very arch expression, she looked up, as she concluded, and said, "They wouldn't let us sing that. They wouldn't let us sing that. They thought we was going to *rise*, because we sung, 'better days are coming.'"

Child's interview was initially published as Lydia Maria Child, "Charity Bowery," in *The Liberty Bell: By Friends of Freedom*, edited by Maria W. Chapman (Boston: American Anti-Slavery Society, 1839), pp. 42–43.

The reader will note that "there's a better day a coming" is the repeated refrain of "The African Hymn." I could not locate the music, so I composed a melody according to styles that were then current.

6. "Nat Turner"
(ca. 1830, composed after Nat Turner's Rebellion of 1831)

I first discovered this song as titled "The Gainin' Ground" in Pete Seeger's *Where Have All the Flowers Gone* (p. 236). I later discovered it in John Greenway's *American Folksongs of Protest* (pp. 92–93) and Russell Ames's *The Story of American Folk Song* (1955, pp. 151–52). All three attribute discovery of the song to Lawrence Gellert. This attribution is confirmed by Gellert in the February 1963 issue of *Mainstream*.

Steven Garabedian shared with me the following notes from his interview with Pete Seeger on June 28, 2002: "He [Seeger] only met 'Larry' Gellert . . . late in Gellert's life during the folk boom years; Gellert was very thin and old at the time—he gave Seeger the lyrics and music to 'Nat Turner,' but the music didn't make sense at all and simply did not fit the lyrics. So, Seeger wrote new music; he did it on an album; Rev. F. D. Kirkpatrick sang it as well."

Garabedian also interviewed Israel Young, proprietor of the Folklore Center in New York City. His notes from that interview are as follows: "First phone conversation, 7/18/02. Izzy tracked down this Gellert song mentioned by Pete Seeger in our conversation, 'Nat Turner'; it's in P. Foner, *American Labor Songs of the Nineteenth Century*, it's in Greenway, it's in Seeger's *Incompleat Folksinger* and *Where Have All the Flowers Gone*; slightly changed as 'Gaining Ground' (p. 263)."

I could not locate a recording of either the Rev. F. D. Kirkpatrick or Seeger versions, nor could I make the Seeger tablature work. I therefore composed a melody that fit styles current at the time.

7. "March On" (date undetermined)

I first discovered this song as number 44 (p. 166) in J. B. T. Marsh's *The Story of the Jubilee Singers with Their Songs* (1880). The song was referred to by both John Lovell in *Black Song: The Forge and the Flame* (1972) and John Wesley Work in *Folk Song of the American Negro* (1915). These references were, however, not complete, and it was only in *The Story of the Jubilee Singers* that I found both full text and tablature.

I later located a version of the song collected by Lawrence Gellert and published in Nancy Cunard's *Negro: An Anthology* (1934). That text reads:

> Oh brethren rise, give praise to glory
> For the year of the Jubilee
> Do you want to be a soldier
> For the year of the Jubilee

Oh what you say brother
Oh what you say brother
Oh what you say brother
About dis wahr

I will die in the field
Stay in the field
Stay in the field brother
Stay in the field
Until the victory
March on and you shall gain the victory
March on an you shall gain the day

We want no cowards in our band
We call for only the strongest men

I intend to fight and never stop
Until I reach mountain top

8. "Children, We All Shall Be Free" (date undetermined)

I first discovered this song as number 6 (p. 130) in J. B. T. Marsh's *The Story of the Jubilee Singers with Their Songs* (1880). The song was referred to by both John Lovell in *Black Song: The Forge and the Flame* (1972) and John Wesley Work in *Folk Song of the American Negro* (1915).

9. "We'll Soon Be Free/My Father, How Long?" (1860s)

I found two versions of the same song. The first was in Thomas Wentworth Higginson's *Army Life in a Black Regiment* (1870). Higginson noted that, for singing this, "the negroes had been put in jail in Georgetown, S.C., at the outbreak of the Rebellion. 'We'll soon be free' was too dangerous an assertion, and though the chant was an old one, it was no doubt sung with redoubled emphasis during the new events. 'De Lord will call us home' was evidently thought to be a symbolical verse; for, as a little drummer boy explained it to me, showing all his white teeth as he sat in the moonlight by the door of my tent, 'Dey tink *de Lord* mean for say *de Yankees*.'" (p. 169). The second version was in Allen, Ware, and Garrison's *Slave Songs of the United States* (1867; section IV, number 112).

For this collection, I made a composite lyric and based the music on that provided in *Slave Songs of the United States*.

10. "The Enlisted Soldiers" (1860s)

I first discovered this song in Fenner, Rathbun, and Cleaveland's *Cabin and Plantation Songs as Sung by the Hampton Students* (1901), which quoted the following recollection of Samuel Chapman Armstrong, commander of the 8th US Colored Infantry regiment: "While recruiting and drilling the 9th Regiment, U.S. Colored troops at Benedict, Maryland, in the winter of 1863–64, the men gathered around the camp-fire would sing by the hour the melodies of the plantation slave life that they had just left—not always very melodious; but late one evening I was startled by a magnificent chorus from nearly a thousand black soldiers, that called me from my tent to listen to its most inspiring strains, and I caught the following words which I called the 'Negro Battle Hymn'" (p. 146).

I found a second reference to this song in Dena J. Epstein's *Sinful Tunes and Spirituals: Black Folk Music to the Civil War* (1977; pp. 293–94). The complete song is not presented in that book, but enough of the lyrics appear to confirm that it was the same song. The circumstances are similar to those recorded by Samuel Chapman Armstrong. Epstein cited her source as "Henry Goddard Thomas, Colonel, 2d Brigade, 'The Colored Troops at Petersburg,' *Century Magazine* 34, n.s. 12 (September, 1887): 778." She noted that Thomas reported this song was sung every night as the troops were preparing for the battle of "The Crater," which took place at Petersburg, Virginia, July 30, 1864.

Of further note, almost 200,000 Black soldiers and sailors fought for the Union in the Civil War. They were joined by an additional 200,000 men and women who served behind the lines in various support functions. In this sense, the alternate title, "The Negro Battle Hymn," represents the culmination of centuries of slave revolts as masses of former slaves emancipated themselves by force of arms.

11. "The Year of Jubalo," "Year of Jubilo," and "Kingdom Coming" (1860s)

I found three versions of this song and present all three in Part II. The first was in John Greenway's *American Folksongs of Protest* (1953). Greenway's attribution reads: "Informant: Merton Knowles, WPA Project Worker: 'Heard it from my mother, it was brought back by returning Union soldiers, and became a part of our folklore.' (Indiana) In Library of Congress, Archive of American Song" (p. 104). The second version was identical to a song by Henry Clay Work entitled "Kingdom Coming." That song was composed and published in 1861 and became popular at that time. It was likely to have been sung by Union troops as was Work's most famous composition, "Marching through Georgia."

The third version was in *The American Slave: A Composite Autobiography*, edited by George Rawick (1972; Vol.3 Series 2 [Texas]). The song was reported by Lorenzo Ezell, a formerly enslaved man from Beaumont, Texas, District 3, who said, as recorded in what is now called African American Vernacular English: "My ol' marster run off and stay in de woods a whole week w'en Sherman men come t'rough. He didn' need to worry 'cause us tek care of eb'ryt'ing. Dey was a funny song w'at us mek up 'bout him runnin' off in de woods. I know it was mek up 'cause my uncle hab a han' in it. It went like dis."

I made a composite of the three versions and consider it a slave song because at least some slaves made it their own. This decision is further justified by what I learned later. After completing the recording of this song, I discovered a version in *Negro Folk Rhymes, Wise and Otherwise* (1922) by Thomas Talley. Talley presented as two separate songs what are clearly parts of one complete song in my collection. (See the slave song lyrics in Part II for comparison.) Talley presented the following:

> MASTER IS SIX FEET ONE WAY
> Mosser is six foot one way, an' free foot tudder;
> An' he weigh five hunderd pound.
> Britches cut so big dat dey don't suit de tailor,
> An' dey don't meet half way 'round.
> Mosser's coat come back to a claw-hammer p'int.
> (Speak sof' or his Bloodhound'll bite us.)
> His long white stockin's mighty clean an' nice,
> But a liddle mō' holier dan righteous.

> YEAR OF JUBILEE
> Niggers, has you seed ole Mosser;
> (Red mustache on his face.)
> A-gwine 'roun' sometime dis mawnin,'
> 'Spectin' to leave de place?
> Nigger Hands all runnin' 'way,
> Looks lak we mought git free!
> It mus' be now de Kingdom Come

In de Year o' Jubilee.
Oh, yon'er comes ole Mosser
Wid his red mustache all white!
It mus' be now de Kingdom Come
Sometime to-morrer night.
Yanks locked him in de smokehouse cellar,
De key's throwed in de well:
It shŏ' mus' be de Kingdom Come.
Go ring dat Nigger field-bell!

It is not unlikely that Henry Clay Work's "Kingdom Coming" was sung by Union soldiers, transmitted to newly liberated people, who thereupon adopted and adapted the song. It then could have been re-learned by other Union soldiers, who brought it back with them to Indiana. This circular motion is common in folk song transmission.

It could, however, have been the other way around, and Work heard a version of a slave song and used it as a basis for his published version. Talley's notes suggest this explanation. Talley writes: "Some of the rhymes are very old indeed. If one will but read 'Master Is Six Feet One Way,' found in our collection, he will find in it a description of a slave owner attired in Colonial garb. It clearly belongs, as to date of composition, either to Colonial days, or to the very earliest years of the American Republic. When we consider it as a slave rhyme, it is far from crudest, notwithstanding the early period of its production" (p. 348).

The complicating factor is the reference to Abraham Lincoln ("Linkum gunboats") in both Work's published version and those found in the Federal Writers Project versions. Indeed, the testimony of the formerly enslaved man recorded in *The American Slave: A Composite Autobiography* indicates that the song was "made up" during the Civil War. This does not necessarily contradict Talley since it's very common for new songs to be built on old songs; in short, the basis for the Civil War-era song was older slave songs.

One further note: in consulting all forty-one volumes of *The American Slave: A Composite Autobiography*, I found certain songs mentioned over a wide geographic range. Many were introduced by stories the informants told that made their origin difficult to ascertain.

12. "Old Massa, He Come Dancin' Out" (1860s)

I found this song in John Greenway's *American Folksongs of Protest* (1953). His attribution reads: "Lib. of Cong. Archive American Folk Song, WPA

Collection. Collected by Merton Knowles of Indiana from his mother, who learned and sang the song after the Civil War" (pp. 104–5). I confirmed this information by consulting George Rawick's *The American Slave: A Composite Autobiography* (1972; vol. 5, series 1, Alabama and Indiana), where I also confirmed that Merton Knowles was formerly enslaved (pp. 69, 108–9).

I could not locate the music, so I composed a melody according to styles current at the time.

13. "Agonizing, Cruel Slavery Days" (ca. 1870s)

I originally found two recordings of this song at the Library of Congress. Accompanying the 1/4" tape recording was a note saying the performer of the song was Elijah Cox, who was ninety-three years old. There was no further information. I copied the lyrics from the audio recording.

By chance, I located the text in volume 3, series 2 (Texas) of *The American Slave: A Composite Autobiography* (1972), edited by George Rawick. The entry reads: "Elijah Cox (Uncle Cox) was free-born in Michigan in 1843 and consequently was not a slave. Association with the ex-slaves, however, after he came to Fort Concho in 1871, furnished him with a broad knowledge of slavery days and he wished to contribute the following song which he learned at Fort Concho, having heard the ex-slaves sing it many times, as it was one of their favorite songs" (pp. 952–53).

I made a composite of the lyrics I'd heard on the audio recording with the lyrics Cox recited to the interviewer in *The American Slave*.

14. "The Dirge of St. Malo" (ca. 1785)

I discovered this song in *The Social Implications of Early Negro Music in the United States* (1969), edited by Bernard Katz, in chapter 6 entitled "Dance in the Place Congo and Creole Slave Songs" by George Washington Cable. The editor's note preceding the chapter reads:

> George Washington Cable, a native of New Orleans who fought in the Confederate Army, was forced to leave the South because his writings expressed his distaste for southern postwar mistreatment of the Negro. Cable, Henry Krehbiel, and the irascible, one-eyed poet and writer, Lafcadio Hearn, at one time collected Creole songs in a project that broke up over the mutual distrust of Cable and Hearn. Some of Cable's Creole songs had already appeared in *Slave Songs of the*

United States, nineteen years before the publication of . . . articles in *The Century Magazine*. (p. 54)

This song is only a fragment, presented in both Louisiana Creole and English. Cable's introduction to the song is worth quoting, as he calls on us to notice:

> the stately tone of lamentation over the fate of a famous negro insurrectionist, as sung by old Madeleine of St. Bernard parish to the same Creole friend . . . , who kindly wrote down the lines on the spot for this collection. They are fragmentary, extorted by littles from the shattered memory of the old crone. Their allusion to the Cabildo places their origin in the days when that old colonial council administered Spanish rule over the province. (p. 54)

Juan St. Malo was indeed an "insurrectionist" and a leader of a group of maroons in Spanish Louisiana. An expeditionary force eventually captured St. Malo, And he was executed in New Orleans in 1784. For further information about St. Malo, the best source I found is Gwendolyn Midlo Hall's *Africans in Colonial Louisiana: The Development of Afro-Creole Culture in the Eighteenth Century* (1992). Hall was kind enough to answer my many inquiries about slave songs in Louisiana.

15. "Rebeldia na Bandabou" (ca. 1795)

I discovered this song in Nanette de Jong's *Tambu* (1992), pp. 43–44. It was composed by slaves in Curaçao to celebrate a slave rebellion that occurred in 1795. The song is performed to this day in the language of Papiamentu, a Portuguese-based creole language that is one of the official languages of Curaçao. In English, the title is "Rebellion at Bandabou."

Chapter 4

ABOLITIONIST SONGS
SOURCES AND DOCUMENTATION

I USED THREE MAIN SOURCES FOR THESE SONGS: *THE ANTI-SLAVERY HARP: A Collection of Songs for Anti-Slavery Meetings* (1848), compiled by William Wells Brown; *The Emancipation Car: Being an Original Composition of Anti-Slavery Ballads Composed Exclusively for the Under Ground Rail Road* (1854), compiled by Joshua McCarter Simpson; and *American Anti-Slavery Songs* (1988) by Vicki L. Eaklor. The original publications from which Eaklor compiled nearly five hundred individual songs included the following: *The Genius of Universal Emancipation* (1821–1839), Benjamin Lundy, editor; *The Liberator* (1831–1865), William Lloyd Garrison, editor; *An Appeal in Favor of That Class of Americans Called Africans* (1833) by Lydia Maria Child; *Songs of the Free and Hymns of Christian Freedom* (1836) by Maria Wright Chapman; *Anti-Slavery Melodies* (1843) by Jairus Lincoln; and *The Liberty Minstrel* (1844) by George W. Clark.

Other sources include songs from *The Sacred Harp* (1844), a songbook using shape-note music notation. "Shape-note" is a choral singing tradition originating in the eighteenth century and subsequently popularized throughout New England and the South. In the recording with my collection, songs deriving from this tradition were performed by a shape-note group in Amherst, Massachusetts, under the direction of Professor Tim Eriksen.

At the wise suggestion of a chorus member, the recording of these songs took place at the David Ruggles Center in Florence, Massachusetts. (Ruggles was a famed abolitionist whose former residence now houses the center.) The day of the recording, Eriksen and I discovered on the wall of the center a poem by David Ruggles called "Woman's Rights." Ruggles set his lyrics to a tune in *The Sacred Harp* that was well known by the group called "The Indian Philosopher" or "Ganges." On the spot, we added the song with Ruggles's lyrics to our repertoire.

It should be noted that some of these texts are set to what were known at the time as minstrel songs, "comic negro songs," or "Ethiopian melodies" intended to mock and degrade Black people. Blackface minstrelsy was repudiated by notable figures such as Frederick Douglass, who condemned the lot as "the 'Virginia Minstrels,' 'Christy's Minstrels,' the 'Ethiopian Serenaders,' or any of the filthy scum of white society, who have stolen from us a complexion denied to them by nature, in which to make money, and pander to the corrupt taste of their white fellow-citizens."[1]

"Dandy Jim" was one such tune. It was used by Joshua McCarter Simpson as a setting for "A Song for Freedom." This choice of music served the double purpose of putting a popular tune to abolitionist use and turning a tune perpetuating the enslavement of Black people into a weapon for their emancipation. Simpson explains this choice in the introduction to his *Original Anti-Slavery Songs* (1852), which preceded *The Emancipation Car* by two years:

> In offering my first little production to the public, I am well aware that many superstitious, prejudiced, and perhaps many good, conscientious, well-meaning christians [sic] will have serious objections to the "Airs" to which my poetry is set. My object in my selection of tunes, is to kill the degrading influence of these comic Negro Songs, which are too common among our people, and change the flow of these sweet melodies into more appropriate and useful channels.

The title of each abolitionist song is followed, in parentheses, by the name of the tune to which it is set. In titles of songs, small adjustments have been made to modernize capitalization, spelling, and punctuation. In Part II, the text of lyrics is shown as it appeared in the most authoritative source, with a few obvious typos corrected.

1. "COME JOIN THE ABOLITIONISTS"
   ("WHEN I CAN READ MY TITLE CLEAR")
   - Author unspecified.
   - Found in *The Liberty Minstrel* (1845), compiled by George W. Clark.

2. "WE'RE COMING! WE'RE COMING!"
   ("KINLOCH OF KINLOCH")
   - Author unspecified.
   - Found in *The Anti-Slavery Harp* (1848), compiled by William Wells Brown.

3. "The Underground Railroad"
   ("Nancy Till")
   - Author Joshua McCarter Simpson.
   - Found in *The Emancipation Car* (1854) by Joshua McCarter Simpson.

4. "A Song for Freedom"
   ("Dandy Jim")
   - Author unspecified.
   - Found in *The Anti-Slavery Harp* (1848), compiled by William Wells Brown.

5. "To the White People of America"
   ("Massa's in the Cold, Cold Ground")
   - Author Joshua McCarter Simpson.
   - Found in *The Emancipation Car* (1854) by Joshua McCarter Simpson.

6. "Song of the 'Aliened American'"
   ("America [My Country, 'Tis of Thee]")
   - Author Joshua McCarter Simpson.
   - Found in *The Emancipation Car* (1854) by Joshua McCarter Simpson.

7. "The Voice of Six Hundred Thousand Nominally Free"
   ("The Marseillaise")
   - Author Joshua McCarter Simpson.
   - Found in *The Emancipation Car* (1854) by Joshua McCarter Simpson.

8. "The Band of Thieves"
   ("Scots Wha Hae")
   - Author Joshua McCarter Simpson.
   - Found in *The Emancipation Car* (1854) by Joshua McCarter Simpson.

9. "Flight of the Bondman"
   ("Silver Moon")
   - Author Elias Smith, dedicated to William Wells Brown and sung by the Hutchinsons.
   - Found in *The Anti-Slavery Harp* (1848), compiled by William Wells Brown.

10. "The True Spirit"
   ("Rosin the Bow")
   - Author Joshua McCarter Simpson.
   - Found in *The Emancipation Car* (1854) by Joshua McCarter Simpson.

11. "Right On"
    ("Lenox")
    - Author unspecified.
    - Found in *The Anti-Slavery Harp* (1848), compiled by William Wells Brown.

12. "Woman's Rights"
    ("Ganges/Indian Philosopher")
    - Author David Ruggles.
    - Found on wall at David Ruggles Center, Florence, Massachusetts.

13. "Liberty"
    ("Liberty")
    - Author unknown; composer Stephen Jenks.
    - Found in *The Sacred Harp* (1844).

14. "What Mean Ye?"
    ("Ortonville")
    - Author unspecified.
    - Found in *American Anti-Slavery Songs* (1988) by Vicki L. Eaklor; from various sources, the earliest being Report of the Boston Female Anti-Slavery Society, 1836.

15. "Stole and Sold from Africa"
    (Addie Graham's version)
    - Author unspecified.
    - Found in The Digital Library of Appalachia, Berea College Collection, performed by Addie Graham.

Afterword

THE CONTEMPORARY RELEVANCE OF SONGS OF SLAVERY AND EMANCIPATION

KALI AKUNO
Executive Director of Cooperation Jackson

THE SLAVE SONGS

THE SONGS OF SLAVERY AND EMANCIPATION IN THIS BOOK, SOME WRITTEN more than two hundred years ago, are not only important historically; they have a direct bearing on today's movements for social and economic transformation. When you hear songs like "Nat Turner" or "Hymn of Freedom," it's almost as if they were written yesterday. They bring inspiration and revolutionary clarity to contemporary struggles. One way the songs do this is by challenging fundamental misconceptions. For example, some would have us believe that the Nat Turner rebellion was not a major source of inspiration for the enslaved. Yet, Nat Turner's form of resistance was in fact praised and celebrated by many. It was contemplated and tried many times over in many places and passed on in stories and in songs that were then buried. *Songs of Slavery and Emancipation* is a groundbreaking work because it brings to light this deeper history of unending resistance, which took many forms.

To this day, many people are misled by a false narrative: that Black people, my ancestors, just accepted their fate and didn't resist, when, in fact, the resistance was constant, multifaceted, nuanced, and complex. This resistance shaped reality. That doesn't mean it ended slavery, but resistance changed the terms and conditions of slavery. These songs make this clear, and they relate directly to what W. E. B. Du Bois called "the great strike." Once the Civil War started, the word spread like wildfire. People immediately forged ahead into motion, went into action, and you could hear these songs in the background. *These songs were the soundtrack of that action.* I can imagine somebody running from Tennessee to part of Ohio, or from somewhere in the Carolinas or Virginia or Maryland heading up to Pennsylvania or to New York, singing these songs.

This helps explain why these songs were so dangerous. Not only are they alive, vibrant songs; they speak to specific issues in history: Nat Turner, Gabriel Prosser, the Haitian Revolution, Black soldiers in the Union Army. History is a powerful weapon. Memory is a powerful weapon. Culture is a powerful weapon. And these songs represent all three. If you are trying to keep a subject, captive population in abject poverty and exploitation, you have to remove all the tools of inspiration, all the tools of organizing that they might possess. You have to strip them bare of that.

These songs also remind us of slavery's level of damage and terror. This continued during Reconstruction and the Jim Crow era right up to the explosive rebellions of the 1960s, which unleashed a new culture of resistance.

There have been efforts to mask the viciousness and cruelty of slavery and its aftermath. For example, *Without Sanctuary*, a picture book of lynching photos and postcards that was published in 2000 in a limited edition to expose the brutality against Black people during Reconstruction and into the twentieth century, is now out of print. In the early decades of the twentieth century, those postcards were printed, collected, and mailed around the country. You could buy them at Woolworth's and in little mom and pop stores throughout the South and beyond. The book and the postcards are now difficult and expensive to get, although the "Without Sanctuary" website still makes its collection of images available. Gradually, the systemic horrors perpetrated then against Black people have, for many, faded into "far away and long ago." In order to maintain an apartheid state, those in power have to obscure documentation of the crimes committed to maintain it.

More importantly, it is imperative to bury the signs of resistance. If they are not erased, somebody is going to pick up them up as tools and think "I can do something with this. I'm inspired to do something with this." They *had* to suppress knowledge of this history of resistance, including the music. That removal is ongoing.

The history of the struggle here in Jackson, Mississippi, has been almost erased, from as recently as the 1970s. A lot of the institutions of resistance have been undermined or destroyed, lost funding, and lost resources. So even that recent institutional history and memory of resistance and how to organize have been nearly wiped out. It's not just that these organizations and the activists who formed them have passed on.

The history of the struggle is not taught in any of Jackson's public schools. The school districts and their curricula have intentionally stamped out that history. The state even tried to adopt a Texas textbook that described enslaved people as "workers and immigrants," as if slavery was a voluntary act. The purpose is to obscure history, to deny racism, to deny the settler colonialism aspect of the United States and push the notion everything is fine. The order of things—who's on top, who's on the bottom—is natural, according to that perspective, and should be perpetuated well into the future So this cultural legacy, particularly calling for freedom, calling for rebellion as many of these songs do, had to be wiped out.

The relevance of these songs to young people today is tremendous. The younger generation is reinventing itself. Part of that reinventing is exploring—"Hey let's look at the history of the Sixties and the Twenties and the Thirties and the 1890s and the 1860s." They're going back and looking for material, looking for inspiration, looking for knowledge of how the struggle was carried on, what we can learn from it, what were the positives, what were the negatives, what were the success stories, why did this fail, and why did it not go forward. *Songs of Slavery and Emancipation* will be a core part of that narrative, of speaking to a younger generation that can carry forward this legacy of resistance for our children, my children and grandchildren, into the future. This project, the book, the two CDs, and the film are coming out at the perfect time.

Very consciously and deliberately, a lot of the young folks whom we work with in Cooperation Jackson are attuned to culture in ways that my generation was not. With hip-hop, for example, we viewed it like a lifestyle, "B-boys" and "B-girls" kind of thing. But many young people now are much more focused on music that is not only an embodiment of our culture but is focused on healing. This generation is putting a lot of emphasis on deep healing of trauma. These songs speak not only to that culture of trauma but how people responded to it. They show clearly that these enslaved Africans were deeply brutalized; yet, despite all that dehumanization, they didn't quit, they didn't bow. They found ways to resist and ways to share in a deep quest for liberation that was unbound and unbroken.

THE ABOLITIONIST SONGS

The other inspirational part of this project is the abolitionist songs. There is a new abolitionist movement today, battling current forms of enslavement: mass incarceration and the overall government and corporate surveillance and monitoring—all the ways in which we are criminalized just for being Black, just for being of African descent.

These songs document an abolitionist movement that was out to destroy chattel slavery. In the main, it did not compromise with it, accept it, or merely try to reform it. Unfortunately, much of the dominant narrative, right down to today, has tried to make it seem that the abolitionists represented the general opinion in the North. It pretends that the North was a land of absolute freedom and the South was a land of slavery, and somehow the North was more civilized or more humane because it ended the slave trade or aspects of slavery earlier than the South. When you really look at how the North benefited economically from slavery in the South, it's clear that this is not true in any fundamental respect. The abolitionists challenged the whole social and economic system based on slavery. And while some only wanted to return my ancestors to the African continent, many of them argued that the whole edifice of this country is built on two pillars: stealing land from the Indigenous people and stealing Black bodies, forcing them to work against their will. In effect, they called the foundations of the United States into question.

And, similarly to why the slave resistance songs have been almost forgotten, the abolitionist songs have often been removed from their context. When you obscure this particular history and the broader vision of many abolitionists, you eliminate important aspects of how people who were not enslaved actually lived and practiced in solidarity with folks who were and what they did to try to realize their own humanity.

You can't talk about abolition without talking about the Underground Railroad, how it was organized, and the risks that folks took at every point along the road to help fellow human beings whom they didn't even know. The helpers just knew that these people were enslaved and thus made whatever contribution they could, whether giving food, putting out a blanket, or giving shelter in their homes for however long. They provided transportation in the night, at tremendous risk to themselves, to get the escaping enslaved people from one place to another. There are parallels today with the sanctuary movement supporting the undocumented, a culture that refuses to collaborate with the state or even recognize its authority to deport people desperately seeking refuge.

Drawing upon that history and its parallels today is empowering. There are moments in our collective history when we have found the courage and the organizational means to be effective in organizing resistance against the oppression of the system. That is the critical thing that I think this music will help inspire and energize.

This leads us to the following question: why did certain institutions give this music up? And that is going to take us into some deeper issues around class divisions within our own movements, within our own families, that we have to dig into and interrogate. Instead of ignoring that, we need to expose it because we have some profound issues to deal with right now. Ignoring these songs and refusing to question why this culture of resistance has been lost are consequential mistakes.

In June 2015, Pope Francis issued a strong encyclical on climate justice, calling action on climate change a moral imperative. Based on it, Cooperation Jackson has made the effort to draw in some of our local churches to have a conversation about climate change and the Sixth Extinction (the sixth time the planet is experiencing the mass extinction of species)—an issue that is paramount for us.

That was around the same time that documentaries about the song "Amazing Grace" came out. Even before that, I knew the history of that song, but I found it amazing how many ministers who knew the song word for word did not know that it had a direct relation to slavery and abolition. You begin to see how the narrative of our resistance gets eliminated when even a song like that, a vibrant song that is a part of our civil rights tradition, loses its substantive message and is considered "just an everyday church hymn." No! It has a much deeper meaning, which has been lost in the very churches that sing it. Why? That's a deep question we need to ask ourselves.

Some of it has to do with the growing reactionary political and cultural movement in the US. But there is also the self-deceptive notion that "we made it. The struggle is over. These songs and cultural creations are just relics of a time when things were tough." This kind of blindness is very dangerous, and it has cost us. I've heard so many people say, "I thought we defeated that. I thought that was over." But what makes people think that? Did they forget that the Klan has been around in Alabama and Mississippi and Louisiana the whole time? Have they forgotten David Duke? Are they aware of the roots of these white supremacist militias around the country? It's a kind of amnesia.

The struggle to end chattel slavery was a multinational project, and keeping knowledge of it alive in the public consciousness is very important. People are asking deep questions such as "Can there be multiracial unity in the twenty-first century?" and "Is that possible?" In fact, it exists everywhere, all the time. The real question is whether there is a multiracial movement large enough, powerful enough, organized enough to combat the more reactionary forces. Here again, reviving history that has been obscured is crucial.

History often gets read as if the outlooks of the wealthy and powerful are the dominant views in society at all times. This is untrue. In the forty to fifty years leading up to the Civil War, there was both massive revolt against chattel slavery and stubborn retrenchment by white supremacists and segregationists. There were massive disagreements both within and between the

North and South. But there is still a narrative of the "Solid South" that asserts all white people in the South agreed with and supported slavery. This is a fabrication. Mississippi provides an example. *Free State of Jones*, a 2016 movie, was based on the true story of Blacks and whites uniting against slavery. In fact, there was massive resistance to the power of the enslavers throughout the entire country. Some of it was large in scale, as the movie describes. Some of it was small and minute, like work stoppages or people freeing themselves, running away, sometimes twenty or thirty times. The lashes they received are seen in photos from the period. But actual stories like that told in *Free State of Jones* are hidden. Many people in this country have never heard of it. There was even controversy around that movie and whether it was going to be shown in Mississippi. Efforts to censor this movie, the open debates about whether it should be shown, and discussions of whether it was appropriate or revisionist history are a matter of public record. The history of the actual episode is also, but we have to know where to look for it.

Songs of Slavery and Emancipation brings a whole era of resistance forward into the twenty-first century. To forget the lessons of the revolt and rebellion of the enslaved or the organizing of the abolitionist networks and the Underground Railroad is to condemn people to the false belief that because one of us is Black and the other is white we can't unite, we don't have anything in common, and we can't work together. And this goes for people of all ethnicities, places of origin, and genders.

We must not forget this history. These songs can make an important contribution. They provide a popular art form that can help people understand all Americans' history and participate in our contemporary struggles. *Songs of Slavery and Emancipation* carries crucial history that enlivens our collective memory and helps keep the spirit of resistance strong and moving forward.

Part II

LYRICS

SLAVE SONGS
IN HISTORICAL SEQUENCE

1. 1784: The Dirge of St. Malo

2. 1795: Rebeldia na Bandabou

3. 1800: Uncle Gabriel, the Negro General

4. 1813: Hymn of Freedom

5. 1820: The Negro's Complaint

6. 1820: Recognition March of the Independance of Hayti

7. 1820s: The African Hymn

8. 1831: Nat Turner

9. 18??: We'll Soon Be Free/My Father, How Long?

10. 18??: March On

11. 18??: Children, We All Shall Be Free

12. 1863: The Enlisted Soldiers, or The Negro Battle Hymn

13. 1864: Old Massa, He Come Dancin' Out

14. 1865: The Year of Jubalo, Year of Jubilo, and Kingdom Coming

15. 1870s: Agonizing, Cruel Slavery Days

Note: Songs 9, 10, and 11 could be as recent as the 1860s.

THE DIRGE OF ST. MALO

Source: *The Social Implications of Early Negro Music in the United States* (1969), edited by Bernard Katz, in chapter 6, "Dance in the Place Congo and Creole Slave Songs" by George Washington Cable, originally published in *The Century Magazine* (XXXI, February 1886, pp. 517–32, and April 1886, pp. 807–23).

Ourrà St. Malo

Aie! zein zens vini fé ouarrà,
Pou Pov St. Malo dans l'embas!
Yé, çassé li avec yé chien,
Yé tiré li ein coup d'fizi.
  .   .   .   .
Yé halé li la cypriére,
So bras yé 'tassé par derrier.
Yé tassé so la main divant,
Yé marré li apé queue choual.
Yé trainein li zouqu'à tout yé blancs.
Yé mandé li qui so compéres.
Pov St. Malo resté pendi!
Zize là li lir' so la sentence,
Et pis li fé dressé potence.
Yé halé choual—çarette parti—
Pov St. Malo resté pendi!
Eine hér soleil deza leveé
Yé laissé so corps balancé
Pou carenco gagnein manzé.

Alas! young men, come make lament
For poor St. Malo in distress!
They chased, they hunted him with dogs,
They fired at him with a gun,
  .   .   .   .
They hauled him from the cypress swamp
His arms they tied behind his back,
They tied his hands in front of him;
They tied him to a horse's tail,
They dragged him up into the town.

Before the grand Cabildo men
They charged that he had made a plot
To cut the throats of all the whites
They asked him who his comrades were;
Poor St. Malo said not a word!
The judge his sentence read to him,
And then they raised the gallows-tree.
They drew the horse—the cart moved off—
And left St. Malo hanging there.
The sun was up an hour high
When on the Levee he was hung;
They left his body swinging there,
For carrion crows to feed upon.

REBELDIA NA BANDABOU

In English translation from Papiamento, "Rebellion at Bandabou."
Source: Nanette de Jong, *Tambu*, pp. 43–44.
Song composed by slaves in Curaçao to celebrate a slave rebellion that occurred in 1795. Song performed to this day by Grupo Trinchera under the direction of Rene Rosalia.
See also: https://www.youtube.com/watch?v=91be4jJBU2U.

(Deklarashon introduktorio)

August 17th when the bell rang

(Habri-Pregon)

There was much tension at Knip (plantation)
The slaves have decided today,
Things will end.
Slaves have decided today:
Liberty will start.
When the bell sounded
There was much tension at Knip.
The slaves have reunited,
And together have decided,
Today there will be rebellion at
Bandabou.

(Serà-Coro with Pregon)

Rebellion at Bandabou.
   At the head there is a captain,
Rebellion at Bandabou.
   Captain Tula is in command.
Rebellion at Bandabou.
   At his side is Pedro Wacao.
Rebellion at Bandabou.
   Luis Mercer is also fighting.
Rebellion at Bandabou.
   Just at the side there is Sablika.
Rebellion at Bandabou.

Men in rebellion,
Rebellion at Bandabou.
Women also in fight.

(Habri-Pregon)

Tambu player come with me
To Porto Marie!
Come with me to
Niger hill!
Barricade at Niger hill!
Pastor Schink wants to break up
the fight
With the Bible or bayonet.
Liberty for everybody!
Break the bell to stop it from
sounding.
Oh mama, rebellion at
Bandabou!

UNCLE GABRIEL, THE NEGRO GENERAL

Sources: Lawrence Gellert, published in *Mainstream*, Vol. 16, No. 2 (February), 1963, p. 19; and *Ethiopian Glee Book*, Christy Minstrels, 1849, p. 120.

1. Oh my boys I'm bound to tell you,
   CHORUS: Oh! Oh!
   Listen a while and I will tell you,
   CHORUS: Oh! Oh!
   I will tell you little 'bout Uncle Gabriel, Oh! boys I've just began
   CHORUS: Hard times in Old Virginia

2. Oh don't you know Old Uncle Gabriel,
   CHORUS: Oh! Oh!
   Oh! he were that old slave General,
   CHORUS: Oh! Oh!
   He war de Chief of de Insurgents,
   Way down in Southampton
   CHORUS: Hard times in Old Virginia

3. 'Twas a little boy betrayed him,
   CHORUS: Oh! Oh!
   A little boy they call Daniel
   CHORUS: Oh! Oh!
   Betrayed him at de Norfolk landing,
   Oh! boys I'm gettin' done
   CHORUS: Hard times in Old Virginia

4. Says he, "Good day Uncle Gabriel."
   CHORUS: Oh! Oh!
   "I am not your Uncle Gabriel,
   CHORUS: Oh! Oh!
   My name it is Jim McCullen.
   Some dey calls me Archey Mullin."
   CHORUS: Hard times in Old Virginia.

5. The whites dey fought and caught him,
   CHORUS: Oh! Oh!
   And to Richmond Court House brought him,
   CHORUS: Oh! Oh!

Twelve men sot upon that jury,
Oh! boys I'm most done,
CHORUS: Hard times in Old Virginia.

6. They promise his life they give him
    CHORUS: Oh! Oh!
If he name white folks with him
    CHORUS: Oh! Oh!
But he ain't even listen, Oh
boys I reckon he 'bout done
CHORUS: Hard times in old Virginia.

7. Dey took him down to de Gallows,
    CHORUS: Oh! Oh!
Dey drive him down, wid four grey horses,
    CHORUS: Oh! Oh!
Brice's Ben, he drove de waggon,
Oh! boys, I'm most done.
CHORUS: Hard times in Old Virginia.

8. And dare dey hung him and dey swung him,
    CHORUS: Oh! Oh!
And dey swung him and dey hung him,
    CHORUS: Oh! Oh!
That was the end of General Gabriel,
Oh! boys I'm just done.
CHORUS: Hard times in Old Virginia.

HYMN OF FREEDOM

Sung to the tune of "Hail Columbia." "Sung by the Negroes on the island opposite Charleston, during the late War with Britain [War of 1812] composed by one of themselves." Presented here in 1813 version.

Hail! Hail! ye Afric clan
Hail! ye oppressed, ye Afric band,
Who toil and sweat in Slavery bound;
(Repeated)

And when your health & strength are gone
Are left to hunger & to mourn.
Let *Independence* be your aim,
Ever mindful what 'tis worth.
Pledge your bodies for the prize
Pile them even to the skies!
    Chorus
    Firm, united let us be,
    Resolved on death or liberty
    As a band of Patriots joined
    Peace & Plenty we shall find.

Look to Heaven with manly trust
And swear by Him that's always just
That no white foe with impious hand
(Repeated)
Shall slave your wives & daughters more
Or rob them of their virtue dear.
Be armed with valor firm & true,
Their hopes are fixed on Heaven & you
That truth & justice will prevail
And every scheme of bondage fail.
    Chorus
    Firm, united &c…

Arise! Arise! shake off your chains
Your cause is just, so Heaven ordains
to you shall Freedom be proclaimed.
(Repeated)

Raise your arms & bare your breasts,
Almighty God will do the rest.
Blow the clarion! a warlike blast!
Call every Negro from his task!
Wrest the scourge from Buckra's hand,
And drive each tyrant from the land,
  Chorus
   Firm, united &c..

THE NEGRO'S COMPLAINT

Sung to the tune of "Old Hundred."
Written by Rev. Thomas Cooper (ca. 1775–ca. 1823) from *The African Pilgrim's Hymns* (1820).
Source: John Lovell, *Black Song: The Forge and the Flame*, pp. 106–7.

Great God dost thou from heav'n above
View all mankind with equal love?
Why dost thou hide thy face from slaves,
Confin'd by fate to serve the knaves?

When stole and bought from Africa,
Transported to America,
Like the brute beasts in market sold,
To stand the heat and feel the cold.

To stand the lash and feel the pain,
Expos'd to stormy snow and rain.
To work all day and half the night,
And rise before the morning light! . . .

Although our skin be black as jet,
Our hair be friz'd and noses flat,
Shall we for that no freedom have,
Until we find it in the grave.

Hath heav'n decreed that Negroes must,
By wicked men be ever curs'd
Nor e'er enjoy our lives like men,
But ever drag the gauling chain.

When will Jehovah hear our cries,
When will the sons of freedom rise,
When will for us a Moses stand,
And free us from a Pharaoh's land.

RECOGNITION MARCH OF THE INDEPENDANCE OF HAYTI

The cover of the sheet music for "Recognition March of the Independance [*sic*] of Hayti" tells us this music was composed "for the occasion" and is "Dedicated to President J.P. Boyer." Presumably, the "occasion" was a celebration or commemoration of President Jean-Pierre Boyer's declaration, on October 20, 1820, reuniting the north and south of the country into the Republic of Haiti. The variant spellings of words reflect the evolution English spelling was undergoing at this time. Webster's first dictionary, for example, was published in 1828 in an attempt to establish American English as a language distinct from its parent, with simplified and phonetic spellings of many words. The name of the country of Haiti similarly underwent changes in spelling until finally settling in its current form.

The composition is notable for several reasons, not the least of which is that it is rarely mentioned in accounts of Francis Johnson's illustrious career. In fact, the only mention of it I could find was in a listing of Johnson's compositions compiled by Professor Dominique-René de Lerma (1928–2015). De Lerma was a noted musicologist and leading researcher of Johnson's life and work. Even in this rare instance, it appears de Lerma was only aware of the existence of the work since he dates its composition "circa 1804." Yet, as noted above, the march could not have been written before at least 1818 when J. P. Boyer first became president of a part of Haiti. Since it was 1820 when Boyer successfully united the whole country, it is much more likely that it was at that date or sometime shortly thereafter that Johnson would have written and dedicated his march.

THE AFRICAN HYMN

Written by the Reverend Shadrack Bassett. "The lyrics were more prophetic than the slaves in northern Virginia could have known," according to Stephen B. Oates in *The Fires of Jubilee: Nat Turner's Fierce Rebellion*, pp. 133–34.

>We shall not always weep and groan
>And wear these slavish chains of woe,
>There's a better day that's coming
>Come and go along with me.
>
>Good Lord, O when shall slavery cease
>And these poor souls enjoy their peace,
>Good Lord, break the power.
>Come and go along with me.
>
>O! come, ye Africans, be wise
>We'll join the armies in the skies!
>We'll ruin Satan's kingdom
>Come and go along with me.
>
>King Jesus now comes riding in,
>He bids his army sound again.
>They will ruin Satan's kingdom
>Come and go along with me.
>
>I will pursue my journey's end,
>For Jesus Christ is still my friend,
>O, may this friend go with me.
>Come and go along with me—
>Go sound the Jubilee.

NAT TURNER

Also known as "Gainin' Ground."
Source: collected by Lawrence Gellert and published in *Mainstream*, vol. 16, no. 2, February 1963, pp. 20–21.
Referred to by Pete Seeger, Russell Ames, and John Greenway.
Ames contributes an additional verse in *Story of American Folksong*, p. 151. It appears with the heading "Virginia 1831" below the three main verses in the lyrics. Ames writes: "With the tightening of all restrictions on them (the slaves) after the rebellion, any singing about Nat Turner had to be well disguised. A song about him has survived, in which there was humorous satire on the masters, who allowed it as kings once allowed jokes on themselves by court fools and jesters, mixed with a pun on Nat Turner's name and veiled references to revolution and change."

>You mought be rich as cream,
>And drive you coach and four horse team;
>But you can't keep the World from moverin' round,
>Nor Nat Turner from gaining ground.
>
>You mought be reader and writer too
>And wiser'n Old Solomon the Jew
>But you can't keep the World from moverin' 'round,
>Nor Nat Turner from gainin' ground.
>
>And your name it mought be Caesar sure
>And got you cannon can shoot a mile or more
>But you can't keep the World from moverin' 'round
>Nor Nat Turner from gainin' ground.
>
>   Virginia 1831
>
>You mought be a Carroll from Carrollton,
>Arrive here night afo' Lawd make creation,
>But you can't keep the world from moverin' around
>And not turn her back from the gaining ground.

WE'LL SOON BE FREE/MY FATHER, HOW LONG?

There are two versions of the same song. The first was in Thomas Wentworth Higginson's *Army Life in a Black Regiment* (p. 169, XXXIV). He described it as follows: "For singing this the negroes had been put in jail in Georgetown, S.C., at the outbreak of the Rebellion. 'We'll soon be free' was too dangerous an assertion, and though the chant was an old one, it was no doubt sung with redoubled emphasis during the new events. 'De Lord will call us home' was evidently thought to be a symbolical verse; for, as a little drummer boy explained it to me, showing all his white teeth as he sat in the moonlight by the door of my tent, 'Dey tink *de Lord* mean for say *de Yankees*.'"

The second version is from *Slave Songs of the United States*, section IV, #112. I made a composite lyric; the music is based on that provided in *Slave Songs of the United States*.

> My father, how long,
> My father, how long,
> My father, how long,
>   'Fore we done sufferin' here?
>
> My mother, how long,
> My mother, how long,
> My mother, how long,
>   'Fore we done sufferin' here?
>
> It won't be long (thrice)
>   'Fore de Lord will call us home
>
> We'll soon be free (Thrice)
>   When Jesus sets me free.
>
> We'll fight for liberty (Thrice)
>   When de Lord will call us home.

MARCH ON

Discovered in *The Story of the Jubilee Singers with Their Songs* by J. B. T. Marsh (No. 44, p. 166).
Song referred to by both John Lovell in *Black Song: The Forge and the Flame* and John Wesley Work in *Folk Song of the American Negro*. These references were, however, not complete, and it was only with *The Story of the Jubilee Singers* that I could locate both full text and tablature.

>   Way over in the Egypt land,
>   You shall gain the victory
>   Way over in the Egypt land,
>   You shall gain the day
>
>   Chorus
>   March on, and you shall gain the victory
>   March on, and you shall gain the day
>
>   When Peter was preaching at the Pentecost
>   You shall gain the victory
>   He was endowed with the Holy Ghost
>   You shall gain the day
>
>   Chorus
>
>   When Peter was flashing in the Sea
>   You shall gain the victory
>   He dropped his net and followed me
>   You shall gain the day
>
>   Chorus
>
>   King Jesus on the mountain top
>   You shall gain the victory
>   King Jesus speaks and the chariot stops
>   You shall gain the day
>
>   Chorus

I later located a version of the song collected by Lawrence Gellert and published in *Negro: An Anthology* (1934) edited by Nancy Cunard and Hugh D. Ford. That text reads:

Oh brethren rise, give praise to glory
For the year of the Jubilee
Do you want to be a soldier
For the year of the Jubilee

Oh what you say brother
Oh what you say brother
Oh what you say brother
About dis wahr

I will die in the field
Stay in the field
Stay in the field brother
Stay in the field
Until the victory
March on and you shall gain the victory
March on an you shall gain the day

We want no cowards in our band
We call for only the strongest men

I intend to fight and never stop
Until I reach mountain top

CHILDREN, WE ALL SHALL BE FREE

Discovered in *The Story of the Jubilee Singers with Their Songs* by J. B. T. Marsh (No. 6, p. 130).
Song referred to by both John Lovell in *Black Song: The Forge and the Flame* and John Wesley Work in *Folk Song of the American Negro*.

Children, we all shall be free
Children, we all shall be free
Children, we all shall be free
When the Lord shall appear

We want no cowards in our band
That from their colors fly
We call for valiant hearted men
That are not afraid to die

Chorus

We see the pilgrim as he lies
With glory in his soul
To Heaven he lifts his longing eyes
And bids this world adieu

Chorus

Give ease to the sick, give sight to the blind
Enable the cripple to walk
He'll raise the dead from under the earth
And give them permission to fly

Chorus

THE ENLISTED SOLDIERS, OR THE NEGRO BATTLE HYMN

Sung by the men of the US Colored Volunteers.
Source: *Cabin and Plantation Songs as Sung by the Hampton Students* (1901), p. 145.

>   Hark! listen to the trumpeters,
>   They call for volunteers,
>   On Zion's bright and flow'ry mount,
>   Behold the officers.
>
>   *Refrain:* They look like men,
>   they look like men,
>   they look like men of war;
>   All armed and dressed in uniform,
>   They look like men of war.
>
>   Their horses white
>   their armor bright
>   With courage bold they stand,
>   Enlisting soldiers for their King,
>   To march to Canaan's land.
>
>   *Ref.*
>
>   It sets my heart quite in a flame
>   A soldier thus to be,
>   I will enlist, gird on my arms,
>   And fight for liberty.
>
>   *Ref.*
>
>   We want no cowards in our band,
>   That will their colors fly;
>   We call for valiant hearted men,
>   Who're not afraid to die.
>
>   *Ref.*

To see our armies on parade
How martial they appear,
All armed and dressed in uniform
They look like men of war.

Ref.

They follow their great General,
The great Eternal Lamb,
His garment stained in His own blood,
King Jesus is His name.

Ref.

The trumpets sound, the armies shout,
They drive the host of Hell,
How dreadful is our God to adore,
The great Immanuel.

Ref.

OLD MASSA, HE COME DANCIN' OUT

Source: *American Folksongs of Protest*, Library of Congress Archive, American Folk Song, WPA Collection, pp. 104–5. Collected by Merton Knowles of Indiana from his mother, who learned and sang the song after the Civil War.

Old massa he come dancin' out
An' he call de blackuns round.
He pleased so well dat he couldn't stand
Wid both feet on de ground.

You, Pomp and Pete and Dinah, too,
You'll catch it now, I swear.
I'll whip you good for mixin' wid
De Yanks when dey was here.

Say, don't you hear dem 'tillery guns,
You niggers, don't you hear?
Ole General Bragg is a mowin' 'em down,
Dem Yankees ober here.

Dar comes our troops in crowds and crowds,
I knows dat red and gray,
But oh! What makes dem hurry so
And trow dere guns away?

Ole massa now keep both feet still
And stare with bofe his eyes.
Till he see de blue coats jest behind
Dat take him wid surprise.

Ole massa busy wadin' round
In swamps up to his knees,
While Dinah, Pomp, and Pete dey look
As if dey mighty pleased.

THE YEAR OF JUBALO, YEAR OF JUBILO, AND KINGDOM COMING

Source: *American Folksongs of Protest*, p. 104. Informant: Merton Knowles, WPA project worker: "Heard it from my mother, it was brought back by returning Union soldiers, and became a part of our folklore." In Library of Congress, Archive of American Folk Song, Indiana. Authenticated by E. Southern, "Greenwood Encyclopedia Black Music," p. 222.

Song so closely resembles "Kingdom Coming" (1862) by abolitionist Henry Clay Work that it is likely to have been brought by Union soldiers to newly liberated slaves who, in turn, made it their own.

This conclusion is supported by finding the song with different lyrics in Vol. 3, Series 2 (Texas) of *The American Slave: A Composite Autobiography*, contributed by Lorenzo Ezell, a former slave from Beaumont, Texas, District 3 (see Ezell's comment with lyrics below).

Here are all three versions of the song: Merton Knowles's version, Lorenzo Ezell's version, and Henry Clay Work's version. Note the different spelling of the word Jubalo/Jubilo.

THE YEAR OF JUBALO

Has anybody seen my massa
With the moustache on his face?
Go long the road some time this mornin'
Like he gwine to leab de place.

REFRAIN:
De massa run, ha! ha!
De darky stay, ho! ho!
It must be now dat de kingdom am a comin'
And de year of jubalo.

He seed a smoke way up de ribber
Where de Linkum gunboats lay;
He took his hat and he left mighty sudden,
And I speck dat he runned away.

He six feet one way, two feet todder,
And he weigh three hundred pound;
His coat so big dat he can't pay de tailor,
An' it won't go half-way around.

De oberseer he gib us trubble
An de dribe us round a spell,
Den we lock him up in the smoke house cellar,
Wid de key throwed in de well.

De whip am lost and de handcuff broken,
An' mass'll get him pay.
He old enough, big enough, out to know better,
Dan to take an' runned away.

YEAR OF JUBILO

Lorenzo Ezell's version. Ezell stated: "My ol' marster run off and stay in de woods a whole week w'en Sherman men come t'rough. He didn' need to worry 'cause us tek care of eb'ryt'ing. Dey was a funny song w'at us mek up 'bout him runnin' off in de woods. I know it was mek up 'cause my uncle hab ahn' in it. It went like dis."

> W'ite folks hab you seed ol' marster
> Up de road wid he mustache on?
> He pick up he hat and he lef' real sudden
> And I b'leeb he's up and gone.
>
> He seed a smoke way up de ribber
> Where de Linkum gunboats lay;
> He took his hat and he left mighty sudden,
> And I speck dat he runned away.
>
> Chorus
> De massa run, ha! ha!
> Us darkies stay, ho! ho!
> It must be now dat de kingdom am a comin'
> And de year of jubalo
>
> He six foot one way, two foot tudder, and he weigh tree hundred pound
> His coat so big, he couldn't pay the tailor, an' it won't go halfway round
> He drill so much dey call him Cap'n, an' he got so dreffel tanned
> I spec' he try an' fool dem Yankees for to tink he's contraband
>
> Chorus
>
> Us black folks feel so lonesome libbing in de loghouse on de lawn
> We move ar tings into massa's parlor for to keep it while he's gone
> Dar's wine an' cider in de kitchen, an' I guess now we'll have some;
> I s'pose dey'll all be cornfiscated when de Linkum sojers come
>
> Chorus

De obserseer he make us trouble, an' he dribe us round a spell;
We lock him up in de smokehouse cellar, wid de key trown in de well
De whip is lost, de han'cuff broken, but de massa'll hab his pay;
He's ole enough, big enough, ought to known better dan to went an' run away

KINGDOM COMING

Henry Clay Work's version of 1862.

Say, darkies, hab you seen de massa, wid de muffstash on his face
Go long de road some time dis mornin', like he gwine to leab de place?
He seen a smoke way up de ribber, whar de Linkum gunboats lay;
He took his hat, and lef' berry sudden, and I spec' he's run away!

CHORUS: De massa run, ha, ha! De darkey stay, ho, ho!
It mus' be now de kindom coming, an' de year ob Jubilo!

He six foot one way, two foot tudder, and he weigh tree hundred pound
His coat so big, he couldn't pay the tailor, an' it won't go halfway round
He drill so much dey call him Cap'n, an' he got so drefful tanned
I spec' he try an' fool dem Yankees for to tink he's contraband

CHORUS

De darkeys feel so lonesome libbing in de loghouse on de lawn
Dey move dar tings into massa's parlor for to keep it while he's gone
Dar's wine an' cider in de kitchen, an' de darkeys dey'll have some;
I s'pose dey'll all be cornfiscated when de Linkum sojers come

CHORUS

De obserseer he make us trouble, an' he dribe us round a spell;
We lock him up in de smokehouse cellar, wid de key trown in de well
De whip is lost, de han'cuff broken, but de massa'll hab his pay;
He's ole enough, big enough, ought to known better dan to went an' run away

CHORUS

AGONIZING, CRUEL SLAVERY DAYS

Library of Congress audio recording, lyrics transcribed. Further lyrics discovered in *The American Slave: A Composite Autobiography*, vol. 3, series 2 (Texas), pp. 952–53.

I am thinking today 'bout the times passed away,
When they tied me up in bondage long ago.
In old Virginia state, is where we separate.
And it fills my heart with misery and woe.
They took away my boy who was his mother's joy.
A baby from the cradle him we raised.
Then they put us far apart and it broke the old man's heart,
In those agonizing, cruel slavery days.

Chorus
Though they'll never come again let us give our praise to Him.
Who looks down where the little children play.
Every night and morn' we'll pray for them that's gone.
In those agonizing cruel slavery days.

At night when all is dark. We hear the watch dog bark
and listen to the murmurs of the wind.
It seemed to say to me, you people must be free.
For the happy 'times are comin' Lord we pray.
My memory will steal o'er that dear old cabin floor and
in the shadows find those passed away
And for them we'll weep and mourn
For our souls were not our own
In those agonizing cruel slavery days.

Repeat Chorus

I'm very old and feeble now my hair is turning gray.
I have traveled o'er the roughest kinds of roads.
Through all the toils and sorrows I have reached the end at last.
Now I'm resting by the way-side with my load.
Forget now and forgive has always been my guide.
For that's what the Golden Scripture says.

But my memory will turn 'round back to when I was tied down,
In those agonizing cruel slavery days.

Repeat Chorus

ABOLITIONIST SONGS
BY COLLECTION

The Anti-Slavery Harp (1848)
1. We're Coming! We're Coming!
2. A Song for Freedom
3. Flight of the Bondman
4. Right On

The Emancipation Car (1854)
5. The Underground Railroad
6. To the White People of America
7. Song of the "Aliened American"
8. The Voice of Six Hundred Thousand Nominally Free
9. The Band of Thieves
10. The True Spirit

The Liberty Minstrel (1845)
11. Come Join the Abolitionists

David Ruggles Center
12. Woman's Rights

The Sacred Harp (1844)
13. Liberty

American Anti-Slavery Songs (1836)
14. What Mean Ye?

Digital Library of Appalachia, Berea College Collection
15. Stole and Sold from Africa

WE'RE COMING! WE'RE COMING!

Sung to tune of "Kinloch of Kinloch" (traditional).
Source: *The Anti-Slavery Harp* by William Wells Brown.
Author: George W. Clark.

> We're coming, we're coming, the fearless and free,
> Like the winds of the desert, the waves of the sea!
> True sons of brave sires who battled of yore,
> When England's proud lion ran wild on our shore!
> We're coming, we're coming, from mountain and glen,
> With hearts to do battle for freedom again;
> Oppression is trembling as trembled before
> The slavery which fled from our fathers of yore.
>
> We're coming, we're coming, with banners unfurled,
> Our motto is FREEDOM, our country the world;
> Our watchword is LIBERTY—tyrants beware!
> For the liberty army will bring you despair!
> We're coming, we're coming, we'll come from afar,
> Our standard we'll nail to humanity's car;
> With shoutings we'll raise it, in triumph to wave,
> A trophy of conquest, or shroud for the brave.
>
> Then arouse ye, brave hearts, to the rescue come on!
> The man-stealing army we'll surely put down;
> They are crushing their millions, but soon they must yield,
> For *freemen* have *risen* and taken the field.
> Then arouse ye! arouse ye! the fearless and free,
> Like the winds of the desert, the waves of the sea;
> Let the north, west, and east, to the sea-beaten shore,
> *Resound* with a *liberty triumph* once more.

A SONG FOR FREEDOM

Sung to tune of "Dandy Jim"—no known composer, published 1844 by A. Fiot (Philadelphia).
Source: *The Anti-Slavery Harp* (1848).
Author: unspecified.

    Come all ye bondmen far and near,
    Let's put a song in massa's ear,
    It is a song for our poor race,
    Who're whipped and trampled with disgrace.

    Chorus:
    My old massa tells me O
    This is a land of freedom O;
    Let's look about and see if 'tis so,
    Just as massa tells me O

    He tells us of that glorious one,
    I think his name is Washington,
    How he did fight for liberty,
    To save a threepence tax on tea.
    Chorus:

    And then he tells us that there was
    A Constitution, with this clause,
    That all men equal are created,
    How often have we heard it stated.
    Chorus:

    But now we look about and see,
    That we poor blacks are not so free;
    We're whipped and thrashed about like fools,
    And have no chance at common schools.
    Chorus: Still, my old massa &

    They take our wives, insult and mock,
    And sell our children on the block,
    Then choke us if we say a word,
    And say that "niggers" shan't be heard.
    Chorus: Still, my old massa &

FLIGHT OF THE BONDMAN

In original: "Dedicated to William W. Brown, and sung by the Hutchinsons (Silver Moon)."
Source: *The Anti-Slavery Harp* (1848).
Author: Elias Smith.
Composer: "Roll On, Silver Moon," Jane Sloman, 1841 (adapted by Mat Callahan).

> From the crack of the rifle and baying of hound,
> Takes the poor panting bondman his flight;
> His couch through the day is the cold damp ground,
> But northward he runs through the night.
>
> Chorus;
>
> O, God speed the flight of the desolate slave,
> Let his heart never yield to despair;
> There is room 'mong our hills for the true and the brave,
> Let his lungs breathe our free northern air!
>
> O, sweet to the storm-driven sailor the light,
> Streaming far o'er the dark swelling wave;
> But sweeter by far 'mong the lights of the night,
> Is the star of the north to the slave.
>
> Chorus:
>
> Cold and bleak are our mountains and chilling our winds,
> But warm as the soft southern gales
> Be the hands and the hearts which the hunted one finds,
> 'Mong our hills and our own winter vales.
>
> Chorus:
>
> Then list to the 'plaint of the heart-broken thrall,
> Ye blood-hounds, go back to your lair;
> May free northern soil soon give freedom to *all*,
> Who shall breathe in its pure mountain air.
>
> Chorus:

RIGHT ON

Sung to tune of "Lenox" by Lewis Edson (1782).
Source: *The Anti-Slavery Harp*.
Author: unspecified.

> Ho! children of the brave,
>   Ho! freemen of the land,
> That hurl'd into the grave
>   Oppression's bloody band;
> Come on, come on, and joined be we
> To make the fettered bondman free.
>
> Let coward vassals sneak
>   From freedom's battle still,
> Poltroons that dare not speak
>   But a their priests may will;
> Come on, come on, and joined be we
> To make the fettered bondman free.
>
> On parchment, scroll and creed,
>   With human life blood red,
> Untrembling at the deed,
>   Plant firm your manly tread;
> The priest may howl, the jurist rave,
> But we will free the fettered slave.
>
> The tyrant's scorn is vain,
>   In vain the slanderer's breath,
> We'll rush to break the chain,
>   E'en on the jaws of death;
> Hurrah! Hurrah! right on go we,
> The fettered slave shall yet be free.
>
> Right on, in freedom's name,
>   And in the strength of God,
> Wipe out the damning stain,
>   And break the oppressor's rod;
> Hurrah! Hurrah! right on go we,
> The fettered slave shall yet be free.

THE UNDERGROUND RAILROAD

Sung to tune of "Nancy Till" (traditional).
Source: *The Emancipation Car* (1854), pp. 147–48.
Author: Joshua McCarter Simpson.

> Don't you hear the steam cars,
>   Don't you hear them hum?
> Get your hat and shoes on—
>   Be ready when they come.
> Master's fast asleep now—
>   I hope he'll not awake;
> For here's an invitation now
>   To go across the Lake.
>
> Chorus
> Come boys, come, and go along with me,
> And I'll take you up where colored men are free
> Come, boys, come—make no delay,
> And I'll take you up to Canada.
>
> I hear old master say,
>   Just a day or two ago,
> That he was going to sell us all,
>   Down to "'Tucky ho;"
> But here's the Underground Horse,
>   A very noble nag;
> "A free ride to colored men,"
>   Is written on his flag.
>
> The Underground Railroad,
>   Is a queer machine;
> It carries many passengers,
>   And never has been seen,
> Old master goes to Baltimore,
>   And mistress goes away,
> And when they see their slaves again
>   They're all in Canada.

Uncle Sam has tried hard
    To find the mystic route;
But well do our engineers
    Know what they are about.
While he is sleeping soundly,
    They are wide awake,
And firing up the engine,
    That runs across the Lake.

The Underground Railroad
    Is doing mighty well;
The number of her passengers
    Is very hard to tell.
When once they ship for Canada,
    It's hard to bring them back,
For "Johnny" runs a strong race,
    And never flies the track.

TO THE WHITE PEOPLE OF AMERICA

Sung to tune of "Massa's in the Cold, Cold Ground" by Stephen C. Foster (1852).
Source: *The Emancipation Car* (1854), pp. 13–14.
Author: Joshua McCarter Simpson.

O'er this wide extended country,
Hear the solemn echoes roll,
For a long and weary century,
Those cries have gone from pole to pole;
See the white man sway his sceptre,
In one hand he holds the rod—
In the other hand the Scripture,
And says that he's a man of God.

Hear ye that mourning?
'Tis your brothers' cry!
O! ye wicked men take warning,
The day will come when you must die.

Lo! Ten thousand steeples shining
Through this mighty Christian land,
While four millions slaves all pining
And dying 'neath the Tyrant's hand.
See the "blood-stained" Christian banner
Followed by a host of saints
While they loudly sing Hosannah,
We hear the dying slave's complaints:

Hear ye that mourning?
Anglo-sons of God,
O! ye Hypocrites take warning,
And shun your sable brothers blood.

In our Legislative members,
Few there are with humane souls,
Though they speak in tones of thunder
'Gainst sins which they cannot control,
Women's rights and annexation,

Is the topic by the way,
While poor Africa's sable nation
For mercy, cry both by night and day.

Hear ye that mourning?
'Tis a solemn sound,
O! ye wicked men take warning,
For God will send his judgment down.

Tell us not of distant Island—
Never will we colonize:
Send us not to British Highlands,
For this is neither just nor wise,
Give us equal rights and chances,
All the rights of citizens—
And as light and truth advances,
We'll show you that we all are men.

Hear ye that mourning?
'Tis your brothers sigh,
O! ye wicked men take warning,
The judgment day will come by and by.

SONG OF THE "ALIENED AMERICAN"

Sung to tune of "America (My Country, 'Tis of Thee)," traditional melody derived by lyricist Samuel Frances Smith from "God Save the Queen."
Source: *The Emancipation Car* (1854), pp. 17–18.
Author: Joshua McCarter Simpson.

My country, 'tis of thee,
Dark land of Slavery,
   In thee we groan,
Long have our chains been worn—
Long has our grief been borne—
Our flesh has long been torn,
   E'en from our bones.

The white man rules the day—
He bears despotic sway,
   O'er all the land.
He wields the Tyrant's rod,
Fearless of man or God,
And at his impious nod,
   We "fall or stand."

O! shall we longer bleed?
Is there no one to plead
   The black man's cause?
Does justice thus demand
That we shall wear the brand,
And raise not voice nor hand
   Against such laws?

No! no! the time has come,
When we must not be dumb,
   We must awake.
We now "Eight Millions Strong,"
Must strike sweet freedom's song
And lease ourselves, our wrong—
   Our chains must break.

THE VOICE OF SIX HUNDRED THOUSAND NOMINALLY FREE

Sung to tune of "The Marseillaise" by Claude-Joseph Rouget de Lisle (1792).
Source: *The Emancipation Car* (1854), pp. 27–28.
Author: Joshua McCarter Simpson.

Come, friends, awake! The day is dawning,
'Tis time that we were in the field;
Shake off your fears and cease your yawning,
And buckle on your sword and shield,
And buckle on your sword and shield,
The enemy is now advancing,
   The Tyrant-Host is great and strong
   But ah, their reign will not be long,
We shrink not at their war-steeds prancing.
   Stand up, stand up my boys,
   The battle field is ours;
Fight on! Fight on! all hearts resolved,
   To break the Tyrant's power.

The men of God have quite deserted
The battle-field and gone their way;
The world will never be converted,
While tyrants bear despotic sway;
While tyrants bear despotic sway;
The infidels are quite astounded,
   And Atheists do speechless stand,
   To see God's image wear the brand,
While with God's word, they thus surrounded,
   Stand up! Stand up! my braves,
   The army ne'er forsake;
March on! March on! all hearts resolved,
   The tyrant's power to break.

We boast not of our might in number;
Our weapons are not carnal steel;
The weight of arms does not encumber
Our progress in the battle field;
Our progress in the battle field;

But truth, the mighty arm of power,
   Shall smite the great Goliath down,
   And pluck from Monarch's head the crown
Which o'er our race has long been towering.
   Be brave! Be brave my boys!
March on! March on! all hearts resolved
   To leave the ranks no more.

'Tis true that we are few in number,
And yet, those few are *brave* and *strong*,
Like Athens' mighty sons of thunder,
Upon the plains of Marathon;
Upon the plains of Marathon;
With courage bold, we'll take our station,
   Against the mighty host of whites,
   And plead like men for equal rights,
And thus exalt our fallen Nation.
    "To arms! To arms! my braves,"
   The sword of truth unsheath.
March on! March On! all hearts resolved,
   On Liberty or death.

THE BAND OF THIEVES

Sung to tune of "Scots Wha Hae" (traditional).
Source: *The Emancipation Car* (1854).
Author: Joshua McCarter Simpson.

Who are those who loud declare
All mankind their rights should share;
But the slaves their chains should wear?
'Tis the band of thieves.

Who are those who rule and reign—
Bind the black man down with chain—
Then his prayer and groans disdain?
'Tis the band of thieves.

Who are those who preach and pray
On the Holy Sabbath day;
Yet for slaves have naught to say?
'Tis the band of thieves.

Who are those who whine and sing
Praises to their Heavenly King;
Yet, will call the slave a "thing"?
'Tis the band of thieves.

Who so gentle meek and mild,
Say that they are undefiled;
Yet will steal their brother's child?
'Tis the band of thieves.

Who are those that's free from strife
Would not quarrel for their life,
Yet will sell their brother's wife?
'Tis the band of thieves.

THE TRUE SPIRIT

Sung to tune of "Rosin the Bow" (traditional).
Source: *The Emancipation Car* (1854), pp. 86–87.
Author: Joshua McCarter Simpson.

Come all ye true friends of your Nation,
Awake from stupidity's grave,
Come join in your country's salvation,
And free the American slave.
    And free the American slave
    And free the American slave
    Come join in your country's salvation,
    And free the American slave.

Come all of you half hearted freemen,
Your honesty now is at stake,
While over the slave you are dreaming,
Your government's standard will break.

We wish not to sever the Union,
But rather in love to unite;
We hold not from our communion.
No man who will strive to do right.

We loathe the bare name of man-stealing,
And all who will aid in its cause,
And we are intent on repealing
That outrageous Fugitive Law.

We'll sacrifice time and our money,
And life, too, if it is required,
While the blood of our brethren is running
We'll flinch not nor ever grow tired.

COME JOIN THE ABOLITIONISTS

Sung to tune of "When I Can Read My Title Clear" (traditional), original lyricist Isaac Watts (1724).
Source: *The Liberty Minstrel* (1845), pp. 96–98.
Author: unspecified.

Come join the Abolitionists,
Ye young men bold and strong,
And with a warm and cheerful zeal,
Come help the cause along:
Come help the cause along,
And with a warm and cheerful zeal,
Come help the cause along

Oh that will be joyful, joyful, joyful,
Oh that will be joyful,
When slavery is no more
When slavery is no more
When slavery is no more
'Tis then we'll sing and offerings bring,
When slavery is no more

Come join the Abolitionists
Ye men of riper years,
And save your wives and children dear
From grief and bitter tears
From grief and bitter tears
And save your wives and children dear
From grief and bitter tears

Oh that will be joyful, joyful, joyful,
Oh that will be joyful,
When slavery is no more
When slavery is no more
When slavery is no more
'Tis then we'll sing and offerings bring,
When slavery is no more

Come join the Abolitionists,
Ye dames and maidens fair;

And breathe around us in our path
Affection's hallowed air.
Oh that will be joyful, joyful, joyful,
Oh that will be joyful,
When woman cheers us on,
When woman cheers us on,
To conquests not yet won
'Tis then we'll sing, and offerings bring,
When woman cheers us on.

Come join the Abolitionists
Ye sons and daughters all;
Of this our own America,
Come at the friendly call.
O that will be joyful, joyful, joyful
O that will be joyful,
When all shall proudly say,
This, this is Freedom's day,
Oppression flee away!
'Tis then we'll sing and offerings bring,
When Freedom wins the day.

WOMAN'S RIGHTS

Sung to tune of "The Indian Philosopher" by Amzi Chapin (c. 1798).
Source: display at the David Ruggles Center, Florence, Massachusetts.
Author: David Ruggles.

>Come heavenly muse, inspire my song
>To whom the arts divine belong,
>   And whom I now invoke
>Say, wait it e'er by fate designed,
>To crush a free, immortal mind
>   Beneath a tyrant's yoke?
>
>Was woman formed to be a slave—
>To sink in thralldom to the grave,
>   And freedom never know?
>Say, must she toil and sweat and bleed
>A pampered lordling's pride to feed,
>   And every joy forgo?
>
>Ah, yes! McDuffie, Southern King,
>Has taught the fact, and made it ring
>   From southern plains to northern hills
>That woman's hands were made to wear
>The accursed chain! Her for to bear
>   Life's heaviest-direst ills.
>
>But, Tyrant King, avaunt I pray;
>Humanity demands a stay
>   Til she address the nation:
>And plead the cause of woman's right,
>By urging on in Pharaoh's spite
>   INSTANT EMANCIPATION.

LIBERTY

Sung to tune of "Liberty" by Stephen Jenks.
Source: *The Musical Harmonist* (1800).
Author: unspecified.

>No more beneath th'oppressive hand
>Of tyranny we groan.
>
>Behold the smiling, happy land
>That freedom calls her own.

WHAT MEAN YE?

Also known as "Where Is Thy Brother?"
Sung to tune of "Ortonville" by Thomas Hastings (1837) from *The Sacred Harp*.
Sources: *Anti-Slavery Melodies* (1843), Hymn 10; *The Liberty Minstrel* (1845),
    p. 182; and *The Harp of Freedom* (1856), p. 318.
Author: unspecified.

    What mean ye that bruise and bind
    My people, saith the Lord,
    And starve your craving brother's mind,
    That asks to hear my word?

    What mean ye that ye make them toil
    Through long and dreary years,
    And shed like rain upon your soil
    Their blood and bitter tears?

    What mean ye that ye dare to rend
    The tender mother's heart;
    Brothers from sisters, friend from friend,
    How dare you bid them part?

    What mean ye, when God's bounteous hand
    To you so much has given,
    That from the slave who tills your land
    You keep both earth and heaven?

    When at the judgement God shall call,
    Where is thy brother? say,
    What mean ye to the Judge of all,
    To answer on that day?

STOLE AND SOLD FROM AFRICA

Source: The Digital Library of Appalachia, Berea Collection.
Notes furnished by Rich Kirby, grandson of Addie Graham: "Addie Graham's repertoire included several extremely common songs such as 'We're Stole and Sold from Africa,' an anti-slavery song which seems to have originated in the antebellum Abolitionist movement. She also sang a number of songs of African American origin, many of which she learned from black railroad builders."

We're stole and sold from Africa
Transported to America
Like hogs and sheep we march in drove
Suffer the heat, endure the cold.

We're almost naked, as you see
Almost bare-footed as we be
Suffer the lash, endure the pain
Exposed to sun, both wind and rain.

See how they take us from our wives
Young children from their mother's side
They take us to some foreign land
Make slaves to wait on gentlemen.

Oh Lord, have mercy and look down
Upon the race of the African kind
Upon our knees pour out our grief
And pray to God for some relief.

Union sailor. Unidentified photographer. Library of Congress Prints and Photographs Division, Liljenquist Family Collection of Civil War Photographs.

1st Sergeant Octavius McFarland, formerly a slave from Missouri. Unidentified photographer. Collection of the Gettysburg National Military Park Museum.

Genius of Universal Emancipation. Benjamin Lundy's newspaper (1821–1839).

Susie King Taylor, born into slavery, became a teacher and nurse. Author of *Reminiscences of My Life in Camp with the 33d United States Colored Troops, Late 1st S.C. Volunteers*, she was the only African American woman to publish a memoir of her wartime experiences. Unidentified photographer. Library of Congress.

African American laborers on wharf, James River, Virginia. National Archives, Mathew Brady Photographs of Civil War-Era Personalities and Scenes, 1921–1940.

"Photograph taken while colored infantry was moving to the battleground." District of Columbia, Company E, 4th U.S. Colored Infantry, at Fort Lincoln. Photo by William Morris Smith, Library of Congress.

African American students enrolled at Berea College, 1901. Berea College, founded in 1855 by abolitionist John Fee, was the first interracial and coeducational college in the South. Berea has faced fierce opposition over the years, from armed, proslavery militias to segregation imposed by the state legislature. Despite physical, financial, and legal risk, Berea College has continued in its mission to educate students of all races. The motto "God has made of one blood all peoples of the earth" has inspired this historic institution for generations. Berea College Special Collections and Archives, RG 8 BC PH Box 94, Folder 4—Student Groups (pre-1904): Black Student Groups, c. 1870–1904.

Gerrit Smith, abolitionist, member of the Secret Six who financially supported John Brown's raid on Harper's Ferry. Photo by Matthew Brady. Brady-Handy photograph collection, Library of Congress, Prints and Photographs Division.

Harriet Tubman, abolitionist, led many slaves to freedom on the Underground Railroad, was a spy and scout for the Union Army, and was later active in the movement for women's suffrage. Unidentified photographer.

"Slavery Is a Hard Foe to Battle," sheet music for a song written by Judson Hutchinson of the Hutchinson Family Singers. Library of Congress, Music Division.

Phillis Wheatley's book of poetry: *Poems on Various Subjects, Religious and Moral* (London, 1773). Houghton Library, Harvard University.

The Liberator, William Lloyd Garrison's newspaper, masthead motto: "OUR COUNTRY IS THE WORLD—OUR COUNTRYMEN ARE MANKIND." Massachusetts Historical Society.

William Lloyd Garrison. Unidentified photographer. Library of Congress.

W. E. B. Du Bois, historian, socialist, cofounder of the NAACP. Photo by Cornelius Marion Battey. Library of Congress, Prints and Photographs Division.

Storming Fort Wagner, Robert Gould Shaw (the battle portrayed in the film *Glory*). Chromolithograph on paper, Kurz & Allison Lithography Company, c. 1880–1899. National Portrait Gallery, Smithsonian Institution.

"Twenty-eight fugitives escaping from the Eastern Shore of Maryland." Illustration from William Still's *The Underground Railroad*, published 1872. Schomburg Center for Research in Black Culture, Manuscripts, Archives, and Rare Books Division, The New York Public Library.

"A Bold Stroke for Freedom." Illustration from William Still's *The Underground Railroad*, published 1872. Schomburg Center for Research in Black Culture, Manuscripts, Archives, and Rare Books Division, The New York Public Library.

Frederick Douglass in 1894, the struggle continues. Address by Hon. Frederick Douglass, delivered in the Metropolitan A.M.E. Church, Washington, DC, Tuesday, January 9, 1894. Daniel Murray Pamphlet Collection, Library of Congress.

John Brown, hanged by the US government in 1859; Two years later Union soldiers marched to battle singing "John Brown's Body." His soul is marching on. Daguerreotype. Collection of the Boston Athenaeum.

The Anti-Slavery Harp: A Collection of Songs for Anti-slavery Meetings. Compiled by William Wells Brown, Boston, 1848. Library of Congress, Music Division.

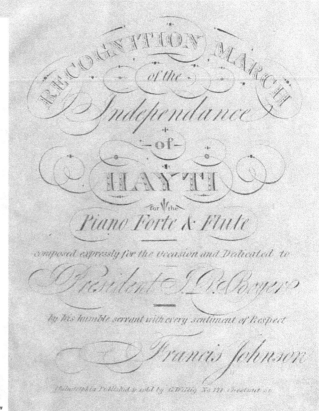

Sheet music for the "Recognition March for the Independance of Hayti."

Joshua McCarter Simpson, abolitionist and author of *The Emancipation Car, Being an Original Composition of Anti-Slavery Ballads, Composed Exclusively for the Under Ground Rail Road*, 1854. Norris Schneider Collection, Ohio History Connection.

Gabriel Prosser (1775–1800), leader of unsuccessful slave revolt in Richmond, Virginia, in 1800. Drawing. Artist unknown.

Lawrence Gellert published *Negro Songs of Protest* and collected "Uncle Gabriel" and "Nat Turner," songs in the present volume.

Vincent Ogé, who led a rebellion in French Saint-Domingue from October to December 1790. The Ogé revolt of 1790 foretold the massive slave uprising of August 1791 that eventually led to the Haitian Revolution. Portrait drawing, 1790. The event was commemorated in a poem "Vincent Ogé" by Oberlin College graduate George Vashon (1824–1878). Vashon was a free man of color, an abolitionist, lawyer, and poet.

James Monroe Trotter, who was born into slavery, served in the Union Army, and published *Music and Some Highly Musical People*. Collection of the Gettysburg National Military Park Museum.

1811 slave uprising on the German Coast near New Orleans.

"Babylon Is Fallen." Henry C. Work, 1863. Greer Music Library Historic Sheet Music Collection, Connecticut College.

Tacky's Revolt, Jamaica, 1760. From *Slavery Images: A Visual Record of the African Slave Trade and Slave Life in the Early African Diaspora*, http://www.slaveryimages.org/s/slaveryimages/item/1211.

Haitian Revolution, 1791–1804. From *Histoire de Napoléon*, by M. De Norvins, 1839, https://www.britannica.com/topic/Haitian-Revolution/images-videos.

Joshua Bryant, "Account of an insurrection of the negro slaves in the colony of Demerara, which broke out on the August 18, 1823."

ACKNOWLEDGMENTS

SONGS OF SLAVERY AND EMANCIPATION IS MADE UP OF THREE COMPONENTS: a book, two hours of recorded music, and a film. Many people contributed, including musicians, technicians, researchers, family, and friends. Among the more than fifty individuals directly involved, there are a number without whom I could not have brought this project to fruition.

With the support of the National Abolition Hall of Fame (NAHOF), Peterboro, New York, and Berea College, Berea, Kentucky, my colleagues and I successfully recorded thirty slave and abolitionist songs. Dorothy Willsey and Norman K. Dann of NAHOF provided crucial practical assistance, introducing us to Alden "Max" Smith. Smith is himself a descendant of enslaved people, and he performed the song "Agonizing, Cruel Slavery Days," composed by recently emancipated people in the decade following the Civil War. This was the first recording we made.

Next, Dorothy Willsey introduced me to President Lyle D. Roelofs of Berea College. Roelofs gave his endorsement and introduced me to Dr. Kathy Bullock, head of both the Berea College Music Department and the Black Music Ensemble. Bullock holds a doctorate in African American music, and her leadership was decisive in bringing together the appropriate group of singers to perform the majority of the slave songs. She also provided choral arrangements, played piano on "Recognition March of the Independance of Hayti," and lent her own powerful voice to the choir.

Kathy Bullock provided further assistance by coordinating with her colleagues in the music department, Professors Al White and Elizabeth DiSavino, who accompanied several of the slave songs and organized performances of several abolitionist songs.

I also received the invaluable assistance of Dr. Timothy Eriksen in Amherst, Massachusetts. Eriksen is the leader of a shape-note singing group, the members of which enthusiastically agreed to participate in this project. It was Eriksen's timely intervention that brought the importance of shape-note singing to my attention, greatly expanding the scope, musically and historically, of the project. (Shape-note is a style of choral singing widely popular in early nineteenth-century New England, and many abolitionists were involved in shape-note singing groups. A Library of Congress description reads: "Nineteenth century American song books that used notes in different shapes to aid singers and teach singing came to be known as 'shape-note hymnals' and the style of singing from these 'shape-note singing.' Christian hymnals using this system were among the most enduring uses of this notation. Among the most popular was *The Sacred Harp* by B. F. White, first published in Georgia in 1844. As a result of this popularity, the style of singing is also sometimes called 'sacred harp.'")

Finally, two people made contributions, musically and administratively, that shaped this project from beginning to end. Eli Smith was one of the first to join in, introducing me to several key musicians and technicians as well as performing himself. Eli's dedication and judgment helped overcome many obstacles encountered along the way. Yvonne Moore was a cofounder of the project, helping both to initiate and determine its course. She furthermore contributed musically with her singing while playing a decisive role in raising the funds necessary to sustain all our efforts. Yvonne's guidance and steadfast commitment kept an unwieldy and complex process on course.

These organizations and individuals made the recording of this music possible. As music, it is beautiful; but as evidence, it is indispensable. These songs are living proof of a body of musical literature, originating among enslaved people and carried forth by supporters of their struggle to abolish slavery, that has too long been denied.

CREDITS FOR FILM AND AUDIO PRODUCTION

Songs of Slavery and Emancipation
Produced and Directed by Art in History and Politics
Mat Callahan
Yvonne Moore
Joe Johnson

Produced in association with
The National Abolition Hall of Fame and Gerrit Smith Estate
& Berea College

Production Assistance
Brian Drolet

Editing
Don Fierro

Cameras
Reto Camenisch
Lily Keber
Don Fierro
Vernon Bentley
Jeff Meadors
Werner Hoffman

Audio Recording
Don Fierro

Musicians by Location
New Orleans, Louisiana
Givonna Joseph
Kamau

Peterboro, New York
Alden "Max" Smith

Berea, Kentucky
Dr. Kathy Bullock
Cherokee Griffiths
Dr. James Dreiling
Al White
Elizabeth DeSavino
Emmanuel Joshua Stokes
Sallesa Dismeaux
Pastor Ray Reed
Whit Whitaker
Keith W. Bullock
Jessica Slaton Greene
Ja'Quaviz Antwain Craig
Oluwatobi Adejumo
Fernando Kittrell II
La'Shelle Q. Allen
Mary Trumbo-Jackson
Jacob Hanshaw

Christella Philippe
Maiesha Simmons
Dr. Eric Charles Brown
Charlotte Thomas
James Sid Riffe
Wilkensley Thervil
Terence Witherspoon
Terri Lynn Davis
Cassaundra Alcorn
Nathaniel Thompson
Nyra Egypt Cullon
Msiba Ann Beard-Grundy
Mark Calkins
Liza White
Hannah From
Jessie Lawson
Cora Allison

Amherst, Massachusetts
Gerald Clark
Liliy Israel
Susan Brearey
John Holbrook
Linda Shea
Tarik Wareh
Patty Wareh
Peter Irvine
Jeremy Galvagni
Allison Steele
Becca Hawkins
Sheila Kelley
Greta Holbrooke
Eliza Cavanaugh
Kit Walsh
Becky Wright
Stina Soderling
Jonas Powell
Tristran Gordon
Liora Goldenshear
Paul Robinson

Wendy Sibbison
Gerald's Mom
Hannah Coyle
Molly Merrett
Sarah Lennox
Lisa Byers-Clark
Nathan Aldrich
Tim Eriksen

New York, New York
Bailey Arnold
Noah Block-Harley
Ali Dineen
Rachel Meyers
Eli Smith

Bern, Switzerland
Mat Callahan
André Pousaz
Helt Oncale
Shannon Callahan
Joe Johnson
Yvonne Moore

Administration
Yvonne Moore
Sherry Thiele
Judy Mott

Special Thanks
Dorothy H. Willsey, President, National Abolition Hall of Fame and Museum
Karol Kucinski, National Abolition Hall of Fame and Museum
Norman K. Dann, Director, Gerrit Smith Estate
Lyle D. Roelofs, President, Berea College
Givonna Joseph, Founder and Director, Opera Creole

Sponsors
Berea College
Förderbeitrag 2017 von Stadt und Kanton Schaffhausen
The Rosa Luxembourg Foundation

Historical and Musical Consultants

Research conducted at the Library of Congress, American Folk Life Center; Tufts University Library; the National Abolition Hall of Fame and Museum; and in conversation with the following historians, folklorists, and musicologists:

Eric Foner	Columbia University
Manisha Sinha	University of Connecticut
James Basker	Gilder Lehrman Institute
Peggy Bulger	American Folk Life Center
Todd Harvey	American Folk Life Center
Steven Garabedian	Marist College
Victor Wallis	Berklee College of Music
Kevin Anderson	U.C. Santa Barbara
Gwendolyn Hall	Michigan State University
Kathy Bullock	Berea College
Tim Eriksen	Wesleyan University
Norman K. Dann	Morrisville State College
Givonna Joseph	Founder & Director, Opera Créole

Appendix

NEGRO SLAVE REVOLTS IN THE UNITED STATES, 1526–1860 (1939)

BY HERBERT APTHEKER

NOTE ABOUT HERBERT APTHEKER (1915–2003) BY MAT CALLAHAN

Herbert Aptheker's pamphlet is presented here in its entirety, exactly as it appeared in 1939. For those unfamiliar with Aptheker, some background might be helpful. I relied on historians Sterling Stuckey and Robin D. G. Kelley, who at different times and in various publications gave their assessments of Aptheker's life and work.

Sterling Stuckey (1932–2018) was a historian and author of many books and the seminal essay "Through the Prism of Folklore."[1] Stuckey noted in an essay devoted to Aptheker that "probably because he was Jewish and a member of the Communist Party," Aptheker was denied regular employment in higher education.[2] Yet his outsider status facilitated friendships with Carter G. Woodson and W. E. B. Du Bois. Those two scholars, preeminent in their field, were largely excluded from the white establishment and, like Aptheker, were effectively barred from teaching at white universities. Stuckey noted that "Aptheker learned far more of their outsider status and that of their people than perhaps any other white historian of his time." Indeed, wrote Stuckey, "certainly by the fifties, no white historian was as greatly respected by African American scholars and artists as was Herbert Aptheker. Well before then, however, he was closely associated with Du Bois and, as early as 1937, shared important experiences with Woodson, the 'father' of Negro history."

The quality Du Bois found most significant in Aptheker's work, Stuckey argued, was expressed in the preface to *Black Folk, Then and Now*, where Du Bois wrote: "The Negro has long been the clown of history; the football of anthropology; and the slave of industry. I am trying to show here why these attitudes can no longer be maintained. I realize that the truth of history lies not in the mouths of partisans but rather in the calm Science that sits in between. Her cause I seek to serve, and wherever I fail, I am at least paying Truth the respect of earnest effort."[3]

From Du Bois's preface to Aptheker's *Documentary History of the Negro People* Stuckey quoted: "It is a dream come true to have the history of the Negro pursued in scientific documentary form."[4] Pioneers such as William C. Nell, William Wells Brown, and George Washington Williams had been met "with tolerance, but with little sympathy or comprehension" since it was assumed, Stuckey continued to quote from Du Bois, that "Africans even in America had no record of thought or deed worth attention." What followed, Du Bois wrote, was "the long hammering of Carter Woodson" and the "researches of a continuous line of students, African American and white, and especially the painstaking and thorough scholarship of Herbert Aptheker."

Stuckey underscored another salutary claim made by Du Bois: that attempts to "excuse the shame of slavery by stressing natural inferiority which would render it impossible for Negroes to make, much less leave, any record of revolt or struggle, any human reaction to utter degradation" could not prevent a growing number of scholars from knowing "of the existence of wide literature which contradicted such assumptions and efforts."[5] Indeed, Stuckey noted, Aptheker rescued "from oblivion and loss the very words of scores of American Negroes who lived slavery, serfdom and quasi-freedom in the United States of America from the seventeenth to the twentieth century." Stuckey added, "For fifteen years, Dr. Aptheker has worked to find and select 450 documents to make an authentic record of what it meant to be a slave . . . and what it meant to be free after the Emancipation Proclamation." Stuckey concluded: "Not usually known to offer much praise, Du Bois hastened 'to greet the day of the appearance of this volume, as a milestone on the road to Truth.'"

Robin D. G. Kelley, Gary B. Nash Professor of American History at UCLA and author of many books, including *Hammer and Hoe: Alabama Communists During the Great Depression*, *Race Rebels: Culture, Politics, and the Black Working Class*, and *Thelonious Monk: The Life and Times of an American Original*, was my other main source for information on Aptheker. Kelley noted, "I think I was about twenty-one years old when I discovered that Herbert Aptheker was not black."[6] Kelley went on to explain how, growing up in Harlem and immersed in local intellectual traditions, he became acquainted, early on, with Aptheker's work. Kelley recalled his family having a copy of Aptheker's *American Negro Slave Revolts* in particular.

While pursuing a graduate degree in history, Kelley discovered that Aptheker was marginalized by the profession. He explained that, "Back in the early to mid-1980s when I first started graduate school, Aptheker was not being taught at the graduate level, and most of the faculty I encountered—at the University of California, Los Angeles, and elsewhere—were indifferent if not downright hostile to his work."[7] Kelley, in fact, was discouraged from including Aptheker's work in the exam lists required by courses in US history. Then, during the written portion of his qualifying examination, Kelley had the following encounter:

> The last question on the exam asked us to write a substantive critical essay on a major historian. I planned to write about Aptheker since I had read so much of his work, but before I started typing I asked one of the faculty proctors if Aptheker falls under the category of "major." "Absolutely not," was the answer, delivered so abruptly I felt embarrassed for even asking the question. I then asked about W. E. B. Du Bois and received a slightly less hostile, though equally negative, response. "He is more of a sociologist than an historian," I was told. So for the final ten pages or so I turned my attention to the late Ulrich B. Phillips. Needless to say, I passed.

Kelley concluded, "In this respect, I was right the first time: Herbert Aptheker is a 'black historian.' He stands in a long tradition of scholars who work with the goal of liberation in mind—a tradition that includes the likes of George Washington Williams, Carter G. Woodson, J. A. Rogers, John Hope Franklin, Rayford Logan, Elizabeth Ross Haynes, William Ferris, Drusilla Dunjee Houston, Benjamin Brawley, St. Clair Drake, William Leo Hansberry, Willis N. Huggins, John Jackson, Louise Kennedy, Charles Wesley, Sadie T. M. Alexander, John Henrik Clarke, and, of course, the grand old man himself: W. E. B. Du Bois."[8] Kelley added, "Had Aptheker repudiated his politics, remained silent on racism in the academy and the world at large, and churned out books primarily for his colleagues, he would have had a comfortable tenured job and a place among the pantheon of 'major' American historians."

NEGRO SLAVE REVOLTS IN THE UNITED STATES, 1526–1860

BY HERBERT APTHEKER

I. INTRODUCTION

The wholly erroneous conception of life in the old South which is still dominant in our movies and novels and textbooks was invented by the slaveholders themselves. They and their spiritual—and even lineal—descendants have written the history of American Negro slavery. These Bourbons have been motivated by a desire to apologize for and, more than that, to justify a barbarous social system. To do this, they have been forced to commit every sin of omission, falsification and distortion. That they have done their job well is attested by the fact that the monstrous myth created by them is believed by most people today.

The apologists and mythologists who are responsible for this distorted picture of the slave system acknowledge as their pioneer and leader the late Professor Ulrich B. Phillips, of Georgia. His attitude clearly presents the approach of the entire school. In one of his early articles (1905), Phillips referred to himself as a person who had "inherited Southern traditions." That by this he meant Bourbon traditions is indicated by his dedication of an early book (1908) "to the dominant class of the South." Since he openly affirms such an allegiance, it is easy to imagine what he says of the old South. To Phillips, under the slave system "severity was clearly the exception, and kindliness the rule." Indeed, at one point he places quotation marks around the word slavery, indicating that harsh word is hardly the proper one with which to label the system he describes.

And the opinions of this "authority" on the people who were enslaved are remarkable to behold. His works are filled with adjectives like stupid, negligent, dilatory, inconstant, obedient—used to describe the Negro. To Phillips the Negro people are cursed by "inherited inaptitude" and are "by racial quality submissive." Thus American slavery emerges as a delightful social system admirably contrived for the efficient and undisturbed subordination of an inferior people.

WHAT WAS AMERICAN SLAVERY?

But the fact of the matter is that American slavery was a horrid form of tyrannical rule which often found it necessary to suppress the desperate expressions of discontent on the part of its outraged victims. The fundamental point to bear in mind is that for ninety per cent of the years of its existence and throughout some ninety per cent of the area it blighted, American slavery was, as Marx stated, "a commercial system of exploitation." That is, American slavery, on the whole, was a staple producing system dependent upon a world market. There was, therefore, no limit to the exploiting drive of the slaveowners. And this system was quite as subject to business cycles, or periods of so-called prosperity, depression and panic, as any other system of private gain dependent upon a world market.

The peculiar feature of this staple-producing agricultural system was the fact that the laborers were owned by, were chattels of, the bosses or slaveholders. And the slaveholders, like employers the world over, were in business—that is, ran cotton or sugar or tobacco plantations—for the gain they could drive out of their workers, whom they literally owned.

So that instead of the delightful picture of a patriarchal institution in which, as a Phillipsian professor recently put it, the slave "was assured of an income proportioned to his necessities and not to his productiveness," one has a large-scale commercial system of exploitation in which the laborers were rationed out, in normal times, a bare minimum of their animal needs. Objection or resistance of any kind made the worker liable to any punishment his boss should decide was proper—sale, branding, lashing, or some other more excruciating form of torture.

Moreover, productiveness was a most important determinant of the amount of the rations. The plantation slaves were divided according to their productivity into full hands, three-quarter hands, half hands and quarter hands. The less productive workers, the children, the aged, many of the women, the less skilled or less strong received less to eat (often fifty or sixty per cent less) than did the more productive workers, or the "prime" field hands, as they were called.

When the depression and panic came to this staple-producing slaveholding system the workers—the slaves—suffered. James Madison explained, in 1819, what conditions affected slaves, and the first item he listed was "the ordinary price of food, on which the quality and quantity allowed them will more or less depend." Robert Hayne, a senator from South Carolina, while lamenting a depression in his native state, in January, 1832, declared that because of it the slaves were "working harder, and faring worse." A Charleston slaveholder, writing in 1811 in the midst of the economic hardships of the moment, stated, "The wretched situation of a large proportion of our slaves is sufficient to harrow up the feelings of the most flinty heart." John Randolph, a Virginia congressman, during the depression of 1814 and early 1815, felt that the slave "will suffer dreadfully" and noted his "tattered blanket and short allowance." At a time when Andrew Jackson was short of funds and depression prevailed, in 1841, he received word from his Mississippi plantation that the slaves "were shivering and starving—provisions out and no shoes."

Other factors tended to worsen the slaves' condition. Soil exhaustion, for example, made the slaveholders drive their workers at a more rapid pace. Improvements expanding the market for plantation products, such as new industrial machines or better transportation facilities, had a like effect. A slave explained this, in the late 1850s, in blaming railroads for increased demand upon his labor, by remarking, "you see it is so much easier to carry off the produce and sell it now; 'cause they take it away so easy; and so the slaves are druv more and more to raise it."

Living Conditions

These factors lowered the slave's general standard of living. But what was that standard? Hours of work were from sun-up to sun-down. Food consisted of corn and occasional meat or fish or molasses, with supplements from gardens, which some slaves were permitted to keep and which they might work in their "spare" time, as on Sundays. Another important supplementary source of nourishment came from what the slaves "took" from their masters. The masters called this stealing, but slaves felt themselves guilty of stealing only if they took the belongings of fellow slaves. Appropriating bread or milk or meat or clothing from the master was "taking," not stealing, for the slaves declared "as we work and raise all, we ought to consume all." Frequent application of this theory into practice was a great annoyance to the slaveholders, who decided that "stealing" was an inherent trait of the Negro. Surely the taking could not result from the slaves' need for more bread and meat and clothes!

Slaveholders, themselves, are the authorities for determining what they spent on their chattels' upkeep. One cotton planter of fifteen years' experience, writing in the leading Southern periodical, that published by J. B. DeBow, declared that the masters' expense was often underestimated. He then proceeded to give what he thought was a proper estimate. The cost of feeding one hundred slaves for one year he said was seven hundred and fifty dollars—seven dollars and fifty cents a year for each slave's food—and this included the expenses of the "hospital and the overseer's table." The remaining items, clothing, shoes, bedding, sacks for gathering cotton, and other articles not enumerated also cost seven dollars and fifty cents per slave per year!

James Madison declared, in 1823, that the annual cost of a slave child in Virginia was from eight to ten dollars, and that the youngster became "gainful to his owner" at about nine or ten years of age. Forty-eight planters of Louisiana informed the United States Secretary of the Treasury in 1846 that the yearly expense of supporting the life of a prime field hand was about thirty dollars, and of others—children, aged, some women—fifteen dollars. A good idea of the habitations of the field hands may be obtained from an article by a Mississippi planter, again in DeBow's publication. The gentleman's purpose in writing the article was to appeal for better slave housing—such as he provided. He owned one hundred and fifty slaves and provided them with twenty-four cabins, each sixteen by eighteen feet. That is, about six slaves "lived" in a hut sixteen by eighteen feet, and this condition was proudly held up for emulation!

The Question of Cruelty

Time and again modern readers are assured, as by Phillips, that cruelty was exceedingly rare under American slavery. The essential argument used is that it is absurd to believe that men would abuse their own slaves—their own property. Normal people, the apologists say, do not maltreat their cows or pianos; then why be cruel to a slave representing a value of several hundred dollars? Thus a biography, published in 1938 by Harvard University (S. Mitchell, *Horatio Seymour*, p. 103), declares that "owners were hardly likely to be cruel or careless with expensive pieces of their own property," just as most folks do not abuse their horses or automobiles.

It may first be remarked that society does find it necessary to maintain institutions for the prevention of cruelty to animals and to children, indicating the not infrequent existence of perverse, insane or malicious people. Slave society was certainly conducive to the production of such persons.

But, entirely apart from this first consideration, cruelty was an integral part of the slave system. The argument of interest would apply were the slaves horses or pianos or automobiles. But they were men and women and children. History certainly teaches us, if it teaches anything at all, that human beings have the glorious urge to be something better than they are at any moment, or to do something new, or to provide their offspring with greater advantages and a happier world than they themselves possess. People who are degraded and despised and sold and bought and arbitrarily separated from all that is familiar and dear will be unhappy. They will be discontented and will *think, at least, of bettering their conditions*. This last idea, if persisted in, was death to the slave institution, and it was precisely because the slaves were property, precisely because they were valuable and profitable, *but rational*, instruments of production, that cruelty was necessary.

Slavery was systematized cruelty. The slaves were machines to be driven as much as possible for the production of profit, and machines of an intelligent nature which had to be terrified and chained and beaten in order for their owners to maintain possession. Specific examples of physical cruelty (taken from unimpeachable sources) are innumerable. At least a few of these, which indicate a general condition, deserve mention.

There was the case of Mr. Symon Overzee of Maryland and his slave, Tony. Tony staged a sit-down strike all his own—surely one of the first in America—way back in 1656. What happened was this: Tony ran away and was retaken with the aid of bloodhounds. He then waited only until his wounds healed and again fled. He was again captured. Flight being now impossible, Tony sat down and refused to rise. He would not work as a slave. Mr. Overzee bound him in an upright position by his wrists and proceeded to beat him. Tony still refused to serve as a slave. Mr. Overzee then poured hot lard over him, and Tony died. This procedure was rather irregular, and Mr. Overzee was brought before a court. He explained the facts and was acquitted by the court because Tony was "incorrigible."

The Grand Jury of Charleston, SC, in 1816, presented "as a most serious evil the many instances of Negro homicide, which have been committed within the city for many years," and went on to refer to "the barbarous treatment of slaves" who were used "worse than beasts of burden." A Mr. John Cooke was actually convicted in 1815 in North Carolina of the wanton murder of a slave under the most monstrous conditions. The Governor pardoned him. Said a native:

> Some thought, as this was the first instance in which a white man had ever been convicted for killing a negro, it would be impolitic to hang him so unexpectedly. And others believing it would be wrong in all respects, to hang a white man for killing a negro. But whatever might have been the motives of his Excellency, we hear no dissatisfaction expressed by any at this act of clemency; yet we think it may be well to caution the unwary against the repetition of the too common practice of whipping negroes to death as . . . executive interposition may not be expected in all cases.

The British Consul in Charleston, SC, wrote in a private letter of January, 1854:

> The frightful atrocities of slave holding must be seen to be described. . . . My next door neighbor, a lawyer of the first distinction, and a member of the *Southern Aristocracy*, told me himself that he flogged all his own negroes, men and women, when they misbehaved. . . . It is literally no more to kill a slave than to shoot a dog.

As a final piece of evidence is offered the statement of a Major in the United States Army, Amos Stoddard, who lived in Louisiana from 1804 to 1809. In 1811 he wrote of that region:

> cruel and even unusual punishments are daily inflicted on these wretched creatures, enfeebled, oppressed with hunger, labor and the lash. The scenes of misery and distress constantly witnessed along the coast of the Delta, the wounds and lacerations occasioned by

demoralized masters and overseers, most of whom exhibit a strange compound of ignorance and depravity, torture the feelings of the passing stranger, and wring blood from his heart. Good God! why sleeps thy vengeance!

Why the Revolts?

Vengeance did not sleep. Bourbon historians, who have made slavery idyllic and the slaves an inferior people, have little place in their works for accounts of this vengeance—this heroic anti-slavery struggle of the Negroes. Thus, for example, Phillips in his latest work, published after his death, declared that "slave revolts and plots were very seldom in the United States"; and two other eminent historians recently said the same thing—John D. Hicks: "Attempts at insurrection were extremely rare"; James G. Randall: "Surprisingly few instances of slave insurrections."

The history of American slavery is marked by the occurrence of at least two hundred *reported* Negro conspiracies and revolts. This certainly demonstrates that organized efforts at freedom were neither "seldom" nor "rare," but were rather a regular and ever-recurring phenomenon in the life of the old South.

Considerable explanation of this rebellious activity has already been given. We have seen that cruelty—that is, actual physical maltreatment—was an essential part of slavery. We have seen that the system, in so-called normal times, provided a bare animal sustenance to its victims. And we have observed the fact that economic disaster seriously depressed the already miserably low standards of the Negroes.

Economic depression had other results of a disturbing nature. It would naturally sharpen the tempers of the slaveowners or of their overseers, whose incomes depended upon the value of the crop they could force the slaves to produce. Bankruptcy and liquidation are, moreover, concomitants of depression and, when property was human beings, its liquidation carried many stories of woe. For it entailed an increase in the leasing or sale of thousands of slaves, which meant the forced separation of brother from sister, child from mother, husband from wife. Surely it is more than a coincidence that the years of severe economic depression coincide with the periods of greatest rebellious activity.

Another factor of considerable importance in arousing concerted slave unrest was the occurrence of an exciting or unusual event. Thus, the landing of a new provincial governor from England in one of the colonies here might lead to a belief on the part of the slaves that they were to be freed, and thereby cause the masters trouble, as occurred in Virginia during 1730. Again, the prevalence of revolutionary philosophy and activity, as from 1770 to 1783, or the rapid spread and growth of an equalitarian religion, as Methodism from 1785 to 1805, or a war against a foreign power, as against Great Britain from 1812 to 1815, or stirring debates in Congress over the question of slavery, as in 1820, or particularly exciting Presidential campaigns as those of 1840 and 1856—all clearly aroused subversive activity on the part of the slaves. The actual outbreak of a slave revolt seems also to have had a contagious effect, so that, for instance, the tremendous struggles for liberation of the slaves of the French West Indies (especially St. Domingo or Haiti) in the 1790s and early 1800s certainly inspired similar attempts in the United States. It is to be noted, too, that attempts at revolt evoked more stringent measures of repression, and the added pinch these created was at times probably important in causing new conspiracies or rebellions.

The more rapid growth of the Negro population as compared to that of the white was also a disturbing factor. This occurred for various reasons. When, in the late seventeenth and early eighteenth centuries, Negro slavery was found to be profitable in certain regions, greed led to an enormous spurt in the importation of slaves. This undoubtedly is an explanation for the considerable slave unrest in South Carolina in the 1730s. The settlement of new and fertile slave areas was likewise followed by a disproportionate growth of the Negro population and consequent slave unrest, as in Mississippi in 1835. Depression, on the other hand, in the great staple producing areas caused them to import less slaves. This meant a severe blow to the prosperity of the slave-raising and slave-exporting regions of the South, with a resultant rapid rise in their slave populations and a more dangerous social condition. This state of affairs prevailed, for instance, from about 1820 to 1831 in eastern Virginia and eastern North Carolina.

Urbanization and industrialization—which were occurring to some extent in the South from about 1840 to 1860—and their creation of a proletarian Negro were also exceedingly dangerous to a slave society. These phenomena were probably important in accounting for some slave outbreaks, especially those of the late 1850s.

SAFEGUARDS OF THE SLAVOCRATS

While the propaganda mill of the slavocratic oligarchy incessantly ground out its falsehoods concerning the innate cowardice and stupidity of the Negro and the delights of being a slave, the same group nevertheless maintained a whole series of devices and laws which it knew was necessary to keep the Negro in bondage.

Armed might was the main instrument of suppression. This comprised large detachments of regular troops of the United States Army, the efficient militia of each of the Southern states, the patrols or mounted bodies of armed men who scoured every piece of land in every county of the South at various intervals from one week to four weeks, the considerable bodies of guards present and active in every Southern city, volunteer military organizations in numerous areas of the South, and the continual presence of at least one armed white, master or overseer, on every plantation.

The activities of the slaves were severely limited. None might possess arms. It was illegal to teach a slave how to read or write. Writing or saying anything with a "tendency" to create unrest among the slaves was a serious crime. No slave might buy or sell or trade anything without his master's permission. Slaves might not assemble without the presence of whites. They could not testify in any court in any case involving whites. Legal restrictions also hit free Negroes, so that their movements from county to county or from state to state were regulated or totally forbidden. They, too, could not testify in any court against a white person. They, as a rule, could not vote, and even their business activities were closely regulated and limited. In the two years immediately preceding the Civil War laws were passed in several Southern states having as their purposes the re-enslavement of free Negroes or their forced evacuation.

Numerous non-legal regulations and customs were important, too, in maintaining subordination. The opinion of a North Carolina judge rendered in 1852 indicated some of these:

> What acts in a slave towards a white person will amount to insolence, it is manifestly impossible to define—it may consist in a look, the pointing of a finger, a refusal or neglect to step out of the way when a white person is seen to approach. But each of such acts violates the rules of propriety, and if tolerated, would destroy that subordination, upon which our social system rests.

A carefully nursed policy of division between the poor whites and the slaves on the basis of race hatred was another very important Bourbon device for retaining his power. Divisions amongst the slaves themselves were also fostered. Thus the domestic slaves were, generally, better treated than the field slaves. It was from this favored group that the slaveholders recruited spies and traitors to whom they gave considerable financial rewards together, often, with freedom—the greatest gift in the power of the "patriarchal" slaveholders!

The slaveholders' religion had, so far as the slave was concerned, one message—be meek. In the words of the Rev. Dr. Nelson, who lived for many years in North Carolina:

> I have been intimately acquainted with the religious opportunities of the slaves—in the constant habit of hearing the sermons which are preached to them. And I solemnly affirm that, during the forty years of my residence and observation in this line, I never heard a single one of these sermons but what was taken up with the obligations and duties of slaves to their masters. Indeed, I never heard a sermon to slaves but what made obedience to masters by the slaves the fundamental and supreme law of religion.

But the slaves had a different religion. Their God had declared that all men were created of one blood, and that the divine rule of doing unto others as one would have others do unto you was the true guide for religious behavior. Their God had cursed man-stealers and had himself taken slaves out of their bondage. Their God had denounced the oppressors and had praised the humble. Their God had declared that the first would be last and the last would be first.

II. THE REVOLTS AND CONSPIRACIES

Before discussing the slave revolts themselves it is important that it be understood that they form but one manifestation of the discontent of the Negro. Revolt was merely one method by which the slaves hoped to obtain their liberty. There were others, each of which merits extensive treatment. One of the most important of these was flight. In the history of slavery many tens of thousands of slaves *succeeded* in escaping from their enslavers. They fled wherever freedom loomed—the destinations varying with the different times and places—to the Dutch, the Indians, the Mexicans, the British armies, the Canadians, the French, the Spanish, to the Northern states and to the swamps and mountains and forests of the South.

Other slaves, particularly those who were leased by their masters for work in towns and cities, were able, by working in their spare time, to accumulate enough money to purchase their freedom (this was possible, of course, only if the master were willing and honest). There is considerable evidence to indicate that this was by no means infrequent, especially in the more northern of the slave states, like Tennessee, Kentucky and Missouri.

Enlistment and faithful service in the armed forces of the nation was another method whereby Negroes at times gained their freedom. Several hundreds, for example, became free in this manner in the two wars against Great Britain. Individual acts of terrorism, self-mutilation and self-destruction (sometimes, as in Charleston, in 1807, mass suicides), sabotage, as shamming illness, "careless" work, destruction of tools and occasionally strikes were other forms of protest against enslavement.

It is, finally, not to be forgotten that Negroes were leaders in the agitational and political movement against slavery, none being more important in these respects than Allen, Jones, Hall, Truth, Purvis, Remond, Garnet, Ruggles, Wright, Still, Tubman, Walker, Ray, Douglass and a host of others.

The Earliest Revolts

The first settlement within the present borders of the United States to contain Negro slaves was the victim of the first slave revolt. A Spanish colonizer, Lucas Vasquez de Ayllon, in the summer of 1526, founded a town near the mouth of the Pedee river in what is now South Carolina. The community consisted of five hundred Spaniards and one hundred Negro slaves. Trouble soon beset the colony. Illness caused numerous deaths, carrying off, in October, Ayllon himself. The Indians grew more hostile and dangerous. Finally, probably in November, the slaves rebelled, killed several of their masters, and escaped to the Indians. This was a fatal blow and the remaining colonists—but one hundred and fifty souls—returned to Haiti in December, 1526.

The first slave plots and revolts in English America did not occur until the latter half of the seventeenth century. This is due to the fact that very few Negroes were there until about 1680. Thus in 1649 Virginia contained but three hundred Negroes, and twenty-one years later the Negroes numbered but two thousand, or some five per cent of the total population. It is also to be noticed that Negroes were not legally enslaved until about 1660, and not enslaved by custom until about 1640. The only crop produced by relatively large-scale labor in the seventeenth century was tobacco, and this was mainly raised by white indentured servants until about 1675.

With the opening of the eighteenth century and the development of large-scale cultivation of rice and indigo as well as tobacco, Negro slavery became important, and frequent and serious revolts occurred. By 1715 about one-third the population of Virginia, the Carolinas and Maryland were slaves (46,000 out of 123,150). Within five years importation of slaves became important in Louisiana also. Georgia adopted slavery by 1750, and four years later the five English provinces of Georgia, the Carolinas, Virginia and Maryland contained a quarter of a million Negro slaves out of a total population of 609,000.

On September 13, 1663 a favorite slave of a Mr. John Smith of Gloucester county, Virginia, betrayed an extensive conspiracy of Negro slaves and white indentured servants. An unknown number of the rebels was executed. The day of the betrayal was set aside by the colonists as one of thanksgiving and prayer to a merciful God who had saved them from extermination. The traitor was given his freedom and 5,000 pounds of tobacco.

There is evidence of several other slave plots in the seventeenth century, probably the most important of which was that of 1687 in Virginia. But, for the reasons made clear by the economic and population data already presented, the really serious uprisings do not occur until the early years of the next century. From that time until final emancipation, one hundred and sixty years later, the history of Negro slavery is filled with heroic and carefully planned mass plots or outbreaks.

It is manifestly impossible within the confines of this booklet to deal with each of these events, or even to exhaustively treat any of the main revolts. We shall, however, attempt to briefly describe the more important uprisings. (A complete list of plots and revolts will be found in the Appendix.)

1709–1730

A joint conspiracy of Negro and Indian slaves was uncovered and crushed in the counties of Surry and Isle of Wight, Virginia, in 1709. The court of investigation declared that "greate numbers" were involved. The next year another extensive conspiracy, this time only of Negro slaves, was again discovered in Surry county. A slave named Peter was the leader. Another slave, Will, was the traitor. His reward was freedom. South Carolina was greatly troubled by slave rebelliousness in 1711. According to the provincial legislature, this kept the inhabitants "in great fear and terror."

A serious uprising occurred in New York City in 1712. A contemporary declared that the plot was formed January 1, "the Conspirators tying themselves to secrecy by Sucking ye blood of each Others hands." Very early in the morning of April 8, about twenty-five Negro slaves set fire to a house, and then, with a few guns, clubs and knives ready, waited for the whites to approach. They did, and about nine were killed and seven severely wounded. The alarm soon spread and soldiers hastened to the disturbance. In about twenty-four hours most of the rebels were captured. Six, however, were not, for they committed suicide; "one shot first his wife and then himself and some who had hid themselves in Town when they went to Apprehend them Cut their own throats."

Twenty-one slaves were executed. According to the account of the Governor:

> some were burnt others hanged, one broke on the wheele, and one hung alive in chains in the town, so that there has been the most exemplary punishment inflicted that could be possibly thought of.

This revolt was important in leading Massachusetts and Pennsylvania to pass effective tariff regulations to cut down the importation of slaves.

An extensive revolt occurred in the drought-stricken and Indian-menaced area of Charleston, SC, in 1720. Precise numbers are unknown but many slaves were banished from the province, some hanged and others burned alive. The summer of 1730 witnessed the suppression of three serious slave outbreaks, one in five counties of Virginia, centering in Williamsburg, one in Charleston, SC, and one in Louisiana.

The unrest in Virginia seems to have been brewing for weeks prior to the main outbreak, for several suspected slaves were early arrested and lashed. Later, on a Sunday, two hundred slaves assembled and chose leaders for an insurrection planned for the near future. Betrayal came, however, and at least four of the leaders were executed. On October 28, 1730 it was ordered that henceforth, in Virginia, all who went to worship the Prince of Peace were to go armed.

Information concerning the Charleston plot of 1730 is far from satisfying, but it is certain that many Negroes were involved. Disagreement as to method among the slaves led to betrayal and the familiar report, "ringleaders executed." One contemporary letter states that "had not an overruling Providence discovered their Intrigues, we had all been in blood."

The unguarded speech of a slave woman who, on being beaten, shouted that Negroes would not be beaten much longer, led to investigation and the disclosure, after torture with fire, of a plot amongst the slaves of Louisiana, in 1730. The leader, Samba, had headed an uprising against whites in Africa and had been shipped to America. He and seven other men were "broke alive on the wheel," and one slave woman was hanged "before their eyes." Two years later the discovery of another plot here led to the hanging of another woman and the breaking of four more men on a wheel. As a further stimulus to contentment, the heads of the four men were strung on poles near the city of New Orleans. Incidentally, some idea of conditions in Louisiana at this time may be gained from the fact that though 7,000 slaves had been imported between 1719 and 1731, in the latter year there were less than 3,500 living.

1739–1741

There were three distinct uprisings in South Carolina in 1739. One of them, which took place in Charleston during March, involved a Spaniard and an Irishman, as well as slaves. The most serious, however, was that led by Cato. This started on a plantation at Stono, some twenty miles west of Charleston, on the ninth of September. The slaves killed the two guards of a magazine, armed themselves and set out for the Edisto river, to the west. Their aim was to escape into Spanish-held Florida, the Governor of which had promised liberty to all fugitive English slaves.

A contemporary wrote: "Several Negroes joyned them, they called out liberty, marched on with colours displayed, and two drums beating." They destroyed and burned everything in their path in this bid for freedom, so that, as an eye-witness said, "The Country thereabout was full of flames."

About thirty whites were killed, but not indiscriminately, for one—"a good man and kind to his slaves"—was spared. Scores of well-armed whites soon overtook the slaves, and in a surprise attack killed fourteen Negroes. In two more days of pursuit and battle twenty more rebels were killed and forty captured. These "were immediately some shot, some hang'd, and some Gibbeted alive." About twenty were yet at large and in another engagement, in which the slaves "fought stoutly for some time," ten more were killed. Apparently ten slaves made good their bid for freedom.

Early in June, 1740, a slave plot, involving at least two hundred Negroes in and about Charleston, was discovered a short time before it was to have matured. On the day set for the outbreak about one hundred and fifty Negroes had gathered but, while yet unarmed, they were surprised and attacked by the whites. Fifty were captured and hanged, ten a day. In this same month the city was swept by a terrific fire, doing well over a million pounds damage and necessitating aid from other colonies. This was at first ascribed to the slaves, but was later denied. The cause is not positively known, but it is certain that in the summer of 1741 at least two slaves were executed for incendiarism in Charleston.

It is this revolutionary activity, and the Negro's habit of running away, that were important considerations impelling statesmen connected with the settlement of Georgia, like Oglethorpe and Egmont, to prohibit Negroes in that colony. This prohibition lasted until 1749. South Carolina itself passed laws in 1740 for the purpose of lessening the danger. Slave importations were taxed, the funds raised to be used for obtaining white Protestant settlers. Rather vague regulations requiring better food and clothes for the slaves were passed. It was also most generously provided that a master was not to work his slave more than fourteen hours a day in the winter or more than fifteen hours a day in the summer!

The slave plot of 1741 in New York City has been dealt with by historians as either a complete frameup resulting from a baseless panic, or as a real and considerable conspiracy. The truth is probably somewhere between those two ideas. Discontent certainly was rife. England was at the moment waging an unpopular and costly war against Spain and New York itself, early in 1741, was momentarily expecting attack. Probably of more importance was the fact that the winter of 1740–41 was a particularly severe one, six feet of snow being common in the city. The suffering among the poor generally and the slaves especially was most acute.

Yet the star witness against the conspirators, Mary Burton, as her own testimony establishes, was a liar, and the methods used to extract confessions from the prisoners, torture or promises of rewards, militate against their complete acceptance.

Nevertheless, beginning in March there were a series of suspicious fires and many contemporaries were convinced that some, at least, of these were set by Negro slaves and by white accomplices. Indeed, the Governor of the Province declared on June 20, "if the truth were ever known, there are not many innocent Negro men, and it is thought that some Negroes of the Country are accomplices and were ready to act there." This last idea undoubtedly arose from the fact that there were frequent and suspicious fires in Hackensack, New Jersey, for which at least two slaves were executed, by burning, on the fifth of May.

Whatever may be the facts as to the justification for the panic aroused among the slaveholders, the results of that panic are unquestionable. About one hundred and fifty slaves and twenty-five whites were arrested. Four whites and thirteen slaves were burned alive. Eighteen Negroes were hanged, two of them in chains, seven who were indicted were not captured, and about seventy were banished.

During the First American Revolution

Abigail, the honest and forthright wife of John Adams, wrote to her husband (himself, at the moment, leading a revolution) in September, 1774, of the discovery of a fairly widespread plot for rebellion among the slaves of Boston. And she closed in this fashion: "I wish most sincerely there was not a slave in the province; it always appeared a most iniquitous scheme to me to fight ourselves for what we are daily robbing and plundering from those who have as good a right to freedom as we have."

The revolutionary activity amongst the colonists certainly brought such ideas forcibly to the minds of the Negro slaves. The commotion enhanced the possibility of gaining freedom without, however, resorting to the desperate expedient of rebellion, and thousands of slaves grabbed the chance by flight and by enlistment in the opposing armies. It is also true that Mrs. Adams' sentiments were held by many other white people, amongst them slaveholders, so that the period of America's First Revolution witnessed hundreds of manumissions of slaves. These factors served as safety valves and cut down the number of plots and revolts. Nevertheless several occurred.

Probably the most important of these was that which rocked Pitt, Beaufort and Craven counties, North Carolina, in July, 1775. Two slaves betrayed the plot on the day set for the outbreak, the eighth of July. Immediately all was military activity. In Craven county alone forty slaves were arrested the first day and questioned before a citizens' committee who found "a deep laid Horrid Tragick Plan" for rebellion. For several days thereafter, throughout the counties mentioned, dozens of slaves were apprehended (some of whom were armed, and some killed resisting arrest). The favorite sentence seems to have been "to receive 80 lashes each [and] to have both Ears crap'd." Rather crude displays of "kindliness" to inflict upon people who, as Professor Philips has stated, were "by racial quality submissive"!

1791–1802

The next period of serious organized disaffection among America's "docile" Negroes extended from 1791 through 1802. These years witnessed a remarkable conjunction of those types of events which were most conducive to slave unrest.

Economic distress was characteristic of the period throughout the South and was most acute in the regions of greatest unrest, Louisiana, North Carolina and Virginia. In the latter two states there was a considerable exodus of impoverished whites seeking better opportunities and this, together with a decline in the exportation of slaves, resulted in a much more rapid growth of the Negro population as compared with the white.

The period was also, of course, one of a great worldwide outburst of revolutionary activity. These were the years of the French Revolution, of the cry "liberty, equality, fraternity," slogans representing precisely those things of which the Negro people, more than any other, were deprived. The year 1791 marked the beginning of the revolution of the Negro slaves in St. Domingo, which, after fourteen years of unsurpassed heroism, culminated in the establishment of an independent Negro republic. Both events filled American newspapers and formed the great topic of conversation in the North and in the South. The latter event, the Negro revolution, directly affected the South, for it caused an exodus of thousands of panic-stricken slaveholders, together with some slaves, into cities like Richmond, Norfolk and Charleston.

The general upsurge of revolutionary feeling gave a considerable impetus to anti-slavery sentiment. In the South this resulted in the freeing of hundreds of slaves by conscience-stricken masters, the growth of anti-slavery groups like the Quakers and Methodists and, indeed, the formation of emancipationist societies in several of the more northern of the slave states. In the North the period was marked by the enactment of gradual emancipation acts so that by 1802 every Northern state (except New Jersey, whose act came in 1804) had provided for the ultimate extinction of slavery.

It is to be noted that even in this early period, the anti-slavery feeling went, in some cases, to the extent of condoning if not urging slave rebellion. This was true of a Boston writer, J. P. Martin, who declared, in 1791, that if the American Revolution was just, then surely a rebellion of slaves would be just. It was true of the Kentuckian, David Rice, who in that state's constitutional convention of 1792 declared that the slaves of St. Domingo were "engaged in a noble conflict." It was true of a prominent citizen of Connecticut, Theodore Dwight, who published his sentiments in 1794. Similar ideas appeared in Northern newspapers of these years, and a Massachusetts Negro leader, Prince Hall, suggested, in 1797, that American Negroes would do well to imitate those of the French West Indies.

Finally, this was the period, beginning about 1795, of the spread of two great staple crops, sugar and cotton, due to the inventions of Boré and Whitney. It was, then, a period of extremely rapid transformation in the economic life of the South. It was a time of the very greatly increased commercialization of slavery. Slavery became more than ever before the foundation of a "big business," a heartless big business whose markets were unlimited and whose workers were completely in the power of the bosses. These laborers represented, indeed, the system's greatest investment, and that investment had to yield profits no matter what it meant in sweat and blood and tears.

Slave uprisings occurred in lower Louisiana in 1791 and in 1792. Details, however, are unknown. The latter year also witnessed very serious trouble during May, June and July, in Norfolk, Portsmouth, Hampton and the counties of Northampton, Greenbrier and Kanawha in Virginia, as well as in the neighborhood of Newbern, North Carolina. Many hundreds of slaves were implicated, scores were jailed, dozens lashed and several executed. There were sporadic attacks on whites, especially on patrols. Clubs, spears and some guns were found in the possession of slaves.

A Mr. Randolph of Richmond overheard three slaves, on the night of July 20, 1793, discussing plans for a forthcoming revolt and even allocating the property they were to seize. "The one who seemed to be the chief speaker said, you see how the blacks has killed the whites in the French Island [St. Domingo] and took it a while ago." Other people, including John Marshall, Chief Justice of the Supreme Court of the United States, reported, as late as November 25, discoveries of plots in Petersburg, Portsmouth, Elizabeth City, and in Powhatan and Warwick counties, Virginia. The familiar story was repeated: mobilization and arming of the militias of the affected areas, the arrest of scores of slaves and the torture and execution of the rebel leaders.

The next major outbreak occurred in 1795 in Pointe Coupée parish in the (then) Spanish colony of Louisiana. The conspiracy was betrayed after disagreement among the leaders as to when to revolt. The militia was immediately armed, and with the aid of regular soldiers the plot was crushed. The slaves resisted arrest, and twenty-five of them were killed. Twenty-three others were executed, and the bodies of nine of these were left hanging near the churches of the region. Many others were severely lashed. It appears certain that at least three whites were implicated with the slaves and were banished from the colony. There is, also, evidence of a slave conspiracy in May of this year in St. Landry parish, Louisiana. A direct result of this rebellious activity in Spanish Louisiana was the banning of the slave trade.

Two months later the depredations of a group of outlawed runaway slaves and the killing of an overseer, led to an intense slave hunt in New Hanover county, North Carolina. At least four of these black Robin Hoods were captured and executed.

Gabriel's Conspiracy

The year 1800 is the most important one in the history of American Negro slave revolts. For it is the birth year of John Brown and of Nat Turner, the year in which Denmark Vesey bought his freedom, and it is the year of the great Gabriel conspiracy.

It is clear that this conspiracy, under the leadership of Gabriel, slave of Thomas Prosser, and of Jack Bowler, another slave (both of Henrico county, Virginia), was well formed by the spring of 1800. Apparently wind of this early reached the authorities, for Virginia's Governor, James Monroe, expressed "fears of a negro insurrection" as early as April 22. Yet, as a contemporary declared, the plot was "kept with incredible Secrecy for several months," and it was not until August 9 that Monroe was warned, in a letter from Petersburg, of a forthcoming revolt. The military authorities were instantly informed of this.

The next disclosure came in the afternoon of the day, Saturday August 30, set for the outbreak. It was made by Mr. Mosby Sheppard, whose two slaves, Tom and, aptly enough, Pharaoh, had told him of the plot. Monroe acted immediately. He appointed three aides for himself, asked for and got the use of the federal armory at Manchester, posted cannon at the capitol, called into service at least six hundred and fifty troops, and gave notice of the conspiracy to every militia commander in the state.

"But," as an eyewitness declared, "upon that very evening just about Sunset, there came on the most terrible thunder, accompanied with an enormous rain, that I ever witnessed in this State." This storm flooded rivers and tore down bridges and made military activity for both the rebels and the slaveholders impossible. A patrol captain did, however, report observing an exodus of slaves out of Richmond, whereas, usually, on Saturdays, the slaves from the countryside flocked into the town.

As a matter of fact on that stormy night at least one thousand slaves had appeared at their agreed rendezvous, six miles outside of Richmond, armed with clubs and swords; but after vainly trying to advance in the face of the flood, the rebels dispersed.

The next day scores of slaves were arrested. About thirty-five Negroes were executed. At least four condemned slaves escaped from prison, and at least one committed suicide. The leader, Gabriel, a twenty-four year old giant of six feet two, was finally captured in Norfolk on September 25 and sent to Richmond. He was tried and condemned, but his execution was postponed for three days, until October 7, in the hope that he would talk. Monroe himself interviewed him, but reported that, "From what he said to me, he seemed to have made up his mind to die, and to have resolved to say but little on the subject of the conspiracy."

Thomas Jefferson pointed out to Monroe that the "other states & the world at large will forever condemn us if we indulge a principle of revenge, or go one step beyond absolute necessity. They cannot lose sight of the rights of the two parties, & the object of the unsuccessful one." Ten condemned slaves were reprieved and banished.

Certain features of this conspiracy merit special attention. It is certain that the motivating drive of the rebels, as one of their leaders said, was "death or liberty." This spirit is also shown by their heroic behavior before the courts and the gallows of the slavocrats. John Randolph, who attended the trials, declared that the slaves "manifested a sense of their rights, and contempt of danger, and a thirst for revenge which portend the most unhappy circumstances." Another lawyer who was present at the trials told an English visitor, Robert Sutcliff, of the courageous actions of the slaves. He declared that when one of the Negroes was asked,

> what he had to say to the court in his defense, he replied, in a manly tone of voice: "I have nothing more to offer than what General Washington would have had to offer, had he been taken by the British officers and put to trial by them. I have ventured my life in endeavouring to obtain the liberty of my countrymen, and am a willing sacrifice to their cause; and I beg, as a favour, that I may be immediately led to execution. I know that you have pre-determined to shed my blood, why then all this mockery of a trial?"

And a resident of Richmond wrote, September 9, 1800: "Of those who have been executed, no one has betrayed his cause. They have uniformly met death with fortitude."

It was this love of liberty which led the slaves to plan no harm to antislavery groups like the Methodists and the Quakers. The French inhabitants were also to be exempt from attack, for they personified to the slaves the ideals of liberty and equality. Poor white women were also in no case to be injured. The slaves expected too, or at least hoped that the poorer whites would join them in their struggle against the slaveholders. They counted, too, on the aid of the nearby Catawba Indians. Testimony offered at the trials directly implicated two Frenchmen, but they were never named and never captured.

It is not known how many slaves were involved in the conspiracy. One witness said 2,000, one 5,000 and one 10,000. The Governor of Mississippi thought 50,000 were implicated. Monroe himself said:

> It was distinctly seen that it embraced most of the slaves in this city [Richmond] and neighbourhood, and that the combination extended to several of the adjacent counties, Hanover, Caroline, Louisa, Chesterfield, and to the neighbourhood of the Point of the Fork; [Columbia in Goochland county was known as Point of the Fork]— there was good cause to believe that the knowledge of such a project pervaded other parts, if not the whole of the State.

(In 1800 there were about 347,000 slaves in Virginia. In the regions specified by Monroe there were about 32,000 slaves.)

Serious unrest came to the surface again in 1802. Indeed, plots had been uncovered in Norfolk just three months after Gabriel's capture, and again in the winter of 1801 in Petersburg. On January 2, 1802, trouble was once more reported from Petersburg and the militia was pressed into service. Five days later two slave conspirators were sentenced to death in Nottoway county, Virginia.

A letter of January 18 from a Negro to another in Powhatan referred to a plot and declared, "Our travelling friend has got ten thousand in readiness for the night." Two slaves were hanged in Brunswick on February 12 (seven years, to the day, before Abe Lincoln saw the light). Two more were executed in April in Halifax, and many arrests were then reported from Princess Anne and Norfolk. A rebel was executed in the latter city in May. The editor of the Norfolk *Herald* thought this conspiracy was more widespread than that of 1800. Fears in Virginia were increased when, in May, plots were reported from North Carolina.

The trouble there was widespread, conspiracies being uncovered in the counties of Camden, Currituck, Bertie, Martin, Pasquotank, Halifax, Warren, Washington, Wake and Charlotte. Hundreds of slaves were arrested, scores lashed, branded and cropped, and about fifteen hanged. The finding of pikes and swords amongst the slaves was several times mentioned. Six Negroes, "mounted on horseback," attacked the jail in Elizabeth City with the aim of rescuing their imprisoned comrades, but their attempt was defeated and four of them were captured. It appears that the leader of the North Carolina rebels was named Tom Copper and that he, with several followers, had been fugitive slaves for months.

There is good evidence that white people were accomplices of the slaves in the Virginia plots of 1802. Thus a Mr. John Scott, while informing the Governor of the trial and execution of slaves in Halifax, stated, "I have just received information that three white persons were concerned in the plot; that they have arms and ammunition concealed under their houses, and were to give aid when the negroes should begin." A slave, Lewis, twice stated at his trial that whites, "that is, the common run of poor white people," were involved. And Arthur Farrar, a slave leader, appealed for support from his fellow slaves with these words:

> Black men if you have now a mind to join with me now is your time for freedom. All clever men who will keep secret these words I give to you is life. I have taken it on myself to let the country be at liberty this lies upon my mind for a long time. Mind men I have told you a great deal I have joined with both black and white which is the common

man or poor white people, mulattoes will join with me to help free the country, although they are free already. I have got 8 or 10 white men to lead me in the fight on the magazine, they will be before me and hand out the guns, powder, pistols, shot and other things that will answer the purpose . . . black men I mean to lose my life in this way if they will take it.

Arthur was hanged in Henrico county on June 18, 1802.

1810–1816

The years 1810–1816 mark the next period of serious concerted slave unrest. Here again the familiar pattern of surrounding conditions is apparent. Severe depression, due to soil exhaustion, to the non-intercourse and embargo acts passed prior to the War of 1812, and the blockade and devastation brought by that war caused acute suffering in the slave states. The excitement incident to the waging of the war itself also affected the slaves.

There were other military events of the period affecting the slave areas, as the revolution in and American annexation of West Florida in 1810, and the slavocratic filibusters from 1811 to 1813, and again in 1816 against Texas and East Florida. Revolutionary struggles in Mexico and in South America (Simon Bolivar started his career in 1810) filled American newspapers. The anti-slavery activity of Bolivar (which was fostered by his Negro ally, Alexandre Petion, President of Haiti) was especially alarming to and anxiously discussed by the rulers of the slave states.

In March, 1810, two communications were found on a road in Halifax county, North Carolina. One was from a slave in Greene county, Georgia, to another slave, Cornell Lucas, of Martin county, NC; another, likewise to and from slaves, had been sent from Tennessee and was intended for Brunswick county, Virginia. The contents of both letters, even as to details, were similar, and one, that to Cornell Lucas, may be quoted in full:

Dear Sir—I received your letter to the fourteenth of June, 1809, with great freedom and joy to hear and understand what great proceedance you have made, and the resolution you have in proceeding on in business as we have undertook, and hope you will still continue in the same mind. We have spread the sense nearly over the continent in our part of the country, and have the day when we are to fall to work, and you must be sure not to fail on that day, and that is the 22d April, to begin about midnight, and do the work at home first, and then take the armes of them you slay first, and that will strengthen us more in armes—for freedom we want and will have, for we have served this cruel land long enuff, & be as secret convaing your nuse as possabel, and be sure to send it by some cearfull hand, and if it happens to be discovered, fail not in the day, for we are full abel to conquer by any means.—Sir, I am your Captain James, living in the state of Jorgy, in Green county—so no more at present, but remaining your sincer friend and captain until death.

General Thomas Blount, a North Carolina Congressman, informed the Governor of Georgia of these letters. This probably explains the passage in the latter's legislative message referring to information he had received "from a source so respectable as to admit but little doubt of the existence of a plan of an insurrection being formed among our domesticks and particularly in Greene county." A resident in Augusta, Georgia (about fifty miles east of Greene county) wrote to a friend April 9, 1810:

The letter from "Captain James" is but a small part of the evidence of the disposition of the Blacks in this part of the country. The most vigorous measures are taking to defeat their infernal designs. May God preserve us from the fate of St. Domingo. The papers here will, for obvious reasons, observe a total silence on this business; and the mail being near closing, I can say no more on the subject at present.

And so far as Georgia is concerned "no more on the subject" is known.

A letter of May 30, 1810, from a Virginia slaveholder, Richard W. Byrd of Smithfield, to the Governor, John Tyler, told of the discovery of insurrectionary schemes among the slaves of his neighborhood and of North Carolina. Many were arrested and lashed. Slave preachers, especially one named Peter, were declared to be the leading rebels. One had declared that "he was entitled to his freedom, and he would be damned, if he did not have it in a fortnight." Early in June at least one slave, Sam, of Isle of Wight, and two others, Glasgow and Charlotte, of Culpeper, were found guilty of conspiracy. The woman was lashed, Sam was banished and Glasgow was executed. At the same time trouble was reported from Norfolk, but details are not known.

At the end of November, 1810, "a dangerous conspiracy among the negroes was discovered" in Lexington, Kentucky. "A great many Negroes were put in jail," according to a resident, but what became of them is not reported.

On the afternoon of January 9, 1811, the people of New Orleans were thrown into the "utmost dismay and confusion" on discovering wagons and carts, straggling into the city, filled with people whose faces "wore the masks of consternation" and who told of having just escaped from "a miniature representation of the horrors of St. Domingo." They had fled from a revolt of slaves, numbering about four hundred, of St. Charles and St. John the Baptist parishes, about thirty-five miles away from the city. These slaves, led by Charles Deslondes, described as a "free mulatto from St. Domingo," rose on the evening of January 8, starting at the plantation of a Major Andry.

They were originally armed with cane knives, axes and clubs. After killing Andry's son and wounding the Major, they took possession of a few guns, drums and some sort of flags, and started marching from plantation to plantation, slaves everywhere joining them. They killed at least one other white man and destroyed a few plantations.

Major Andry, according to his own statement, organized about eighty well-armed planters and, on the ninth of January, attacked the slaves, "of whom we made great slaughter." Many, however, escaped this first attack and continued their depredations. Andry ordered "several strong detachments to pursue them through the woods, and, he wrote on January 11, "at every moment our men bring in or kill them."

Meanwhile, in New Orleans, Governor Claiborne had, on January 9, appointed seven aides for himself, called out the militia and forbidden male Negroes from going at large. Brigadier-General Wade Hampton immediately left that city with four hundred militiamen and sixty United States Army men for the scene of action. Major Milton left Baton Rouge at about the same time with two hundred more soldiers.

These forces, very early in the morning of the tenth, attacked the rebellious slaves and decimated them. Sixty-six were killed or executed on the spot, sixteen were captured and sent to New Orleans, and seventeen were reported as missing and were "supposed generally to be dead in the woods, as many bodies have been seen by the patrols." All those tried in New Orleans were executed, at least one, a leader named Gilbert, by the firing squad; and their heads were strung at intervals from the city to Andry's plantation. Hampton reported on January 12 that Milton had been for the time being posted in the neighborhood to aid "various companies of the citizens, that are scouring the country in every direction." At the same time a company of light artillery and one of dragoons were sent up the river to suppress "disturbances that may have taken place higher up."

Governor Claiborne, writing January 19, said he was "happy to find...so few Slaves are now in the woods. I hope this dreadful Insurrection is at an end and I pray God! we may never see another." What else occurred cannot be said, but this paragraph from a Louisiana paper is suggestive:

We are sorry to learn that a ferocious sanguinary disposition marked the character of some of the inhabitants. Civilized man ought to remember well his standing, and never let himself sink down to a level with the savage; our laws are summary enough and let them govern.

A law of April 25, 1811, provided for the payment by the Territory of twenty-nine thousand dollars as some compensation to the masters whose slaves were killed.

Repeatedly plots were uncovered and crushed during the War of 1812. Those of most interest occurred in Louisiana in 1812 and in South Carolina in 1813.

In New Orleans, August 18, 1812, "it was discovered that an insurrection among the negroes was intended." The militia was immediately ordered out and was kept in service until the end of the month. White men and free Negroes were implicated with the slaves. One of these white men, Joseph Wood, was executed on September 13. "All the militia of the city were under arms—strong patrols were detailed for the night." It is clear that another of the whites involved in this plot was named Macarty, and that he was jailed, but what became of him or of the slave rebels, is not known.

There is evidence of unrest among the slaves of South Carolina in 1812 and of the existence of a widespread secret slave society there in 1813. The members of this group waited, vainly, for British aid to afford an opportunity to effectively strike for freedom. A song, said to have been written by a slave, and sung by these conspirators at their meetings, has been preserved. Its last stanza and chorus are:

> Arise! arise! shake off your chains!
> Your cause is just, so Heaven ordains;
> To you shall freedom be proclaimed!
> Raise your arms and bare your breasts,
> Almighty God will do the rest.
> Blow the clarion's warlike blast;
> Call every Negro from his task;
> Wrest the scourge from Buckra's hand,
> And drive each tyrant from the land!
>
> Chorus: Firm, united let us be,
>   Resolved on death or liberty!
>   As a band of patriots joined,
>   Peace and plenty we shall find.

Early in 1816 Virginia was rocked by an indigenous John Brown, one George Boxley. In appearance he was anything but like Brown, but in ideas the two men were well nigh identical. Boxley was about thirty-five years old, six feet two inches tall, with a "thin visage, of a sallow complexion, thin make, his hair light or yellowish (thin on top of his head, and tied behind)—he stoops a little in his shoulders, has large whiskers, blue or grey eyes, pretends to be very religious, is fond of talking and speaks quick." Contemporaries were in doubt as to "whether he is insane or not," since he openly "declared that the distinction between rich and poor was too great; that offices were given rather to wealth than to merit; and seemed to be an advocate for a more leveling system of government. For many years he had avowed his disapprobation of the slavery of the Negroes, and wished they were free." It was believed that his failure to be elected to the state legislature sometime prior to the War of 1812 his declining economic fortunes, and his failure to advance in position while fighting in that war had embittered him.

Be that as it may, late in 1815 George Boxley decided to attempt to free the slaves and formed a conspiracy in Spotsylvania, Louisa and Orange counties. A slave woman betrayed it, and early in 1816 about thirty slaves were arrested. Boxley, after vainly trying to organize a rescue party, fled. He finally surrendered and was imprisoned but, with the flame of a candle and a file smuggled to him by his wife, he escaped, in May. Though a reward of one thousand dollars was offered for him he was never captured. About six slaves were hanged and the same number banished.

A favorite, but unnamed, slave betrayed a plot involving many Negroes in and around Camden, South Carolina, one month after Boxley's escape. The fourth of July was the day selected for the outbreak, which was to have been started by setting fire to several houses. Espionage was used to uncover the ramifications of this widespread conspiracy. A letter from Camden, dated July 4, stated that the slaves had been plotting since December, 1815, and that the local jail "is filled with negroes. They are stretched on their backs on the bare floor, and scarcely move their heads; but have a strong guard placed over them.... The negroes will never know who betrayed them, for they tried to engage all for a great distance round."

The legislature purchased, for one thousand one hundred dollars, the freedom of the traitor and passed a law giving him fifty dollars a year for the rest of his life. At least six rebel leaders were hanged.

Two major expeditions were carried out in 1816 against large settlements of outlawed fugitive slaves, one in South Carolina, the other in Florida. The maroons were attacked in the first case by the state militia, and in the second by infantry and artillery units of the regular United States army. About three hundred Negroes and a few whites were killed in these engagements.

1821–1831

From 1821 through 1831 there were incessant reports of slave unrest throughout the South. And, once more, that decade was marked by severe economic depression. Suffering was increased, too, by natural calamities such as drought in the southeast in 1826, in the southwest in 1827 and again in the southeast in 1830. Excessive rains ruined crops in South Carolina and Louisiana in 1829. Because of this depression there was a much more rapid increase of the slave population than the white population in the eastern slave states.

Revolutionary sentiments and slogans were in the air, and Southern papers were filled with praise for revolutionists in Turkey, Greece, Italy, Spain, France, Belgium, Poland, South America, the West Indies and Mexico. (It was only home-grown rebels who were referred to as "banditti" by the local press.) Slave uprisings in Brazil, Venezuela, Martinique, Puerto Rico, Cuba, Antigua, Tortola and Jamaica also found their way into the local press and conversation. The decade witnessed, too, an upsurge in the anti-slavery movement in England (which freed her colonial slaves in 1833), in Mexico (which abolished slavery in 1829), and in the border slave states and the northern states of America.

The activities of large numbers of outlawed fugitive slaves, aided by free Negroes, assumed the proportions of rebellion in the summer of 1821 in Onslow, Carteret and Bladen counties, North Carolina. There were, too, plans for joint action between these maroons and the field slaves against the slaveholders.

Approximately three hundred members of the militia of the three counties saw service for about twenty-five days in August and September. About twelve of these men were wounded when two companies accidentally fired upon each other. The situation was under control by the middle of September, and although the militia "did not succeed in apprehending all the runaways & fugitives, they did good by arresting some, and driving others off, and suppressing the spirit of insurrection." A newspaper report of May, 1824, disclosed that the "prime mover" of this trouble, Isam, "alias General Jackson," was among those who escaped at the time, for he is there reported as dying from lashes publicly inflicted at Cape Fear, North Carolina.

Denmark Vesey

The conspiracy in and around Charleston, SC, of 1822 was one of the most, if not the most, extensive in American history. It was led by a former slave, Denmark Vesey, who had purchased his freedom in 1800.

Vesey, like most of the other rebels, was deeply religious. In justifying his plans to his numerous followers he read to them "from the bible how *the children of Israel were delivered out of Egypt from bondage.*" Antislavery speeches uttered in Congress during the Missouri debates of 1820–21 were also known to and encouraged the conspirators.

If Vesey's companion were to bow "to a white person he would rebuke him, and observe that all men were born equal, and that he was surprised that any one would degrade himself by such conduct; that he would never cringe to the whites, nor ought any who had the feelings of a man." He had not heeded the urgings of the slaveowners that free Negroes go to Africa, "*because he had not the will,* he wanted to stay and see what he could do for his fellow-creatures," including his own children, who were slaves. (These quotations are from the official record of the trials and all emphases are as in the original.)

Most of the other Negroes felt as Vesey did. Two of the rebels told a slaveholders' court, "They never spoke to any person of color on the subject, or knew of any one who had been spoken to by the other leaders, who had withheld his assent." Nevertheless, the leaders feared betrayal, and it came. One of them, Peter Poyas, had warned an agent, "Take care and don't mention it to those waiting men who receive presents of old coats, etc., from their masters, or they'll betray us." The traitor was Devany, favorite slave of Colonel Prioleau.

Vesey had picked the second Sunday in July as the day to revolt. Sunday was selected because on that day it was customary for slaves to enter the city, and July because many whites would then be away. The betrayal led him to put the date ahead one month, but Vesey could not communicate this to his country confederates, some of whom were eighty miles outside the city. Peter Poyas and Mingo Harth, the two leaders first arrested, behaved "with so much composure and coolness" that "the wardens were completely deceived." Both were freed on May 31, but spies were put on their trails. Another slave, William, gave further testimony and more arrests were made. The most damaging of these was the arrest of Charles Drayton, who agreed to act as a spy. This led to complete exposure.

One hundred and thirty-one Negroes were arrested in Charleston, and forty-seven condemned. Twelve were pardoned and transported, but thirty-five were hanged. Twenty were banished and twenty-six acquitted, although the owners were asked to transport eleven of these out of the state. Thirty-eight were discharged by the court. Four white men, American, Scottish, Spanish and German, were fined and imprisoned for aiding the Negroes by words of encouragement.

Although the leaders had kept lists of their comrades, only one list and part of another were found. Moreover, most of the executed slaves followed the advice of Poyas, "Die silent, as you shall see me do," and so it is difficult to say how many Negroes were involved. One witness said 6,600 outside of Charleston, and another said 9,000 altogether were implicated. The plan of revolt, comprising simultaneous attacks from five points and a sixth force on horseback to patrol the streets, further indicated a very considerable number of rebels.

The preparations had been thorough. By the middle of June the Negroes had made about two hundred and fifty pike heads and bayonets and over three hundred daggers. They had noted every store containing arms and had given instructions to all slaves who tended or could easily get horses as to when and where to bring the animals. Even a barber had assisted by making wigs as a disguise for the slaves. Vesey had also written twice to St. Domingo, telling of his plans and asking for aid.

After the arrests of the leaders many of the slaves planned their rescue, and an attempt to revolt in the city was suppressed by state troops. It was felt necessary to bring in Federal troops during the time of the executions.

There was trouble outside Charleston in July. Early that month three slaves were executed in Jacksonboro, forty miles west of the city. In August the Governor offered a reward of two hundred dollars for the arrest or killing of about twenty armed Negroes harassing the planters. In September a guarded report came of the discovery and crushing of a slave plot in Beaufort, SC; "The Town council was in secret session. Particulars had not transpired." They rarely did. Tighten restrictive laws, get rid of as many free Negroes as possible, keep the slaves ignorant, and your powder dry, hang the leaders, banish others, whip, crop, scourge scores, and above all keep it quiet, or, if you must talk, speak of the slaves' "contentedness" and "docility"!

The Norfolk *Herald* of May 12, 1823, under the heading "A Serious Subject," called attention to the activities, reaching revolt, of a growing number of pugnacious outlawed slaves in the southern part of Norfolk county, Virginia. The citizens of the region were in "a state of mind peculiarly harrassing and painful," for no one's life or property was secure. The Negroes had already obtained arms and had killed several slaveholders and overseers. Indeed, one slaveholder had received a note from these amazing men suggesting it would be healthier for him to remain indoors at night—and he did.

A large body of militia was ordered out to exterminate these outcasts and "thus relieve the neighbouring inhabitants from a state of perpetual anxiety and apprehension, than which nothing can be more painful." During the next few weeks there were occasional reports of the killing or capturing of outlaws, culminating June 25 in the capture of the leader, Bob Ferebee. It was declared that he had been an outlaw for six years. Bob Ferebee was executed on the twenty-fifth of July.

The inhabitants of Edgecombe county, North Carolina, were much distraught in December 1825, "by the partial discovery of an insurrectionary plot among the blacks." The slaves seem to have believed that the national government had set them free. The patrol was strengthened, the militia called out and the unrest crushed; but what that meant in human terms is not known.

Early in September 1826, seventy-five slaves—chained on a slave-ship going down the Mississippi, with the boat one hundred miles south of Lexington, Kentucky—in some way broke their chains, killed their four guards and another white passenger and managed to get into Indiana. All the rebels "except one or two" were captured, five were hanged, some banished from the country and the rest sold south. The same year, twenty-nine slaves on board the domestic slave-ship, *Decatur*, revolted, killed the captain and mate, and commanded another white to take them to Haiti. The boat was captured and taken into New York, where in some way every one of the slaves escaped. One, however, William Bowser, was later captured and executed in New York City on December 15, 1826.

A lady in Georgia wrote, in June, 1827, that a "most dangerous and extensive insurrection of the blacks was detected at Macon a few days since." Three hundred slaves and one white man were involved, but no further particulars are known. Later that same month came the report of the destruction of a considerable group of slave outlaws in Alabama. These maroons had been exceedingly troublesome and were constantly gaining new recruits. They planned to build a fort just prior to their annihilation, and then "a great number of Negroes in the secret were to join them." In the attack, during which the Negroes "fought desperately" with what poor weapons they had, three slaves were killed, several escaped, and others were wounded and captured. One white was wounded.

The years 1829 and 1830 were filled with rebellious activities. Space permits but the barest mention of the outstanding events. Large-scale slave incendiarism was common, most notably in Augusta and Savannah, Georgia, in 1829, and in New Orleans and Cambridge, Maryland, in 1830. But, of course, the slaves did not restrict themselves to fire.

In February 1829, slaves of several plantations forty miles north of New Orleans revolted. Militia suppressed the outbreak. At least two of the leaders were hanged. The Secretary of War wrote to the local commanding officer,

Colonel Clinch, on March 17, 1829, to hold himself ready to aid the Governor of Louisiana, "on account of the insurrectionary spirit manifested by the black population in that state."

Probably in this same month a widespread conspiracy was uncovered in the neighbourhood of Georgetown, South Carolina. The militia of the region was reinforced by troops and arms forwarded from Charleston. That the trouble was serious becomes clear from a letter of April 17, sent by the Attorney-General of the state to the military commander, General Allston, on the scene. The official comments that while the proceedings were not yet "bloody" he feared the General would "hang half the country. You must take care and save negroes enough for the rice crop." The leaders of this plot, all slaves, were Charles Prioleau, Nat, Robert and Quico. Quico was banished. What became of the others is not known.

The agitation of western Virginia for a greater share in the governing of the state, which was accompanied by much talk about liberty and equality, culminated in the constitutional convention of 1829–30. The excitement affected the slaves and inspired them to concerted efforts for freedom. Alarm pervaded Richmond, and the counties of Mathews, Isle of Wight, Gloucester and Hanover. Fears were intensified with the report of the killing of one white and the wounding of another in Hanover County on July 4, 1829, by about eight slaves. Patrols, militia and volunteer military bodies were pressed into service and crushed, for the time being, the "spirit of dissatisfaction and insubordination," to quote the Governor of Virginia.

In August 1829, a drove of sixty slaves, men and women, were marching on their way to be sold in the deep South when, between Greenup and Vanceburg, Kentucky, two of the slaves apparently began to fight with each other. One of the white drivers came at them with a whip, and immediately all the slaves dropped their filed chains. Two of the white drivers were killed, but a third, with the aid of a slave woman, succeeded in escaping and obtained assistance; all the slaves were soon captured. What became of them is not known.

The same county in Kentucky, Greenup, witnessed, early in December, the execution of four slaves who had rebelled while being sent south and had killed their master. According to Southern newspapers the slaves "all maintained to" the last, the utmost firmness and resignation to their fate. They severally addressed the assembled multitude, in which they attempted to justify the deed they had committed. One of the condemned slaves, the instant before being launched into eternity shouted, "death—death at any time in preference to slavery."

By this same month of December 1829, copies of the revolutionary pamphlet denouncing slavery, written by a free Negro of Boston, David Walker (and first published in September) were found amongst slaves and some whites in Louisiana, Georgia, North Carolina and Virginia. This evoked tremendous fear and led to increased police and military measures. It also definitely seems to have inspired slave plots, particularly in Wilmington, North Carolina, in September 1830.

Going back, however, to December 1829, we find that Negroes aboard the domestic slave-trader, *Lafayette* (!), bound for sale at New Orleans from Norfolk, revolted, with the aim of reaching St. Domingo. The slaves stated that a similar effort was to be made by Negroes on another boat from the same port. The slaves "were subdued, after considerable difficulty, and twenty-five of them were bolted down to the deck, until the arrival of the vessel at New Orleans."

Early in April 1830, a conspiracy was uncovered in New Orleans, and at least two slaves were hanged. Plots were discovered in and around Dorchester, Maryland, in July. In October a conspiracy involving at least one hundred Negroes, including some who were free, was crushed in Plaquemines parish, Louisiana, by the local militia. In November plots were reported from Nashville, Tennessee, and from Wilmington, North Carolina.

On December 14, 1830, the inhabitants of Sampson, Bladen, New Hanover, and Duplin counties, North Carolina, petitioned the legislature for aid because their "slaves are become almost uncontroulable." Ten days later the residents of Newbern, Tarborough and Hillsborough in the same state were terrified by slave unrest. And "the inhabitants of Newbern being advised of the assemblage of sixty armed slaves in a swamp in their vicinity, the military were called out, and surrounding the swamp, killed the whole number." A resident of Wilmington, NC, reported, on January 7, 1831, that: "There has been much shooting of negroes in this neighborhood recently, in consequence of symptoms of liberty having been discovered among them. These inhuman acts are kept profoundly secret." In Mississippi, too, on the day, in 1830, of the birth of the humble Prince of Peace, slave conspiracies were reported, particularly in Jefferson County.

The disaffection and unrest continued into the early months of 1831. Because of this and at the urgent requests of local authorities, the United States government sent two companies of infantry to New Orleans, and five more companies to Fort Monroe, in Virginia.

Nat Turner

The terror prevalent in the South due to this rebellious activity was soon transformed into hysteria as the result of the actions of a slave named Nat

Turner. He had been born October 2, 1800, and lived all his life in Southampton county, Virginia. When, in August, 1831, he led a rebellion, he was officially described as follows:

> 5 feet 6 or 8 inches high, weighs between 150 and 160 pounds, rather bright complexion, but not a mulatto, broad shoulders, large flat nose, large eyes, broad flat feet, rather knock-kneed, walks brisk and active, hair on the top of the head very thin, no beard, except on the upper lip and the top the chin, a scar on one of his temples, also one on the back of his neck, a large knot on one of the bones of his right arm, near the wrist, produced by a blow.

Nat Turner was an intelligent and gifted man who could not reconcile himself to life as a slave. His religion offered him a rationalization for his rebellious feeling and, having taught himself how to read, he immersed himself in the stories of the Bible. His personality and keen mentality made him influential among his fellow-slaves and even with some neighboring poor whites.

In 1826 or 1827 he ran away, as his father had done successfully, and stayed away one month. Yet doubts overwhelmed him, and he felt that perhaps he "should return to the service of my earthly master." He did, but the other slaves "found fault, and murmured against me, saying that if they had my sense they would not serve any master in the world." In the spring of 1828 Turner, while working the fields, was finally convinced that he was to take up Christ's struggle for the liberation of the oppressed, "for the time was fast approaching when the first should be last and the last should be first."

The solar eclipse of February 12, 1831, was his sign. This fact has led chauvinistic historians to ridicule the "negro intelligence" (whatever that may mean) of Turner. The fact is that his (what would today be called) superstitious nature was common in his day among all people. Southerners still, generally, carried on agriculture according to the signs of the Zodiac. In 1833 under William Miller, a white citizen of New York, thousands of people were to be firmly convinced that the end of the world and the second coming of Christ were just around the corner. Indeed, that eclipse of 1831 itself led a white minister in New York City to prophesy that the whole city "South of Canal-Street would sink," and some folks actually moved to the upper part of the city.

Following the eclipse, Turner told four slaves it was time to prepare for rebellion. Significantly they selected July 4 as the day on which to strike for freedom. But Turner was ill on that day and he waited for another sign. This came on August 13 in the peculiar greenish blue color of the sun. A meeting was called for Sunday, August 21.

> Turner arrived last and noticed a newcomer.
> I saluted them on coming up, and asked Will how came he there, he answered, his life was worth no more than others, and his liberty as dear to him. I asked him if he meant to obtain it? He said he would, or lose his life. This was enough to put him in full confidence.

Such were the "bandits," as the slavocrats called them, that Nat Turner led.

In the evening of that Sunday this group of six slaves started on their crusade against slavery by killing Turner's master, Joseph Travis, together with his family. Within twenty-four hours some seventy Negroes, several mounted, had covered an area of twenty miles and had killed every human being (with an important exception), about sixty in all, that they came upon. The exception was a family of non-slaveholding poor whites who, as the Governor of Virginia sarcastically but truthfully declared, were hardly any better off than the rebels.

When within three miles of the Southampton county seat, Jerusalem (now called Courtland), there was, against Turner's advice, a fatal delay, and the Negroes—whose guns, according to the Richmond *Compiler* of August 29, were not "fit for use"—were overwhelmed by volunteer and state troops. Soon hundreds of soldiers, including cavalry and artillery units of the United States Army, swarmed over the county and, together with the inhabitants, slaughtered over one hundred slaves. Some, in the agony of death, "declared," to quote an eyewitness, "that they was going happy fore that God had a hand in what they had been doing." The killings and torturings ended when the commanding officer, General Eppes, threatened martial law.

Thirteen slaves and three free Negroes were immediately (and legally) hanged. According to Governor Floyd, "all died bravely indicating no reluctance to lose their lives in such a cause." Turner, himself, though he never left the county, was not captured until October 30. By November 5, after pleading not guilty, for, as he said, he did not feel *guilty*, he was sentenced to "be hung by the neck until you are dead! dead! dead!" on the eleventh of November. And on that day Nat Turner went calmly to his death.

The South was panic-stricken. Disaffected or rebellious slaves were, in the winter of 1831, arrested, tortured or executed in other counties of Virginia, in Delaware, Maryland, North Carolina (where at least three slaveholders died from fear!), Tennessee, Kentucky, South Carolina, Georgia, Alabama, Mississippi and Louisiana. The terror in the latter state was increased when it was discovered, according to Major-General Alexander Macomb, commanding officer of the United States Army, writing October 12, 1831, that "the coloured people in the (West Indian) Islands, had a correspondence with the Blacks of Louisiana, tending to further their insurrectionary dispositions."

There is evidence, too, that the unrest extended to poor whites as well as Negroes, at least in Virginia and North Carolina. A letter to Governor Stokes of North Carolina, from Union county, dated September 12, 1831, declared that the slave rebels there were "assisted by some rascally whites." A militia colonel of Hyde county told the same Governor on September 25 that non-slaveholding whites were refusing to join in slave-suppression activity for they said "they have no slaves of their own and ought not to be interrupted about the slaves of others." Finally, a Baltimore newspaper of October 15, 1831, stated that so far as North Carolina was concerned the "extensive and organized plan to bring about desolation and massacre ... was not altogether confined to slaves."

The Governor of Virginia, in his legislative message of December 6, 1831, darkly hinted that the unrest was "not confined to the slaves." Indeed, there exists a letter from a white man, Williamson Mann, to a slave, Ben Lee, dated Chesterfield county, August 29, 1831, which confirms this. The letter makes it clear that several whites, among whom a Methodist by the name of Edmonds is especially mentioned, were plotting to aid the slaves. Mr. Mann hoped the anti-slavery efforts might succeed so that "we poor whites can get work as well as slaves."

1835–1840

The slaveholders of Madison and Hinds counties, Mississippi (where the Negro population had recently increased at a tremendous rate), became uneasy in June, 1835, due to rumors of an impending uprising. In that month a lady of the former county reported to her neighbors that she had overheard one of her slaves say, "she wished to God it was all over and done with; that she was tired of waiting on the *white folks*, and wanted to be her own mistress the balance of her days, and clean up her own house."

A favorite slave was sent among the others as a spy and soon accused one Negro. This slave, "after receiving a most severe chastisement" confessed that a plot for a revolt had been formed and implicated the slaves of a Mr. Ruel Blake, as well as that man himself. One of Mr. Blake's slaves was severely whipped, "but refused to confess anything—alleging all the time, that if they wanted to know what his master had told him, they might whip on until they killed him, that he promised that he would never divulge it."

Other slaves were tortured and it was finally discovered that there was a general plot of the slaves in the neighborhood and that a number of white men were implicated. During July about fifteen slaves and six white men were hanged. Among the white men were at least two, Joshua Cotton and William Saunders, who were notorious criminals and were interested in rebellion only for plunder's sake. It appears, however, that at least two of the white men, A. L. Donovan and R. Blake, actually hated slavery.

In October, 1835, an extensive conspiracy, said to have been instigated by white lumbermen, was unearthed and crushed in Monroe county, Georgia. This same month a plot involving at least one hundred slaves was discovered in Texas, which at the moment was rebelling against Mexico. The (slave) rebels were arrested, "many whipped nearly to death, some hung, etc." The slaves had planned to divide the land once they had conquered their masters. In December, 1835, a confidential slave betrayed a plot in East Felidana, Louisiana. At least two whites were found to be implicated and were hanged. What happened to the slaves does not appear.

It is certain that great excitement prevailed in Tennessee and Georgia in 1836 due to reports of conspiracies and uprisings, but further details are lacking.

A conspiracy for rebellion among the slaves of Rapides parish, Louisiana, which a slaveholder described as "perfectly-planned," was betrayed in October, 1837. About forty slave leaders were arrested and at least nine of these, together with three free Negroes were hanged. After two companies of United States troops entered the zone of trouble the Negroes were "completely subdued." The betrayer of this plot was freed in 1838 and given five hundred dollars by the state to aid him in settling in some distant community.

The depression year of 1840 was very troublesome. Widespread slave disaffection was reported from Washington, DC, from Southampton county, Virginia, from "some part of North Carolina," from Alabama and, especially, from Louisiana. The unrest in Louisiana centered in Iberville, Lafayette, St. Landry, Rapides and Avoyelles parishes. Many hundreds of slaves and several white men were arrested and scores of Negroes were legally and extra-legally killed. The massacre seems to have been most terrible in Rapides parish and it was only after a regiment of soldiers arrived "that the indiscriminate slaughter was stayed."

The Pre-Civil War Decade

The question of slavery agitated the nation during the decade prior to the Civil War as never before. This was the period of *Uncle Tom's Cabin* and the

Impending Crisis, of the attack on Senator Sumner and the Dred Scott Decision, of the Kansas-Nebraska debates and the Kansas War, of the exciting elections of 1856 and 1860, and of a hundred other events forcing the slavery issue into the limelight. This reached the minds of the slaves. Moreover, an especially acute economic depression in the middle of the period, 1854–56, reached their stomachs. These, undoubtedly, are the two main reasons for the very great concerted slave unrest of the decade. Here only the most important plots and uprisings may be described.

A free Negro, George Wright, of New Orleans, was asked by a slave, Albert, in June, 1853, to join in a revolt. He declared his interest and was brought to a white man, a teacher by the name of Dyson, who had come to Louisiana in 1840 from Jamaica. Dyson trusted Wright, declared that one hundred whites had agreed to aid the Negroes in their bid for freedom, and urged Wright to join. Wright did—verbally.

He almost immediately betrayed the plot and led the police to Albert. The slave at the time of arrest, June 13, carried a knife, a sword, a revolver, one bag of bullets, one pound of powder, two boxes of percussion caps and eighty-six dollars. The patrol was ordered out, the city guard strengthened, and twenty slaves and Dyson were instantly arrested.

Albert stated that twenty-five hundred slaves were involved. He named none. In prison he declared that "all his friends had gone down the coast and were fighting like soldiers. If he had shed blood in the cause he would not have minded the arrest." It was indeed reported by the local press that "a large number of negroes have fled from their masters and are now missing," but no actual fighting was mentioned. Excitement was great along the coast, however, and the arrest of a white man, a cattle driver, occurred at Bonnet Clare. A fisherman, Michael McGill, testified that he had taken Dyson and two slaves carrying what he thought were arms to a swamp from which several Negroes emerged. The Negroes were given the arms and disappeared.

The local papers tended to minimize the trouble, but did declare that New Orleans contained "numerous and fanatical" whites, "cutthroats in the name of liberty—murderers in the guise of philanthropy." They commended the swift action of the police and called for further precautions and restrictions. The last piece of information concerning this is an item telling of an attack by Albert upon the jailer in which he caused "the blood to flow." The disposition of the rebels is not reported.

The year 1856 was one of extraordinary slave unrest. In the summer a large group of maroon Negroes in Bladen and Robeson counties, North Carolina, became very daring and dangerous, successfully fighting off attacks by armed slaveholders. In September a conspiracy involving over two hundred slaves, together with a white man named William Mehrmann and many of "the lower class of the Mexican population," was discovered in Colorado county, Texas. The whites were forced to leave, and each of the two hundred slaves arrested was severely whipped, two dying under the lash. Three were hanged.

In October a plot involving some three hundred slaves and a few white men was reported from Ouchita and Union counties, Arkansas, and across the border in the parishes of Union and Claiborne in Louisiana. Early in November "an extensive scheme of negro insurrection" was discovered in Lavaca, DeWitt and Victoria counties, Texas. A letter from Victoria, of November 7, declared that the "negroes had killed off all the dogs in the neighbourhood, and were preparing for a general attack" when betrayal came. Whites were again implicated, one being "severely horsewhipped" and the others banished. What became of the slaves is not reported. A week later an extensive conspiracy for rebellion was disclosed in St. Mary parish, Louisiana. Many slaves together with three whites and a free Negro were arrested. The slaves were lashed, and at least one of the whites together with the free Negro were hanged.

During this same month of November plots were uncovered, always with a few whites implicated, in Fayette, Obion and Montgomery counties, Tennessee, in Fulton, Kentucky, and in New Madrid and Scott counties, Missouri. Again in December conspiracies were reported, occasionally outbreaks occurred, and slaves and whites were arrested, banished, tortured, executed in virtually every slave state.

It is clear that news of this mass discontent was censored. Thus a Georgia paper, the Milledgeville *Federal Union*, admitted it had "refrained from giving our readers any of the accounts of contemplated insurrections." Similarly the New Orleans *Daily Picayune* stated it had "refrained from publishing a great deal which we receive by the mails, going to show that there is a spirit of turbulence abroad in various quarters." Later it confessed that the trouble in Kentucky, Arkansas, Tennessee, Mississippi, Louisiana and Texas amounted "very nearly to positive insurrection." Finally, the Washington correspondent of the New York *Weekly Tribune* stated on December 20 that the "insurrectionary movement in Tennessee obtained more headway than is known to the public—important facts being suppressed in order to check the spread of the contagion and prevent the true condition of affairs from being understood elsewhere." Next week the same correspondent declared that he had "reliable information" of serious trouble in New Orleans leading to the hanging of twenty slaves, "but the newspapers carefully refrain from any mention of the facts."

To the areas already mentioned as disturbed by slave disaffection may be added Maryland, Alabama, the Carolinas, Georgia and Florida. Features of the plots are worth particular notice. Arms were discovered among the slaves in, at least, Tennessee, Kentucky and Texas. Preparations for blowing up bridges were uncovered. Attacks upon iron mills in Kentucky were started but defeated. At least three slaveholders were killed in the same state. The date for the execution of four slaves in Dover, Tennessee, was pushed ahead for fear of an attempt at rescue, and a body of one hundred and fifty men was required to break up the same number of slaves marching to Dover for that very purpose.

A letter, passed along by whites as well as slaves, found December 24, 1856, on a slave employed by the Richmond and York railroad in Virginia, is interesting from the standpoint of white cooperation. It indicates, too, a desire for something more than bare bodily freedom. It reads:

> My dear friend: You must certainly remember what I have told you— you must come up to the contract—as we have carried things thus far. Meet at the place where we said, and dont make any disturbance until we meet and d'ont let any white man know any-thing about it, unless he is trust-worthy. The articles are all right and the country is ours certain. Bring all your friends; tell them, that if they want freedom, to come. D'ont let it leak out; if you should get in any difficulty send me word immediately to afford protection. Meet at the crossing and prepare for Sunday night for the neighbourhood—
>
>   P.S. Dont let anybody see this—
>   Freedom—Freeland
>   Your old friend
>   W. B.

Another interesting feature of the plots of November and December, 1856, is the evidence of the effect of the bitter Presidential contest of that year between the Republican, Frémont, and the Democrat, Buchanan. The slaves were certain that the Republican Party stood for their liberation, and some felt that Colonel Frémont would aid them, forcibly, in their efforts for freedom. "Certain slaves are so greatly imbued with this fable that I have seen them smile when they were being whipped, and have heard them say that, 'Frémont and his men hear the blows they receive.'" One unnamed martyr, a slave iron worker in Tennessee, "said that he knew all about the plot, but would die before he would tell. He therefore received 750 lashes, from which he died."

The story of John Brown's raid has so often been told that it need not be repeated in any detail. Suffice it to say that on the night of October 16, 1859, old John Brown led twelve other white men and five Negroes (four of whom, Copeland, Leary, Anderson, Green, were escaped slaves; one, Newby, a free Negro) in an attack upon the armory in Harper's Ferry, Virginia (now West Virginia). The armory was taken, but Brown and his comrades were trapped and besieged. On October 18 a force of United States marines, led by Colonel Robert E. Lee, overpowered the rebels, seriously wounding Brown himself. The seven survivors of the battle were tried, convicted and hanged, Brown going to his death on December 2, 1859.

John Brown had in mind the establishment of centers of armed Negroes in the mountains of Virginia to which the slaves might flee and from which liberating forays might be conducted. The raid itself would not have been possible without the encouragement and financial aid offered by white and Negro abolitionists like Smith, Parker, Higginson, Sanborn, and Gloucester, Douglass, Still, Garnet.

To draw the lesson from the raid's failure that the slaves were docile, as so many writers have done, is absurd. And it would be absurd even if we did not have the record of the bitter struggle of the Negro people against enslavement. This is so for two main reasons: first, Brown's attack was made in the northwestern part of Virginia where slavery was of a domestic, household nature and where Negroes were relatively few; secondly, Brown gave the slaves absolutely no foreknowledge of his attempt. (Frederick Douglass, the great Negro leader, warned Brown that this would be fatal to his purpose.) Thus the slaves had no way of judging Brown's chances or even his sincerity, and in that connection it is important to bear in mind that slave stealing was a common crime in the old South.

Panic seized the slavocracy. Rumors of plots and revolts flew thick and fast, many undoubtedly false or exaggerated both by terror and by anti-"Black Republican" politicians. Bearing this in mind, however, there yet remains good evidence of real and widespread slave disaffection following Brown's attempt.

Serious trouble, taking the form of incendiarism, disturbed the neighborhood of Berryville, Virginia, in November, 1859. In December, Negroes in Bolivar, Missouri, revolted and attacked their enslavers with sticks and stones. A few whites were injured and at least one slave was killed. Later, according to a local paper:

> A mounted company was ranging the woods in search of negroes. The owner of some rebellious slaves was badly wounded, and only

saved himself by flight. Several blacks have been severely punished. The greatest excitement prevailed, and every man was armed and prepared for a more serious attack.

Still later advices declared that "the excitement had somewhat subsided." What this "subsidence" meant in human suffering is unknown.

The years from 1860 through 1864 were filled with slave revolts and conspiracies. These have been described in detail in the writer's work, *The Negro in the Civil War* (New York, 1938). Here it need merely be stated that, in these years, poor whites were almost invariably implicated as allies of the Negro slaves. Furthermore, at times, the plots very definitely had aims other than the end of slavery, such as distribution of the land, the work animals and the tools to the common people of the South. And the entire South was involved, from Maryland to Florida, from Kentucky to Texas.

III. EFFECTS OF THE REVOLTS AND CONSPIRACIES

There are few phases of ante-bellum Southern life and history that were not in some way influenced by the fear of, or the actual occurrence of, slave uprisings. In some cases the influences were plainly of a minor, if not of a merely formal nature. Such was surely the case when Southerners appealed in 1803 for the annexation of Louisiana in order to take it out of the hands of a possibly hostile and apparently revolutionary France, which might use that possession as a means of arousing slave rebellion in the United States. Similar arguments were used to justify the annexation of Texas and Florida.

Another argument, however, used in the Louisiana annexation case and in every subsequent territorial advance of the slavocracy, to the effect that the South needed new lands in order to lessen the danger of slave rebellion by checking the concentration of Negroes within a limited area, seems to have been a fairly important consideration in the minds of Southern leaders.

The possibility of slave rebellion, the necessity of guarding one-third of the population, and the inadvisability of arming that proportion of the population, created serious military difficulties for the United States and later, and particularly, for the Confederate States. When, for example, during the Revolution, South Carolina learned that the Continental Congress was seriously contemplating the wholesale arming of the slaves to fight the British (with future manumission understood), she threatened to withdraw from the contest with England and return to a colonial status. And, in other ways, throughout the Revolutionary War and the War of 1812, the United

States was made keenly aware of military weakness due to the fear of servile disaffection. Similarly, as has been shown in the work previously referred to, this fear, and its not infrequent justification in actual outbreak, was a major military disadvantage to the Confederate States.

During years of national peace the military might of the United States government was concentrated in the Southern region, undoubtedly because of fear of rebellion. The use of this might for purposes of slave suppression occurred in Virginia in 1800, in Louisiana in 1811, in Florida in 1816 and 1820, in South Carolina in 1822, in Virginia in 1831, in Louisiana in 1837, in Florida again during the Second Seminole War from 1836–43, and in Virginia in 1859.

The South itself was, so far as about one-third of its population was concerned, a huge fortress in which prisoners were held, at hard labor, for life. Like any other fortress it was exceedingly well guarded. Militarism was a dominant characteristic of the region and was noticed by virtually every visitor. As an English traveler, Francis Baily remarked in 1796, every white man was a soldier. The carrying of some type of weapon was a universal characteristic of Southern white men. Well-trained militia companies and volunteer military units were numerous, patrols were everywhere, armed overseers were on all plantations, guards and standing armies (like the seventy soldiers maintained by Richmond after Gabriel's conspiracy of 1800) abounded in the cities. Slavery was a chronic state of warfare, and all men who were not Negroes were, *by law*, part of the standing army of oppressors.

The violence and militarism, the chronic state of war, were most important factors in arousing opposition to the slave system amongst non-slaveholders. This is especially true of the Quaker element in the South; mass migrations of those devout people occurred particularly after periods of serious slave unrest. This was especially true in the years from about 1795–1805 and again from 1828–32, when thousands of Quakers from Virginia to Georgia removed from the South into Pennsylvania and the Northwest. It is also to be noted that there is evidence of migrations of other non-slaveholders, during serious slave unrest, from the very simple motive of fear. Why remain in an area subject to intermittent upheavals?

It has been mentioned that all white male citizens of the South were subject to patrol duty. The brunt, however, of this arduous duty fell upon the poor whites, not only because they were most numerous, but also because the wealthier whites easily paid the fine of from one dollar to five dollars for failure to perform patrol duty. This was of course impossible to the poor whites, and this class distinction aroused bitterness, especially since patrolling was often dangerous and rarely pleasant. Another grievance of non-slaveholding whites arose from the fact that they were taxed (in common, of course, with slaveholders; though in some states, as North Carolina, the tax system favored the slaveholders) to support the slave suppression apparatus. Moreover, masters whose slaves were executed by the state were reimbursed the approximate value of the slave and this, again, added to the non-slaveholders' tax bills.

Fear of slave disaffection was a factor in the widespread Southern opposition to urbanization and industrialization. Undoubtedly of greatest importance in keeping the pre-war South rural and agrarian was the fact that the institution of slavery froze billions of dollars of capital into human beings. Nevertheless the fear that proletarianized Negroes, congregated in common centers, would be more difficult to hold in enslavement was widespread, and did much to discourage large-scale manufacturing.

It has been shown that the prevalence of revolutionary sentiments and slogans invariably reached the consciousness of America's slaves and affected their behavior. The slavocrats were keenly aware of this. The irreconcilability of a progressive political philosophy with the persistence of plantation slavery was well understood in the South. The fear that the former would lead to the destruction of the latter did much to hasten the South in its repudiation of Jeffersonian equalitarian doctrines. A Virginia aristocrat back in 1794 pointed out that the democrats favored the common, poor people and asked, "Who so poor as our slaves, who therefore so fit to participate in the spoils of the rich and to direct the affairs of the nation?" This is certainly a factor explaining the dominance of anti-Jeffersonianism in cities like Richmond and Charleston, and in the early substitution by the South of a superior "race" and property-rule philosophy for the Jeffersonian ideas of equality and democracy.

Slave rebellion at times frightened the ruling class into granting some concessions, as the establishing of legal minima of provisions for the Negroes. This occurred in South Carolina in 1740 and in Louisiana in 1795. More often it led the Bourbons to pass laws restricting or forbidding the foreign or the domestic slave trade. Other factors than fear were often behind such laws, as the desire to boost the price of the slaves already in the state, or, particularly from 1770 to about 1790, the widespread influence of the Jeffersonian concepts of individual freedom and economic independence, leading to opposition to slavery and, especially, to the slave trade. Yet the aim of cutting down slave outbreaks appears to have been the dominant motive. The period of the most numerous and most drastic anti-slave trade laws coincides with that period of most serious slave unrest, 1791–1802. These enactments (passed by the Federal government in 1794, 1800; by South Carolina in 1792, 1794, 1796, 1800, 1801; North Carolina, 1794; New Jersey, 1798; Maryland, 1796; Louisiana,

1796), indeed, had they not usually been quickly repealed and always laxly enforced, might well have caused the death of slavery.

As a matter of fact, other acts or bills having this, the end of slavery in view, were passed or nearly passed, throughout the nation during the 1790s. During that decade of depression and unprecedented slave unrest (in the West Indies as well as here), the slaveholders of the border areas came the closest they were ever to come to the peaceful abolition of slavery. Manumission was made easier in Maryland (1796), in New Jersey (1798), Kentucky (1708, 1800), Tennessee (1801). Serious, though futile, attempts were made in Maryland and Kentucky in 1799 to enact laws for gradual emancipation. The Territory of Mississippi had the same experience in 1798, and in 1802 a bill to forbid the importation into that Territory, for any purpose, of all male Negro slaves, passed the House but was defeated in the Council by two votes. These years, too, mark the enactment of emancipation laws in the Northern states. To the conventional reasons for this—relatively small number of slaves and unprofitableness of slavery in the North—is to be added the fear aroused by the examples of mass slave rebellion in the South, as well as a taste of this at home in the widespread arson activities of slaves in New York, Philadelphia, Newark, and Elizabeth, New Jersey, in 1796.

But the great plantation oligarchs of eastern Virginia and North Carolina, of South Carolina, Georgia and Louisiana, never seriously considered the elimination of slavery. With the return of prosperity in about 1802 (earlier in Louisiana) and the tremendous spurt in cotton and sugar production (together with, in 1803, the annexation of Louisiana), slavery became fastened upon the South.

Slavery was, then, not to be abolished but rather encouraged and fostered. Unrest was to be expected but a policy of blood and iron would, nevertheless, maintain the institution. To quote a Virginia slaveholder of 1800: "In a word, if we will keep a ferocious monster in our country, we must keep him in chains."

The forging and refurbishing of these chains always followed slave rebellions. Every conceivable legal device was made use of to keep the Negroes in bondage. The whole system of oppression has been mentioned—military might, chauvinism, enforced ignorance, and the denial of freedom of speech, of press, of petition and of religion so far as the slave question was concerned.

Fear of slave rebellion was also the motivating force behind the movement for the colonization of free or freed Negroes in some area (Africa was favored) outside the United States. One of the earliest proposals of that kind was made in 1772 by a citizen of New Jersey after the discovery of a slave plot there. From then on every conspiracy or uprising renewed propaganda for the idea. There was considerable agitation for it after the Gabriel conspiracy in Virginia in 1800, but the Colonization Society was not formed until December, 1816, a year, it will be remembered, of considerable unrest.

Its essential purpose was well stated by John Randolph, speaking at its first meeting in Washington. He declared that the aim of the movement was "to secure the property of every master to, in, and over his slaves." It was to do this by removing the free Negroes who were "one of the greatest sources of the insecurity" of slaveholding since, by their very existence, "they excited discontent" among the slaves.

Periods of increased slave discontent were periods of increased activity for this Society (until about 1835 when its impotence was clear to all). Yet, although most "respectable" channels of propaganda were friendly to it, and although wealthy individuals and Southern states liberally provided it with funds, the movement was a total failure. In its first (and most active) sixteen years of existence the Society managed to colonize only 2,203 Negroes. The essential reason for its utter failure was, from its beginning, the bitter and well-nigh unanimous opposition of the Negro people to any movement seeking to remove them from their native land and, by doing that, more securely enslave their brethren.

Colonization depended only upon persuasion. But, especially following serious manifestations of unrest, legal and extra-legal forces were brought to bear to make life in the South miserable for the free Negroes, and so force them to leave. All sorts of laws depriving these Negroes of civil and economic rights were passed with this in mind. Threats of violence were also not infrequent and, especially after the Turner revolt, caused the removal of many free Negroes. Just before the Civil War the desperate slavocracy was moving toward the enslavement of all free Negroes. Arkansas, in 1859, ordered all free Negroes to leave under pain of being sold into slavery, and both Florida and Georgia enacted laws requiring the enslavement of all "idle" or "vagrant" free Negroes. This created a mass exodus of free Negroes (what would today be called a "refugee problem"). Within three years many of these exiles were marching back into Arkansas and Florida and Georgia with guns on their shoulders and the song, "John Brown's Body," on their lips.

Walt Whitman once declared that "where liberty draws not the blood out of slavery, there slavery draws the blood out of liberty." The slavocrats knew this and applied it first in their own bailiwick. For in the slave South freedom was but a shadow. By the 1820s the Bourbons had avowedly turned against the Declaration of Independence and denounced it as a ridiculous, and dangerous, concoction of glittering generalities. Of course one-third of the population of the South was beyond its pale, but, and here's the point, to keep them beyond the pale it was necessary to vitiate everyone's freedom, it was necessary to "draw the blood out of slavery." First came the free Negroes and then the non-slaveholding whites. Their religion, their speech, their writings, their teachings had to conform to the slave system. If not they were forced to leave, lashed, tarred and feathered, or killed.

And you in the North are to say nothing. Slavery is our affair; we demand non-intervention. But this "non-intervention" (the thoroughly modern term was then used) is only to work one way. You are not to interfere in our affairs, but we may in yours; we demand that you curb your "fanatics," stop denouncing slavery, stop sheltering fugitives, continue supporting an army to be used to overawe and suppress our slaves. We refuse to accept your petitions against slavery or, indeed, any petition having the faintest connection with slavery (so that the Congress of the United States actually tabled the Declaration of Independence when offered as a petition!), and we refuse to transmit your anti-slavery writings through the mail. Your Negro seamen are dangerous to us and we refuse to admit them into our ports. In a word, we may and will do what we think is necessary for the security of our slave property. If that restricts your activities or liberties, it is just too bad.

This inevitable broadening of the anti-slavery struggle into a battle for the maintenance of the democratic rights of the white people, as well as the obtaining of those rights for the Negro people, was probably the most important strengthening force of the entire Abolitionist movement. And one of the great causes of this nationalization of the anti-slavery crusade was the fear of slave rebellions and the measures taken to prevent or subdue their occurrence.

At least one other important effect of the slave rebellions is apparent. This is the added drive that they directly gave to the Abolitionist movement. The slavocrats were forever prating about the docility of their slaves, their lack of desire for freedom, and the delightful conditions of slavery. But here, time and again, came news of slaves conspiring and dying in an effort to leave the blessed state of Southern "patriarchal" slavery. Peculiar activity for docile men and women! Peculiar activity for human beings who did not want freedom!

Thus, Abolitionists would declare, following a revolt: "Insurrections are the natural and consequent productions of slavery—experience has proved this in all ages and in all nations where slavery has existed. Slavery ought to be, must be, and shall be abolished in these United States." Or, in the inimitable words of William Lloyd Garrison, addressed to slaveholders after Nat Turner's outbreak:

Ye patriotic hypocrites! ... ye Christian declaimers for liberty! ye valiant sticklers for equal rights among yourselves! ye haters of aristocracy! ye assailants of monarchy! ye republican nullifiers! ye treasonable disunionists! be dumb! Cast no reproach upon the conduct of the slaves, but let your lips and cheeks wear the blisters of condemnation!

There is, too, clear evidence of the inspiration which immortal John Brown drew from Nat Turner (one of the old man's heroes) and from the widespread slave discontent manifested in 1856. Both added to his hatred of slavery and his respect for the Negro people, and were influential in moving him to strike his noble and world-shaking blow against human bondage.

American slavery was a barbarous tyranny. It impoverished the land and the common people, Negro and white, of the South, tore away their freedom and attempted to destroy the liberty of all American citizens.

Its history, however, is not merely one of impoverishment, deprivation, and oppression. For imbedded in the record of American slavery is the inspiring story of the persistent and courageous efforts of the Negroes (aided, not infrequently, by the poor whites) to regain their heritage of liberty and equality, to regain their right to the elemental demands of human beings.

The effects of this struggle were national and world-shaking in its day. An awareness of its history should give the modern Negro added confidence and courage in his heroic present-day battle for complete and perfect equality with all other American citizens. And it should make those other Americans eager and proud to grasp the hand of the Negro and march forward with him against their common oppressors—against the industrial and financial overlords and the plantation oligarchs who today stand in the way of liberty, equality and prosperity.

That unity between the white and Negro masses was necessary to overthrow nineteenth-century slavery. That same unity is necessary now to defeat twentieth-century slavery—to defeat fascism.

SUGGESTED READING

The material in this booklet was mainly culled from highly dispersed, rare and out-of-the-way sources, such as contemporary newspapers, journals, diaries and memoirs. Much was obtained from manuscripts in the New York Public Library, the Congressional Library in Washington, and the Virginia (Richmond), North Carolina (Raleigh), and South Carolina (Columbia) state libraries and archives. Detailed references to these sources are impossible here.

Fairly complete references to published works on the subject will be found in the footnotes to the article by Harvey Wish in the *Journal of Negro History* (1937) XXII, pp. 299–320, and to the articles by the present writer in *Science and Society* (1937, 1938) I, pp. 512–38; II, pp. 386–92. The book published in Boston, December, 1938—*Slave Insurrections in the United States, 1800–1865*, by Joseph C. Carroll—also contains considerable references, but the work is so full of errors, both of commission and of omission, that it cannot be unqualifiedly recommended.

SLAVE PLOTS AND REVOLTS WITHIN THE PRESENT AREA OF THE UNITED STATES

The following table is a minimum list. Good contemporary evidence has been seen for each of the plots listed. Some alleged plots referred to in certain secondary works are not given here either because the references were erroneous or doubtful. Censorship was strong and it is highly probable that some plots were never reported. At times, too, slave disaffection was reported in such general terms that it is difficult to know whether concrete plots were behind the generalities. Such cases are not listed below. It is, furthermore, to be borne in mind that the table is, naturally, limited to the knowledge of its compiler. It is entirely possible that he missed some plots or even some uprisings. An asterisk indicates that at least two plots or revolts were reported within the given year and the indicated area.

Date	Locality
1526	S. C.
1663	Va.
1672	Va.
1680s	Va., N. Y., Md.
1687	Va.
1690s	Va., Mass.
1694	Va.
1702	N. Y., S. C.
1705	Md.
1708	N. Y.
1709	Va.
1710	Va.
1711	S. C.
1712	N. Y.

1713	S. C.
1720	S. C., Mass.
1721	S. C.
1722	Va.
1723	Va., Conn., Mass.
1730	Va., S. C., La.
1732	La.
1733	S. C.
1734	S. C., N. J.
1737	S. C., Pa.
1738	S. C.
1739	S. C.,* Md.
1740	S. C.
1741	N. Y., N. J.
1744	S. C.
1747	S. C.
1755	Va.
1759	S. C.
1760	S. C.
1761	S. C.
1765	S. C.
1766	S. C.
1767	Va.
1768	Mass.
1771	Ga.
1772	N. J.
1774	Ga., Mass.
1775	N. C., S. C.
1776	Ga.
1778	N. Y.
1779	Ga., N. J.
1782	Va.
1783	N. C.
1786	Ga., Va.
1787	S. C.
1791	La.
1792	La., N. C., Va.
1793	Va., S. C.
1795	La.,* N. C.
1796	N. C., S. C., Ga., N. J., N. Y.

APPENDIX: NEGRO SLAVE REVOLTS IN THE UNITED STATES, 1526-1860   187

1797	Va., S. C.
1798	S. C.
1799	Va.
1800	Va., N. C., S. C.
1801	Va.
1802	Va.,* N. C.
1803	N. C., Pa.
1804	Ga., La., Pa.
1805	N. C., S. C., Va., Md., La., Ga.
1807	Miss.
1808	Va.
1809	Va., La.
1810	Va., Ga., Ky., N. C., Tenn.
1811	Va., La.*
1812	Va., La., Ky.
1813	D. C., S. C., Va.
1814	Md., Va.*
1816	Va., S. C.*
1817	Md.
1818	N. C.
1819	Ga., S. C.
1820	Fla., Va.
1821	N. C.
1822	S. C.*
1823	Va.
1824	Va.
1825	N. C.
1826	Miss.

There were also scores of revolts on slave ships, both domestic and foreign. At least two of these, that on the foreign trader *Amistad* (1839) and that on the domestic trader *Creole* (1841) attracted nationwide and, indeed, international attention. In both cases the rebels secured their liberty.

NOTES

INTRODUCTION

1. Besides the classic collections, such as William Francis Allen, Charles Pickard Ware, and Lucy McKim Garrison, *Slave Songs of the United States* (1867; New York: Dover, 1995); John W. Work, *American Negro Songs: 230 Folk Songs and Spirituals, Religious and Secular* (New York: Crown, 1940); J. Rosamond Johnson and James Weldon Johnson, *The Book of American Negro Spirituals* (New York: Viking Press, 1925), see, for example, Dena J. Epstein, *Sinful Tunes and Spirituals: Black Folk Music to the Civil War* (Urbana: University of Illinois Press, 2003); John Lovell Jr., *Black Song: The Forge and the Flame* (New York: MacMillan, 1972); Leroi Jones (Amiri Baraka), *Blues People: Negro Music in White America* (1963; New York: Perennial, 2002); Sterling Stuckey, *Slave Culture: Nationalist Theory and the Foundations of Black America* (New York: Oxford University Press, 1987); Shane White, *The Sounds of Slavery: Discovering African American History through Songs, Sermons, and Speech* (Boston: Beacon Press, 2006), as well as the recordings Alex Foster and Michel Larue, *Songs of the American Negro Slaves* (Folkways Records 1960) and Harry Belafonte, *The Long Road to Freedom: An Anthology of Black Music* (Sony Legacy 2002) and the accompanying booklet in the Appendix. Ironically, there were far more abolitionist songs published in the nineteenth century than the twentieth, but there has been very little contemporary scholarly research on the subject. The most comprehensive work remains Vicki L. Eaklor, *American Anti-Slavery Songs: A Collection and Analysis* (Westport, CT: Greenwood Press, 1988).

2. Herbert Aptheker, *Negro Slave Revolts in the United States, 1526–1860* (New York: International Publishers, 1939). At the time, Aptheker was a twenty-three-year-old history graduate student at Columbia University and a member of the Communist Party. He had just completed a master's thesis on Nat Turner's rebellion in 1831 and published a two-part article on the history of slave revolts in the US in the Marxist journal *Science and Society*. The article was the basis for Aptheker's pamphlet as well as his doctoral dissertation, which he completed and published four years later under the title *American Negro Slave Revolts*. See Aptheker, "American Negro Slave Revolts," *Science & Society* 1, no. 4 (Summer 1937): 512–38; Aptheker, "More on American Negro Slave Revolts," *Science & Society* 2, no. 3 (Summer 1938): 386–91; and Aptheker, *American Negro Slave Revolts* (New York: Columbia University Press, 1943).

3. Benson J. Lossing, *The Pictorial Field Book of the War of 1812* (New York: Harper & Brothers, 1869), 690. John Hammond Moore has elaborated a bit more on the song's

provenance and origins in a short note, "A Hymn of Freedom—South Carolina, 1813," *Journal of Negro History* 50, no. 1 (January 1965): 50–53.

4. Manisha Sinha, *The Slave's Cause: A History of Abolition* (New Haven: Yale University Press, 2016), 2.

5. Samuel Floyd Jr., with Guthrie Ramsey and Melanie Zeck, *The Transformation of Black Music: The Rhythms, the Songs, and the Ships of the African Diaspora* (New York: Oxford University Press, 2017).

6. Sylviane A. Diouf, *Servants of Allah: African Muslims Enslaved in the Americas* (New York: New York University Press, 2013); Michael Gomez, *Exchanging Our Country Marks: The Transformation of African Identities in the Colonial and Antebellum South* (Chapel Hill: University of North Carolina Press, 1998) and *Black Crescent: African Muslims in the Americas* (New York: Cambridge University Press, 2005); and Allan D. Austin, *African Muslims in Antebellum America: Transatlantic Stories and Spiritual Struggles* (New York: Routledge, 1997).

7. Reverend Thomas Wentworth Higginson, "Negro Spirituals," *The Atlantic* 19 (June 1867): 687.

8. Sidney Bechet, *Treat It Gentle: An Autobiography* (New York: Da Capo Press, 2002), 48.

9. Sinha, *Slave's Cause*, 2.

10. C. L. R. James, *The Black Jacobins: Toussaint l'Ouverture and the San Domingo Revolution* (1938; New York: Vintage Books, 1989); Laurent Dubois, *Avengers of the New World: The Story of the Haitian Revolution* (Cambridge, MA: Harvard University Press, 2005) and *A Colony of Citizens: Revolution and Slave Emancipation in the French Caribbean, 1787–1804* (Chapel Hill: University of North Carolina Press, 2004); Carolyn Fick, *The Making of Haiti: The Saint-Domingue Revolution from Below* (Knoxville: University of Tennessee Press, 1990); Ada Ferrer, *Freedom's Mirror: Cuba and Haiti in the Age of Revolution* (New York: Cambridge University Press, 2014); Sibylle Fischer, *Modernity Disavowed: Haiti and the Cultures of Slavery in the Age of Revolution* (Durham, NC: Duke University Press, 2004); Robin Blackburn, *The Overthrow of Colonial Slavery, 1776–1848* (New York: Verso Books, 1988); Jeremy D. Popkin, *You Are All Free: The Haitian Revolution and the Abolition of Slavery* (New York: Cambridge University Press, 2010); and Jane G. Landers, *Atlantic Creoles in the Age of Revolutions* (Cambridge, MA: Harvard University Press, 2010).

11. Michel-Rolph Trouillot wrote eloquently about how the Haitian Revolution was simply inconceivable to the (white) Western world. See his *Silencing the Past: Power and the Production of History* (Boston: Beacon Press, 2015).

12. For a brilliant account of the impact of the revolution throughout the Atlantic and the role of radical Black seamen, see Julius S. Scott, *The Common Wind: Afro-American Currents in the Age of the Haitian Revolution* (New York: Verso Books, 2018).

13. Gwendolyn Midlo Hall, *Africans in Colonial Louisiana: The Development of Afro-Creole Culture in the Eighteenth Century* (Baton Rouge: Louisiana State University Press, 1995), 343–74.

14. Hall, *Africans in Colonial Louisiana*, 203–36; Gilbert C. Din, *Spaniards, Planters, and Slaves: The Regulation of Slavery in Louisiana, 1763–1803* (College Station: Texas A&M Press, 1999), 89–115; Sylviane A. Diouf, *Slavery's Exiles: The Story of the American Maroons* (New York: New York University Press, 2014), 161–85; and Katrina Hazzard-Donald, *Mojo Workin': The Old African-American Hoodoo System* (Urbana: University of Illinois Press, 2013), 80–82.

15. Din, *Spaniards, Planters, and Slaves*, 114.

16. Diouf, *Slavery's Exiles*, 185.

17. Diouf, *Slavery's Exiles*, 185.

18. Douglas R. Egerton, *He Shall Go Out Free: The Lives of Denmark Vesey* (Madison: University of Wisconsin Press, 1999); Egerton, "Of Facts and Fables: New Light on the Denmark Vesey Affair," *South Carolina Historical Magazine* 105 (January 2004): 8–48; Michael P. Johnson, "Denmark Vesey and His Co-Conspirators," *William & Mary Quarterly* 58, no. 4 (October 2001): 915–76; Robert L. Paquette, "From Rebellion to Revisionism: The Continuing Debate about the Denmark Vesey Affair," *Journal of the Historical Society* 4 (Fall 2004): 8–48; and James O'Neil Spady, "Power and Confession: On the Credibility of the Earliest Reports of the Denmark Vesey Slave Conspiracy," *William & Mary Quarterly* 68 (April 2011): 287–304.

19. Ethan J. Kytle and Blain Roberts, *Denmark Vesey's Garden: Slavery and Memory in the Cradle of the Confederacy* (New York: The New Press, 2018); and David Robertson, *Denmark Vesey* (New York: Vintage Books, 1999), 115.

20. The song can be found in William Wells Brown, *The Anti-Slavery Harp: A Collection of Songs for Anti-Slavery Meetings* (Boston: Bela Marsh, 1848), 17–18.

21. Sinha, *Slave's Cause*, 204–8; Peter P. Hinks, *To Awaken My Afflicted Brethren: David Walker and the Problem of Antebellum Slave Resistance* (University Park: Pennsylvania State University Press, 1997); and David Walker, *David Walker's Appeal: To the Coloured Citizens of the World, but in Particular, and Very Expressly, to Those of the United States of America* (New York: Hill and Wang, 1995).

22. The best account of the Cincinnati Riot of 1829 and its aftermath is Nikki M. Taylor, *Frontiers of Freedom: Cincinnati's Black Community, 1802–1868* (Athens: Ohio State University Press, 2005), 50–79. On the antebellum Black freedom movement in the North, see Patrick Rael, *Black Identity and Black Protest in the Antebellum North* (Chapel Hill: University of North Carolina Press, 2002); Graham Russel Gao Hodges, *David Ruggles: A Radical Black Abolitionist and the Underground Railroad in New York City* (Chapel Hill: University of North Carolina Press, 2010); Eric Foner, *Gateway to Freedom: The Hidden History of the Underground Railroad* (New York: W. W. Norton, 2015); and Steven Kantrowitz, *More Than Freedom: Fighting for Black Citizenship in a White Republic* (New York: Penguin Press, 2013).

23. Herbert Aptheker, *Nat Turner's Slave Rebellion, Including the 1831 "Confessions"* (New York: Dover, 2006), 138.

24. See Christopher Tomlins, *In the Matter of Nat Turner: A Speculative History* (Princeton, NJ: Princeton University Press, 2020); and Patrick H. Breen, *This Land Shall Be Deluged in Blood: A New History of the Nat Turner Revolt* (New York: Oxford University Press, 2016).

25. Mat Callahan discusses this song and its genesis in greater depth below. In addition to the citations he provides from Lawrence Gellert, Russell Ames, and Pete Seeger, see Bruce Darden, *People Get Ready! A New History of Gospel Music* (London: Continuum Books, 2004), 82.

26. The most thorough and nuanced account of first and second wave abolitionism can be found in Sinha, *Slave's Cause*. See also Richard J. M. Blackett, *Building an Anti-Slavery Wall: Black Americans in the Atlantic Abolitionist Movement* (Baton Rouge: Louisiana State University Press, 1983); Maurice Jackson, *Let This Voice Be Heard: Anthony Benezet, Father of Atlantic Abolitionism* (Philadelphia: University of Pennsylvania Press, 2010); John Stauffer, *The Black Hearts of Men: Radical Abolitionists and the Transformation of Race* (Cambridge,

MA, 2002); and Shirley J. Yee, *Black Women Abolitionists: A Study in Activism, 1828–1860* (Knoxville: University of Tennessee Press, 1992). For an Atlantic perspective, see Christopher Brown, *Moral Capital: Foundations of British Abolitionism* (Chapel Hill: University of North Carolina Press, 2006); Seymour Drescher, *Abolition: A History of Slavery and Antislavery* (Cambridge, UK: Cambridge University Press, 2009); and Robin Blackburn, *The Overthrow of Colonial Slavery, 1776–1848* (London: Verso, 1988).

27. Henry Mayer, *All on Fire: William Lloyd Garrison and the Abolition of Slavery* (New York, 1998); R. J. M. Blackett, *Building an Antislavery Wall: Black Americans in the Atlantic Abolitionist Movement, 1830–1860* (Baton Rouge, 1983), 52–69; and Sinha, *Slave's Cause*, 214–26.

28. W. Caleb McDaniel, *The Problem of Democracy in the Age of Slavery: Garrisonian Abolitionists and Transatlantic Reform* (Baton Rouge: Louisiana State University Press, 2013). For excellent accounts of the Constitution and the question of slavery, see David Waldstreicher, *Slavery's Constitution: From Revolution to Ratification* (New York: Farrar, Straus and Giroux, 2009); and George William Van Cleve, *A Slaveholders' Union: Slavery, Politics, and the Constitution in the Early American Republic* (Chicago: University of Chicago Press, 2010).

29. See Joel Olsen, *The Abolition of White Democracy* (Minneapolis: University of Minnesota Press, 2004), 42–44.

30. Foner, *Gateway to Freedom*, 69–90.

31. Quoted in Aaron D. McClendon, "Sounds of Sympathy: William Wells Brown's 'Anti-Slavery Harp,' Abolition, and the Culture of Early and Antebellum American Song," *African American Review* 47, no. 1 (Spring 2014): 89; and Eaklor, *American Anti-Slavery Songs*, xxi.

32. George W. Clark, *The Liberty Minstrel* (New York: Leavitt & Alden, 1844), xxx. While the editors and compilers of *Slave Songs of the United States* (1867) praised Black music for its originality and moral power, they still added the caveat that "the chief part of the negro music is civilized in its character—partly composed under the influence of association with the whites, partly actually imitated from their music." See William Francis Allen, Charles Pickard Ware, and Lucy McKim Garrison, eds., *Slave Songs of the United States* (1867; Chapel Hill: University of North Carolina Press, 2011), 10.

33. Clare Midgley, *Women Against Slavery: The British Campaigns, 1780–1870* (New York: Routledge, 1995), 37; and Robin Blackburn, *The Overthrow of Colonial Slavery, 1776–1848* (London: Verso Books, 1988), 139. See also Barbara E. Lacey, "Visual Images of Blacks in Early American Imprints," *William and Mary Quarterly* 53, no. 1 (January 1996): 137–80.

34. Clark, *Liberty Minstrel*, 56.

35. William Wells Brown, *The Anti-Slavery Harp: A Collection of Songs for Anti-Slavery Meetings* (Boston: Bela Marsh, 1848), 24–25.

36. "Dandy Jim from Caroline" (1844), copy available from Library of Congress, https://www.loc.gov/resource/sm1844.391720.0/?sp=3.

37. Brown, *Anti-Slavery Harp*, 38–39. See also Aaron D. McClendon, "Sounds of Sympathy: William Wells Brown's 'Anti-Slavery Harp,' Abolition, and the Culture of Early and Antebellum American Song," *African American Review* 47, no. 1 (Spring 2014): 95–96; and Ivy G. Wilson, *Specters of Democracy: Blackness and the Aesthetics of Politics in the Antebellum U.S.* (New York: Oxford University Press, 2011), 59–61.

38. Clark, *Liberty Minstrel*.

39. See Corey M. Brooks, *Liberty Power: Antislavery Third Parties and the Transformation of American Politics* (Chicago: University of Chicago Press, 2016); and Eric Foner, *Free Soil,*

Free Labor, Free Men: The Ideology of the Republic Party Before the Civil War (New York: Oxford University Press, 1995).

40. Henry Highland Garnet, *Memorial Discourse* (Philadelphia: Joseph M. Wilson, 1865), 51.

41. While the framers, abolitionists, liberal jurists, and Republicans debated whether or not enslaved Africans were property or persons held in service, the Africans themselves answered neither. More than half a century earlier, an enslaved man named Prince Hall petitioned his master for his freedom based on the principles of the Declaration of Independence. Hall's 1777 petition argued that Africans were human beings, "unjustly dragged, by the cruel hand of Power," and victims of a crime, stolen "in Violation of the Laws of Nature & of Nation & in defiance of all the tender feelings of humanity, brought hither to be sold like beasts of burden, & like them condemned to slavery for Life." Prince Hall's petition has been reprinted many times and circulates widely on the internet, but it is noteworthy that it circulated widely in popular form during the 1850s, appearing in William C. Nell, *The Colored Patriots of the American Revolution* (Boston: Robert F. Wallcut, 1855), 47.

42. R. J. M. Blackett, *The Captive's Quest for Freedom: Fugitive Slaves, the 1850 Fugitive Slave Law, and the Politics of Slavery* (Cambridge, UK: Cambridge University Press, 2018)

43. Quoted in Sinha, *Slave's Cause*, 502.

44. See Blackett, *Captive's Quest for Freedom*; Carol Wilson, *Freedom at Risk: The Kidnapping of Free Blacks in America, 1780–1865* (Lexington, Ky., 1994), 54; Lois E. Horton, "Kidnapping and Resistance: Antislavery Direct Action in the 1850s," in David W. Blight, ed., *Passages to Freedom: The Underground Railroad in History and Memory* (Washington, 2004), 149–73; and Earl M. Maltz, *Fugitive Slave on Trial: The Anthony Burns Case and Abolitionist Outrage* (Lawrence: Kansas University Press, 2010).

45. Eaklor, *American Anti-Slavery Songs*, 209. Unfortunately, little is known of Joshua McCarter Simpson. For more, see Matthew Sandler's excellent *The Black Romantic Revolution: Abolitionist Poets at the End of Slavery* (New York: Verso Books, 2020).

46. "John Brown's Provisional Constitution" (1858), https://famous-trials.com/johnbrown/614-browconstitution.

47. There are too many biographies of John Brown to cite, but here are some of the best books: David S. Reynolds, *John Brown, Abolitionist: The Man Who Killed Slavery, Sparked the Civil War, and Seeded Civil Rights* (New York: Vintage, 2009); Evan Carton, *Patriotic Treason: John Brown and the Soul of America* (New York: Atria Books, 2006); and Tony Horowitz, *Midnight Rising: John Brown and the Raid That Sparked the Civil War* (New York: Henry Holt, 2011). I'm still partial to W. E. B. Du Bois's classic *John Brown*, ed. David Roediger (1909; New York: The Modern Library, 2001).

48. This idea is beautifully elaborated in the "Epilogue" of Evan Carton's *Patriotic Treason*.

CHAPTER 1: FINDING THE SONGS

1. In 2006, Aptheker's daughter accused him of abusing her as a child.

2. Julie McCown, a graduate student, discovered the poem in the Yale University Library. See https://sites.newpaltz.edu/nyrediscovered/2013/09/17/jupiter-hammon-of-lloyds-neck-long-island-african-american-poet-of-the-revolutionary-era/.

3. Madeline Lewis, a history major at Columbia University, made the discovery among the Gay Papers at Columbia University. She brought them to the attention of Eric Foner, who credits her discovery in his *Gateway to Freedom* (W. W. Norton, 2015).

4. *Slaves Songs of the United States*, section IV., #112 (New York: Dover, 1995), 93.

5. Bernard Katz, ed., *The Social Implications of Early Negro Music in the United States* (Arno Press and the New York Times, 1969), vii.

6. Katz, *Social Implications*, 134–35.

7. Katz, *Social Implications*, 133.

8. Du Bois used the phrase in his famous 1903 book, *The Souls of Black Folk*. It is worthy of note that Du Bois was not the first to use "sorrow songs" to describe the "Negro spiritual." Frederick Douglass made similar reference in his *Narrative of the Life of Frederick Douglass*: "I have often been utterly astonished, since I came to the north, to find persons who could speak of the singing, among slaves as evidence of their contentment and happiness. It is impossible to conceive of a greater mistake. Slaves sing most when they are most unhappy. The songs of the slave represent the sorrows of his heart; and he is relieved by them, only as an aching heart is relieved by its tears. At least, such is my experience."

9. *The Interesting Narrative of the Life of Olaudah Equiano, or Gustavus Vassa, the African, Written by Himself* (London, 1789). Nine editions were published during his lifetime, and it was translated into Dutch and German.

10. James Basker, *Amazing Grace* (Yale University Press, 2002), xlvii–xlviii.

11. Biographical information about Simpson is available at the following websites: https://www.poetryfoundation.org/poets/joshua-mccarter-simpson and https://henryburke1010.tripod.com/id78.html/id78.html. If the reader is able to locate a copy of Simpson's *Original Anti-Slavery Songs* or *The Emancipation Car* (two editions), these contain autobiographical information. They are, unfortunately, hard to find.

12. Joshua McCarter Simpson, *Original Anti-Slavery Songs* (Zanesville, printed for the author, 1852), 3.

13. Notable exceptions include David Suisman, *Selling Sounds* (Harvard University Press, 2009); Karl Hagstrom Miller, *Segregating Sounds* (Duke University Press, 2010); Brian Roberts, *Blackface Nation* (University of Chicago Press, 2017); and Steven Garabedian, *A Sound History* (University of Massachusetts Press, 2020).

14. Frederick Douglass, *The North Star*, Rochester. October 27, 1848.

15. Douglass, *North Star*.

16. "Reds, Whites, and the Blues: Lawrence Gellert, 'Negro Songs of Protest,' and the Leftwing Folksong Revival of the 1930s and 1940s," *American Quarterly* 57 (March 2005): 179–206.

17. A notable exception, and one often overlooked, is Thomas Talley, who in 1922 published a book called *Negro Folk Rhymes, Wise and Otherwise: With a Study*. Talley taught biology and chemistry at Fisk University. A serious student of music, Talley began collecting Black traditional songs in rural Tennessee, many of which he'd heard in his youth. As an African American born in 1870 in the midst of Reconstruction, Talley was in an excellent position to gather the music of formerly enslaved people, who were, in some cases, his neighbors and fellow congregants. See song notes for more.

18. Benson John Lossing, *Harper's Encyclopaedia of United States History* (Harper & Brothers Publishers, 1905), 211.

19. John Hammond Moore, "A Hymn of Freedom-South Carolina, 1813," *Journal of Negro History*, January 1965.

CHAPTER 2: HISTORY, GEOGRAPHY, LANGUAGE, AND MUSIC

1. I located two relevant poems. The first was by African American lawyer and abolitionist George Vashon (1824–1878) called "Vincent Ogé," dedicated to Ogé, the leader of a slave rebellion in Saint-Domingue that foretold the Haitian Revolution a year later in 1791. The second poem is "Oh Liberty, I Wait for Thee" by the Cuban revolutionary poet Gabriel de la Concepción Valdés, known as Placido. Placido was executed for conspiring to overthrow the Spanish authority on that island June 28, 1844. See https://afrocubaweb.com/eugenegodfried/placidoenglish.htm.

2. There is a wealth of material on the Stono Rebellion (also known as Cato's Rebellion), beginning with Aptheker's pamphlet included in this book (see Appendix). Other sources are listed at https://en.wikipedia.org/wiki/Stono_Rebellion.

3. James Basker, *Amazing Grace* (Yale University Press, 2002), xxxvi.

4. John Lovell Jr., *Black Song: The Forge and the Flame* (Macmillan Co., 1972), 106.

5. Eileen Southern, *The Music of Black Americans: A History* (W. W. Norton, 1971), 70.

6. According to *A Century of Population Growth, from the First Census of the United States to the Twelfth, 1790–1900*, published by the Departments of Commerce and Labor, Bureau of the Census, the 1790 population of the United States (thirteen states) was 3,929,625. Of these, 3,172,444 were white, and 757,181 were "Negro" of whom 59,557 were free and 697,624 were enslaved.

7. According to the Unites States Census Bureau, in the 1860 census there were 3,953,760 enslaved and 488,070 free Black people.

8. According to the US National Archives and Records Administration: "By the end of the Civil War, roughly 179,000 black men (10% of the Union Army) served as soldiers in the U.S. Army and another 19,000 served in the Navy. Nearly 40,000 black soldiers died over the course of the war—30,000 of infection or disease. Black soldiers served in artillery and infantry and performed all noncombat support functions that sustain an army, as well. Black carpenters, chaplains, cooks, guards, laborers, nurses, scouts, spies, steamboat pilots, surgeons, and teamsters also contributed to the war cause. There were nearly 80 black commissioned officers. Black women, who could not formally join the Army, nonetheless served as nurses, spies, and scouts, the most famous being Harriet Tubman who scouted for the 2d South Carolina Volunteers" (https://www.archives.gov/education/lessons/blacks-civil-war).

9. Dena J. Epstein, *Sinful Tunes and Spirituals: Black Folk Music to the Civil War* (University of Illinois Press, 1981), 345.

10. Quoted in Sterling Stuckey, "Through the Prism of Folklore: The Black Ethos in Slavery," *The Massachusetts Review* 9, no. 3 (Summer 1968): 434–35, n. 49.

11. Eileen Southern and Josephine Wright, *African-American Traditions in Song, Sermon, Tale and Dance, 1600s–1920* (Greenwood Press, 1990), 149.

12. See Appendix for more on Aptheker, his scholarship, and the conditions under which he worked.
13. The quality of Aptheker's research is demonstrated by his discovery of the "Hymn of Freedom." See song notes for a fuller description.
14. *Born in Slavery: Slave Narratives from the Federal Writers' Project, 1936–1938* is the name of a particular collection, one of several created under the FWP's direction. For more details see https://www.loc.gov/rr/program/bib/newdeal/fwp.html.
15. George Rawick, *The American Slave: A Composite Autobiography* (Greenwood Publishing, 1979), vol. 3, series 2 (Texas), 952–53.

CHAPTER 3: SLAVE SONGS: SOURCES AND DOCUMENTATION

1. The complete title is *The Ethiopian Glee Book, Complete, Containing the Songs Sung by the Christy Minstrels with Many Other Popular Negro Melodies*. The book's author is purported to be "Gumbo Chaff, A.M.A., First Banjo Player to the King of Congo." Such an assertion was common to the entire blackface minstrelsy tradition, suggesting that this song was "authentic" African American music. The book was dedicated, in what is now called African American Vernacular English, "To all de Bobolashun and Antislabery 'cieties truout de world dis Book am most 'specfully 'scribed by de orther."

CHAPTER 4: ABOLITIONIST SONGS: SOURCES AND DOCUMENTATION

1. Frederick Douglass, *The North Star*, Rochester, October 27, 1848, http://utc.iath.virginia.edu/minstrel/miaro3bt.html.

APPENDIX: *NEGRO SLAVE REVOLTS IN THE UNITED STATES, 1526–1860* (1939) BY HERBERT APTHEKER

1. Sterling Stuckey, "Through the Prism of Folklore," *The Massachusetts Review* 9, no. 3 (Summer 1968): 417–37.
2. Sterling Stuckey, "From the Bottom Up: Herbert Aptheker's *American Negro Slave Revolts* and *A Documentary History of the Negro People in the United States*," in *African American History and Radical Historiography: Essays in Honor of Herbert Aptheker*, ed. Herbert Shapiro (MEP Publications, 1998).
3. Quoted in Stuckey, "From the Bottom Up."
4. Quoted in Stuckey, "From the Bottom Up."
5. Stuckey, "From the Bottom Up."
6. Robin D. G. Kelley, "Afterword," *Journal of American History*, June 2000, 168–71.
7. Kelley, "Afterword."
8. Kelley, "Afterword."

SELECTED BIBLIOGRAPHY

SONGBOOKS OR BOOKS CONTAINING SONGS

Allen, William Francis, Charles Pickard Ware, and Lucy McKim Garrison. *Slave Songs in the United States*. Dover Publications, 1995. First published by A. Simpson & Co., New York, 1867.

Basker, James, ed. *Amazing Grace: An Anthology of Poems about Slavery, 1660–1810*. Yale University Press, 2005.

Brown, William Wells, compiler. *The Anti-Slavery Harp: A Collection of Songs for Anti-Slavery Meetings*. Bela Marsh, 1848.

Chapman, Maria Weston. *Songs of the Free and Hymns of Christian Freedom*. Isaac Knapp, 1836.

Child, Lydia Maria. *The Freedmen's Book*. Ticknor and Fields, 1865.

Clark, George W. *The Liberty Minstrel*. Leavitt & Alden, 1845.

Cunard, Nancy, and Hugh D. Ford, eds. *Negro: An Anthology*. Continuum Publishing Co., 1996. First published in 1934.

de Jong, Nanette. *Tambu*. Indiana University Press, 1992.

Eaklor, Vicki Lynn. *American Anti-Slavery Songs*. Greenwood Press, 1988.

Epstein, Dena J. *Sinful Tunes and Spirituals: Black Folk Music to the Civil War*. University of Illinois Press, 1981.

Equiano, Olaudah. *The Interesting Narrative of the Life of Olaudah Equiano, or Gustavus Vassa, the African, Written by Himself*. Middletown, DE, 2016. First published in 1789. https://en.wikisource.org/wiki/The_Interesting_Narrative_of_the_Life_of_Olaudah_Equiano,_or_Gustavus_Vassa,_the_African.

Fenner, Thomas P., Frederic G. Rathbun, and Miss Bessie Cleaveland. *Cabin and Plantation Songs as Sung by the Hampton Students*. G. P. Putnam's Sons, The Knickerbocker Press, 1901.

Fisher, Miles Mark. *Negro Slave Songs in the United States*. Carol Publishing Group, 1990. First published by Cornell University Press, 1953.

Fowke, Edith, and Joe Glazer. *Songs of Work and Freedom*. Roosevelt University, 1960.

Gellert, Lawrence. *Me and My Captain*. Hours Press, 1939.

Gellert, Lawrence. *Negro Songs of Protest*. American Music League, 1936.

Greenway, John. *American Folksongs of Protest*. A. S. Barnes & Co., Perpetua edition, 1960.

Higginson, Thomas Wentworth. *Army Life in a Black Regiment*. Penguin Classics, 1997. First published by Fields, Osgood & Co., 1870.

Johnson, James Weldon, and J. Rosamund Johnson. *The Books of American Negro Spirituals.* Da Capo Press, 1969. First published in two volumes by Viking Press, 1925 and 1926.

Katz, Bernard, ed. *The Social Implications of Early Negro Music in the United States.* Arno Press and the New York Times, 1969.

Krehbiel, Henry Edward. *Afro-American Folksongs: A Study in Racial and National Music.* G. Schirmer, 1914.

Lincoln, Jairus. *Anti-Slavery Melodies.* Elijah B. Gill, 1843.

Lomax, Alan. *Folk Songs of North America.* Doubleday and Co., 1960.

Lomax, John A., and Alan Lomax. *Negro Folk Songs as Sung by Leadbelly.* Macmillan Co., 1936.

Look Away: 56 Negro Folk Songs. Cooperative Recreation Service, 1963.

Lossing, Benson J. *A Pictorial Field-Book of the War of 1812.* Harper & Brothers, 1868. https://archive.org/details/fieldbookswar18120010ssrich/page/n11/mode/2up.

Lovell, John, Jr. *Black Song: The Forge and the Flame.* Macmillan Co., 1972.

Marsh, J. B. T. *The Story of the Jubilee Singers with Their Songs.* Houghton, Mifflin and Co., Riverside Press, 1880.

Odum, Howard, and Guy B. Johnson. *The Negro and His Songs: A Study of Typical Negro Songs in the South.* University of North Carolina Press, 1925.

Odum, Howard, and Guy B. Johnson. *Negro Workaday Songs.* University of North Carolina Press, 1926.

Parish, Lydia. *Slave Songs of the Georgia Sea Islands.* University of Georgia Press, 1992. First published by Creative Age Books, 1942.

Scarborough, Dorothy. *From a Southern Porch.* G. P. Putnam's Sons, Knickerbocker Press, 1919.

Simpson, Joshua McCarter. *The Emancipation Car, Being an Original Composition of Anti-Slavery Ballads Composed Exclusively for the Underground Railroad.* Zanesville, E.C. Church, 1854. Reprinted by Mnemosyne Publishing Co., 1969.

Simpson, Joshua McCarter. *Original Anti-Slavery Songs.* Printed for the author, 1852.

Southern, Eileen. *The Music of Black Americans: A History.* W. W. Norton & Co., 1971.

Southern, Eileen, and Josephine Wright. *African-American Tradition in Song, Sermon, Tale and Dance 1600–1920: An Annotated Bibliography of Literature, Collections, and Artworks.* Greenwood, 1990.

Talley, Thomas W. *Negro Folk Rhymes, Wise and Otherwise: With a Study.* Macmillan Co., 1922.

Trotter, James Monroe. *Music and Some Highly Musical People.* Lee and Shepard, 1878.

White, Newman I. *American Negro Folk Songs.* Harvard University Press, 1928.

Work, Henry Clay. *Songs of Henry Clay Work.* J. Little & Ives Co., n.d. https://duckduckgo.com/?q=Songs+of+Hery+Clay+Work&t=newext&ia=web.

Work, John W. *American Negro Songs.* Dover Publications, 1998. First published by Crown Publishers, 1940.

Work, John Wesley. *Folk Song of the American Negro.* Press of Fisk University, 1915.

HISTORY AND LITERARY BOOKS

Albert, Octavia V. Rogers. *The House of Bondage or Charlotte Brooks and Other Slaves.* Hunt & Eaton, 1891.

Aptheker, Herbert. *American Negro Slave Revolts*. International Publishers, 1983. First published by International Publishers, 1943.

Aptheker, Herbert. *Essays in the History of the American Negro*. International Publishers, 1954.

Aptheker, Herbert. *Negro Slave Revolts in the United States, 1526–1860*. International Publishers, 1939.

Baptist, Edward. *The Half That's Never Been Told*. Basic Books, 2014.

Basker, James. *American Anti-Slavery Writings: Colonial Beginnings to Emancipation*. Library of America, 2012.

Beckert, Sven. *Empire of Cotton*. Vintage Books, 2015.

Blackburn, Robin. *The American Crucible*. Verso, 2011.

Blackburn, Robin. *Marx and Lincoln: An Unfinished Revolution*. Verso Books, 2011.

Childs, Lydia Maria. *An Appeal in Favor of That Class of Americans Called Africans*. Allen and Ticknor, 1833.

Childs, Matt D. *The 1812 Aponte Rebellion in Cuba and the Struggle Against Atlantic Slavery*. University of North Carolina Press, 2006.

Cone, James. *The Spirituals and the Blues*. Orbis Books, 1991.

Douglass, Frederick. *My Bondage and My Freedom*. Dover Publications, 1969. First published by Miller, Orton & Mulligan, 1855.

Dubois, Laurent. *Avengers of the New World: The Story of the Haitian Revolution*. Belknap Press, 2005.

Dubois, Laurent. *Haiti: The Aftershocks of History*. Picador, 2013.

Du Bois, W. E. B. *Black Folk Then and Now*. Oxford University Press, 2007.

Du Bois, W. E. B. *Black Reconstruction in America, 1860–1880*. Free Press, 1998. First published by Harcourt, Brace, 1935.

Du Bois, W. E. B. *John Brown*. Kraus-Thompson Organization Limited, 1973. First published by George W. Jacobs & Co., 1909.

Du Bois, W. E. B. *The Souls of Black Folk*. Dover Publications, 1994. First published by A. C. McLurg and Co., 1903.

Foner, Eric. *Gateway to Freedom*. W. W. Norton, 2015.

Foner, Eric. *Reconstruction: America's Unfinished Revolution, 1863–1877*. 2014.

Fortier, Alcée. *Louisiana Studies, Literature, Customs and Dialects, History and Education*. F. F. Hansell & Bro., 1894.

Garabedian, Steven P. *A Sound History: Lawrence Gellert, Black Musical Protest, and White Denial*. University of Massachusetts Press, 2020.

Geggus, David. *The Haitian Revolution*. Hackett Publishing, 2014.

Grant, Joanne, ed. *Black Protest*. Fawcett Premier, 1983.

Hall, Gwendolyn Midlo. *Africans in Colonial Louisiana: The Development of Afro-Creole Culture in the Eighteenth Century*. Louisiana State University Press, 1992.

Hinks, Peter, and John McGivian, eds. *The Encyclopedia of Anti-Slavery and Abolition*. Greenwood Publishers, 2006.

Hurmence, Belinda, ed. *My Folks Don't Want Me to Talk About Slavery*. John F. Blair Publishing, 2004.

Hurston, Zora Neale. *Mules and Men*. Harper Perennial, 1990. First published by J. B. Lippincott, 1935.

James, C. L. R. *The Black Jacobins*. Vintage Books, 1989.
Kemble, Frances Anne. *Journal of a Residence on a Georgia Plantation in 1838–1839*. Harper & Brothers Publishers, 1863.
Kulikoff, Allan. *Tobacco and Slaves*. University of North Carolina Press, 1986.
Lambert, John. *Travels Through Lower Canada, and the United States of North America, in the Years 1806, 1807, and 1808, Vol. II*. Richard Phillips, London, 1810.
Levine, Lawrence. *Black Culture and Black Consciousness*. Oxford University Press, 1977.
Linebaugh, Peter, and Markus Rediker. *The Many-Headed Hydra: The Hidden History of the Revolutionary Atlantic*. Revised ed. Verso Books, 2012.
Litwack, Leon F. *Trouble in Mind: Black Southerners in the Age of Jim Crow*. Alfred A. Knopf, 1998.
Lomax, Alan. *The Land Where the Blues Began*. Pantheon Books, 1993.
Lossing, Benson John. *Harper's Encyclopedia of United States History*. Harper & Brothers Publishers, 1905.
Miller, Karl Hagstrom. *Segregating Sounds*. Duke University Press, 2010.
Oates, Stephen B. *The Fires of Jubilee: Nat Turner's Fierce Rebellion*. Harper Perennial, 2016.
Popkin, Jeremy D. *A Concise History of the Haitian Revolution*. Wiley-Blackwell, 2012.
Price, Richard, ed. *Maroon Societies: Rebel Slave Communities in the Americas*. 2nd ed. Johns Hopkins University Press, 1979.
Rasmussen, Daniel. *American Uprising: The Untold Story of America's Largest Slave Revolt*. Harper Perennial, 2012.
Rawick, George, ed. *The American Slave: A Composite Autobiography*. 41 vols. Greenwood Press, 1972.
Reader, John. *Africa: A Biography of the Continent*. Vintage Books, 1999.
Roberts, Brian. *Blackface Nation: Race, Reform, and Identity in American Popular Music, 1812–1925*. University of Chicago Press, 2017.
Sacks, Howard L., and Judith Rose. *Way Up North in Dixie: A Black Family's Claim to the Confederate Anthem*. University of Illinois Press, 2003.
Sinha, Manisha. *The Slave's Cause: A History of Abolition*. Yale University Press, 2016.
Southern, Eileen, ed. *Readings in Black American Music*. W. W. Norton, 1971.
Sublette, Ned. *The World That Made New Orleans*. Lawrence Hill Books, 2009.
Suisman, David. *Selling Sounds*. Harvard University Press, 2009.
Thomas, Hugh. *The Slave Trade*. Simon & Schuster. 1997.
Urbainczyk, Theresa. *Slave Revolts in Antiquity*. University of California Press, 2008.
Walker, David. *Walker's Appeal to the Colored Citizens of the World*. Printed for the author, 1829.
A Wesleyan Methodist. *Methodist Error or, Friendly Christian Advice to Those Methodists Who Indulge in Extravagant Emotions and Bodily Exercises*. D. & E. Fenton, 1819.
White, Shane, and Graham White. *The Sounds of Slavery*. Beacon Press, 2005.
Williams, Eric. *Capitalism and Slavery*. University of North Carolina Press, 1944.
Yar-Shater, Ehsan, ed. *The History of al-Tabari: The Revolt of the Zanj*. University of New York Press, 1992.

ARTICLES, ESSAYS, DISSERTATIONS

Brough, Mr. *Mr. Brough's Musical Lecture of the United States of America*. Printed by R. Carrick, Dublin, Ireland, 1847.

Cimbala, Paul A. "Fortunate Bondsmen: Black 'Musicianers' and Their Role as an Antebellum Southern Plantation Slave Elite." *Southern Studies* 18, no. 3 (Fall 1979).

Epstein, Dena J. "Slave Music in the United States before 1860: A Survey of Sources (pts. 1 & 2)." *Music Library Association NOTES*, Spring & Summer 1963.

Lomax, Alan. AFS L 3: Afro-American Spirituals, Work Songs, and Ballads. Archive of American Folk Song, Library of Congress Music Division.

Mabry, Tyler Grant. "Seizing the Laurels: Nineteenth-Century African American Poetic Performance." PhD diss., University of Texas at Austin, 2011.

National Abolition Hall of Fame. *Changing America: The Emancipation Proclamation, 1863 and the March on Washington, 1963*.

Roberts, Brian. *"Slavery Would Have Died of That Music": The Hutchinson Family Singers and the Rise of Popular-Culture Abolitionism in Early Antebellum-Era America, 1842–1850*. American Antiquarian Society, 2006.

Willey, Jackie Vernon. "Writing and Rebellion in Placido's Poetry." Master's thesis, Vanderbilt University, 2010.

INDEX

Page numbers in **bold** indicate song lyrics.

abolitionist movements: described, 35; divisions in, 17–21; 1850s, 22; in exile, 14; Garrisonians, 15–17; impact of, 46; literature, 34–35; militancy, 21–22; modern, 74; northern, 14, 75; second wave, 15; women in, 16

abolitionist songs: as communication tool, 17–18; contemporary relevance of, 74–77; *vs.* slave songs, 8, 47; sources and documentation, 68–69; themes and characteristics of, 17–18, 21. *See also* slave songs; *and individual songs*

"Ada" (Sarah Forten), 16, 59

African American History and Radical Historiography (Shapiro), 50

African American music, 31, 48, 49, 53

African Americans, 6–7, 46, 194nn6–8. *See also* free Black people

African cultures, 5–6

"African Hymn, The" (Bassett), 45, 59–60, **92**

African Methodist Episcopal Church (AME), 11–12, 45

African Pilgrim's Hymns, The (Cooper), 45, 58–59

Africans in Colonial Louisiana (Hall), 43, 67

age of revolution in Haiti, 8, 35, 45

"Agonizing, Cruel Slavery Days," 31–32, 52, 66, **106–7**

Akuno, Kali, 72

Allen, Richard, *A Collection of Spiritual Songs and Hymns Selected from Various Authors*, 45

Allen, William Francis, *Slave Songs of the United States*, 29–30, 48–49, 62–63, 191n32

Amazing Grace (Basker), 34, 44

"Amazing Grace," 36, 52, 76

"America (My Country, 'Tis of Thee)," 22, 36, 70, 118

American Anti-Slavery Society (AASS), 16

American Anti-Slavery Songs (Eaklor), 54, 68, 71

American Civil War, 46, 63, 194n8

American Colonization Society (ACS), 12

American folk music, 3, 39

American Folksongs of Protest (Greenway), 32, 51–52, 61, 63, 65–66

American Labor Songs of the Nineteenth Century (Foner), 61

American Slave, The (Rawick), 51–52, 64–66

Ames, Russell, *Story of American Folksong*, 61, 93

"Am I Not a Man and a Brother?," 18

Amistad mutiny, 20, 26

Anderson, Osborne Perry, 24

Anti-Slavery Harp, The (Brown), 18, 68, 69–71

Anti-Slavery Melodies (Lincoln), 68

antislavery movements. *See* abolitionist movements

Appeal in Favor of That Class of Americans Called Africans, An (Child), 68

Appeal to the Colored Citizens of the World (Walker), 13–14

INDEX

Aptheker, Herbert, *Negro Slave Revolts in the United States, 1526–1860*, 4, 25–27, 40, 50–51, 56, 188n2
"Arise! Arise! shake off your chains!," 26–27, 57–58, **88–89**
Armstrong, Samuel Chapman, 63
Army Life in a Black Regiment (Higginson), 29–30, 46, 62, 94

"Ballot, The," 19
band leaders, 31–32, 59
"Band of Thieves, The" (Simpson), 70, **121**
banjos, 5, 53
Banneker, Benjamin, 25, 55
Baptists, 45
Baraka, Amiri (LeRoi Jones), 53
Basker, James, *Amazing Grace*, 34, 44
Bassett, Shadrack, "The African Hymn," 45, 59–60, **92**
Bechet, Sidney, *Treat It Gentle*, 3, 8
Bibb, Henry, 22
Bible, 6–7, 42
Birney, James, 19
Birth of a Nation (film), 41
Black Convention Movement, 14, 15
blackface minstrelsy, 36–37, 47, 49, 68–69, 195n1 (chap. 3)
Black Reconstruction (Du Bois), 48
Black Song (Lovell), 33, 47, 58–59, 61, 62
Bolerium Books, 25
Boston Female Anti-Slavery Society, 71
Bowery, Charity, 59–60
Bowler, Jack, 155
Boyer, Jean-Pierre, 31, 91
"Bride's Farewell," 18
Britain, 19, 21, 43–45
Brown, John, 7, 22, 23–24, 55
Brown, William Wells: *The Anti-Slavery Harp*, 18, 68, 69–71; "Colonization Song: To the Free Colored People" (attr.), 13; "Fling Out the Anti-Slavery Flag," 18
"Bury Me in a Free Land" (Harper), 55

Cabin and Plantation Songs as Sung by the Hampton Students (Fenner), 48, 63, 98

Cable, George Washington, 33, 66–67
Callahan, Mat, 4–5, 8, 24
Canada, 14, 19, 21, 26
Cary, Mary Ann Shadd, 16
Cato's Rebellion (1739), 44
Chapin, Amzi, "The Indian Philosopher," 68, 71, 125
Chapman, Maria Wright: *The Liberty Bell*, 60; *Songs of the Free and Hymns of Christian Freedom*, 68
Charleston, South Carolina, 6, 12, 57–58
Child, Lydia Maria: abolitionist, 16; *An Appeal in Favor of That Class of Americans Called Africans*, 68; "Charity Bowery" interview, 59–60; *The Freedmen's Book*, 40, 54–55, 57
"Children, We All Shall Be Free," 46, 62, **97**
Christianity, 6–7, 42. See also churches
Christy's Minstrels, 37, 38, 56, 195n1 (chap. 3)
churches, 11–12, 29, 45, 59, 76
Cincinnati, Ohio, 14
civil rights movement, 46
Civil War, 46, 63, 194n8
Clark, George W., *The Liberty Minstrel*, 17–18, 19, 68–69
Cockburn, George, 40, 57–58
Collection of Spiritual Songs and Hymns Selected from Various Authors, A (Allen), 45
colonization, 12–13
"Colonization Song: To the Free Colored People" (Brown, attr.), 13
"Come Join the Abolitionists," 69, **123–24**
comic Negro songs. See blackface minstrelsy
Concepción Valdés, Gabriel de la (Placido), 194n1
Constitution, US, 16, 19, 23–24
Cooper, Thomas: *The African Pilgrim's Hymns*, 45, 58–59; "The Negro's Complaint," 33–34, 45, 58–59, **90**; "Old Hundred," 33–34, 45, 58, 90
Cooperation Jackson, 74, 76
Copeland, John, Jr., 24
Cox, Elijah, 52, 66

Crandall, Prudence, 16
Creole language, 43
Creole mutiny, 20, 26
Cunard, Nancy, 61–62
Curaçao, 43, 67, 84

"Dandy Jim from Caroline," 18, 69, 70, 111
"Darling Nelly Gray," 36
David Ruggles Center, 68, 71, 125
"Declaration of Liberty by the Representatives of the Slave Population, A" (Brown), 23
"Deep River," 27, 52
de Jong, Nanette, *Tambu*, 67
de Lerma, Dominique-René, 91
Din, Gilbert C., 10
Diouf, Sylviane A., 10
"Dirge of St. Malo, The," 9–10, 33, 43, 66–67, **82–83**
Douglass, Frederick: and the AASS, 16; abolitionist, 22; on blackface minstrelsy, 37, 69; hero, 25; on the Hutchinsons, 36–37; and John Brown, 23–24; *Narrative of the Life of Frederick Douglass, an American Slave*, 3, 47; writer, 53, 55
Douglass, Sarah Mapps, 16
Dred Scott decision (1857), 22–23
drums/drumming, 5, 43
Du Bois, W. E. B., 25, 33, 48, 72
Dunmore's Proclamation (1775), 45

Eaklor, Vicki Lynn, *American Anti-Slavery Songs*, 54, 68, 71
Eastern Shore (Maryland), 59
emancipation: champions of, 33; compensation proposals for, 15; Emancipation Proclamation, 43; self-emancipation, 63; support for, 47; theme in songs, 7–8, 45, 69
Emancipation Car, The (Simpson), 21–22, 35, 68, 70–71
Emerson, Irene and John, 22–23
Emmet, Dan, 38
"Enlisted Soldiers, The," 63, **98–99**
Epstein, Dena J.: on blackface minstrelsy, 47; *Sinful Tunes and Spirituals*, 52–54, 63; "Slave Music in the United States before 1860: A Survey of Sources," 53, 59–60
Equiano, Olaudah, 34
Eriksen, Tim, 38, 54, 68
"Essay on Slavery" (Hammon), 28–29
Ethiopian Glee Book, The, 56, 195n1 (chap. 3)
Ethiopian melodies. *See* blackface minstrelsy
"Eyes on the Prize (Hand on the Plow)," 30
Ezell, Lorenzo, 64, 101, 103–4

Federal Writers Project, 30–32, 51, 195n14
Fenner, Thomas P., *Cabin and Plantation Songs as Sung by the Hampton Students*, 48, 63, 98
fiddles, 5, 53
Fires of Jubilee, The (Oates), 59
Fisk Jubilee Singers, 49
"Flight of the Bondman" (Smith), 70, **112**
"Fling Out the Anti-Slavery Flag" (Brown), 18
Folk Song of the American Negro (Work), 48, 61, 62
"Follow the Drinkin' Gourd," 30
Foner, Eric, 29, 34, 50
Foner, Philip, *American Labor Songs of the Nineteenth Century*, 61
Forsyth, John, 40, 57
Forten, Charlotte L., 55
Forten, Sarah "Ada," 16, 59
Foster, Stephen, 38
France, 9, 21, 44
free Black people, 11–13, 14, 15, 16–17, 21, 46
Freedmen's Book, The (Child), 40, 54–55, 57
freedom songs, 3, 4, 5–6, 8
Free Soil Party, 19–20
Free State of Jones (film), 77
Fugitive Slave Law (1850), 20–21

Gabriel. *See* Prosser, Gabriel
"Gainin' Ground." *See* "Nat Turner"
Garabedian, Steven, 38–40, 56–57, 61
Garnet, Henry Highland, 20, 24

Garrison, Lucy McKim, *Slave Songs of the United States*, 29–30, 48–49, 62–63, 191n32
Garrison, William Lloyd, 15–17, 19, 68
Garrisonians, 15–17
Garrison Juvenile Choir, 17
Gateway to Freedom: The Hidden History of the Underground Railroad (Foner), 29
Gay, Sydney Howard, 29
Geggus, David, *The Haitian Revolution*, 43
Gellert, Lawrence, 32, 38–39, 50, 56, 61
General Colored Association (GCA), 14
General Strike/the great strike, 7, 72
Genius of Universal Emancipation, The (newspaper), 68
"Go Down, Moses," 7, 8, 27, 52
Gone with the Wind (novel), 41
Graham, Addie, 71, 128
"Grave of the Slave, The" (Johnson), 59
Great Britain, 19, 21, 43–45
Green, Shields, 24
Greenway, John, *American Folksongs of Protest*, 32, 51–52, 61, 63, 65–66
Gregoire, Henri, 44
Grimké, Angelina and Frances, 16

"Hail Columbia," 40–41, 57–58
Haiti, 31–32, 91
Haitian Revolution, 8–9, 11, 12, 32, 45, 194n1
Haitian Revolution, The (Geggus), 43
Hall, Gwendolyn Midlo, *Africans in Colonial Louisiana*, 43, 67
Hammer and Hoe (Kelley), 50
Hammon, Jupiter, "Essay on Slavery," 28–29
Handy, James A., *Scraps of African Methodist Episcopal History*, 59
Harding, Vincent, *There Is a River*, 56–57
Harper, Frances E. W., "Bury Me in a Free Land," 55
Harpers Ferry raid (1859), 23
Harvey, Todd, 30
Hearn, Lafcadio, 66
Higginson, Thomas Wentworth: abolitionist, 7, 22; *Army Life in a Black Regiment*, 29–30, 46, 62, 94

historical revisionism, 25–26, 35, 41, 73–74
Horton, George, *The Hope of Liberty*, 55
Hutchinson, Jesse, Jr., 17
Hutchinson Family Singers, 36–37, 70
"Hymn of Freedom," 4, 41, 56–58, 72, **88–89**
"Hymn of Freedom—South Carolina, 1813, A" (Moore), 57
hymns, 34, 40, 42, 45, 57–58, 60

Incompleat Folksinger, The (Seeger), 61
"Indian Philosopher, The" (Chapin), 68, 71, 125
instruments, 5–6, 31, 53
"I Want to Go Home," 7

Jackson, George Pullen, 47
"Jacob's Ladder," 30
Jazz Singer, The (film), 37
Jefferson, Thomas, 9
"Jefferson's Daughter," 18
Jew's harp, 5
"John Brown's Body," 23–24
Johnson, Francis: "The Grave of the Slave," 59; musician, 49; "Recognition March of the Independance [sic] of Hayti," 31, 47, 59, 91
Johnson, Guy B., 47
Johnson, James Weldon, 30, 33, 53
Jones, LeRoi (Amiri Baraka), 53
"Jump Jim Crow," 37

Kansas-Nebraska Act (1854), 22
Katz, Bernard, *The Social Implications of Early Negro Music in the United States*, 32–33, 66
Kelley, Robin D. G., *Hammer and Hoe*, 3, 50
Kent bugle, 31
"Kingdom Coming" (Work), 8, 63–65, **105**
"Kinloch of Kinloch," 69
Kirkpatrick, F. D., 61
Knowles, Merton, 51–52, 63, 66
Krehbiel, Henry, 30, 66

Labor Songs of the Nineteenth Century (Foner), 61

languages, 3–4, 43–45
Leary, Lewis Sheridan, 24
"Lenox," 71
Liberator, The (newspaper), 16, 17, 54, 59, 68
"Liberty," 71, **126**
"Liberty Battle Song," 19
Liberty Bell, The (Chapman), 60
Liberty Minstrel, The (Clark), 17–18, 19, 68–69
Liberty Party, 19
"Liberty Voters Song, The," 19
Library of Congress, 28, 30–32, 35, 51, 52
Lincoln, Abraham, 55, 65
Lincoln, Jairus, *Anti-Slavery Melodies*, 68
Lind, Jenny, 38
literacy, 14, 42–43, 45
Locke, Alain, 33
Loguen, Jermaine W., 22
Lossing, Benson John, *Pictorial Field-Book of the War of 1812*, 4, 40, 58
L'Ouverture, Toussaint, 55
Lovell, John, Jr.: *Black Song*, 33, 47, 58–59, 61, 62; "The Social Implications of the Negro Spiritual," 33; writer, 53
Lowell, James Russell, 17
Lundy, Benjamin, 68

"Marching through Georgia" (Work), 64
"March On," 47, 61–62, **95–96**
maroons, 9, 10, 33, 67
Marryat, Frederick, *Poor Jack*, 56
"Marseillaise, The," 22, 36, 54, 70, 119
Marsh, J. B. T., *The Story of the Jubilee Singers with Their Songs*, 48, 61
"Mary, Don't You Weep," 30
Maryland, 59
"Massa's in the Cold, Cold Ground," 70
Methodists, 11, 44–45
Miller, Jeremiah, 59
minstrel songs. *See* blackface minstrelsy
Mississippi, 14, 77
Missouri Compromise (1820), 20, 23
Monroe, James, 11
Moore, John Hammond, 40, 57
Mott, Lucretia, 16

Music and Some Highly Musical People (Trotter), 49
music industry, 37, 49
"My Father, How Long?," 7, 29–30

"Nancy Till," 70
Narrative of the Life of Frederick Douglass, an American Slave (Douglass), 3, 47
"Nat Turner," 15, 32, 38–39, 61, 72, **93**
Nat Turner's Rebellion (Southampton Insurrection, 1831), 14–15, 42, 60, 72
"Negro Battle Hymn, The," 7–8, 63, **98–99**
Negro Folk Rhymes, Wise and Otherwise (Talley), 64–65, 193n17
"Negro Hymn of Freedom." *See* "Hymn of Freedom"
Negro Slave Revolts in the United States, 1526–1860 (Aptheker), 4, 25–27, 40, 50–51, 56, 188n2
Negro Songs of Protest (Gellert), 38–39
Negro spirituals, 17, 29, 33, 49
"Negro's Complaint, The" (Cooper), 33–34, 45, 58–59, **90**
Newby, Dangerfield, 24
New York Vigilance Committee, 21
"No Master, Never" (Simpson), 21
"No More Auction Block for Me," 7

Oates, Stephen B., *The Fires of Jubilee*, 59
"Ode to James Birney," 19
"Oh Liberty, I Wait for Thee" (Placido), 194n1
"Old Hundred" (Cooper), 33–34, 45, 58, 90
"Old Massa, He Come Dancin' Out," 8, 32, 51, 65–66, **100**
Old Testament, 6–7
oral tradition, 29
Original Anti-Slavery Songs (Simpson), 21, 35–36, 69
"Ortonville," 71
"Ouarra St. Malo" (poem), 9

Papiamentu language, 43, 67, 84
Parker, William, 22
Paul, Susan, 16

Pictorial Field-Book of the War of 1812 (Lossing), 4, 40, 58
Placido, "Oh Liberty, I Wait for Thee," 194n1
Planter (ship), 55
poetry, 9, 17, 28–29, 34, 55, 194n1
Pointe Coupée conspiracy, 9–10
Poor Jack (Marryat), 56
"Pop Goes the Weasel," 21
Potts, Howard, 52
Prosser, Gabriel, 10–11, 32
"Provisional Constitution and Ordinance for the People of the United States" (Brown), 23–24

Quakers, 18, 44–45

racial stereotypes, 4, 47
Rawick, George, *The American Slave*, 51–52, 64–66
"Rebeldia na Bandabou" ("Rebellion at Bandabou"), 43, 67, **84–85**
rebellions, 8–10, 14–15, 20, 23, 25–26, 44
"Recognition March of the Independence [*sic*] of Hayti" (Johnson), 31, 47, 59, 91
Reconstruction, 39, 41, 46, 48, 73
"Reds, Whites, and the Blues" (Garabedian), 38–39
religion, 6–7
Republicanism, 9
revolutionary songs, 21, 27, 33, 36, 72, 93
"Right On," 18, 71, **113**
Robeson, Paul, 25
"Roll, Jordan, Roll," 4, 30, 52
Royal African Company, 44
Ruggles, David, "Woman's Rights," 68, 71, **125**
"Run, Nigger, Run," 6, 52

Sacred Harp, The, 38, 54, 68, 71
San Malo, Juan. *See* St. Malo, Juan
"Scots Wha Hae," 36, 54, 70
Scott, Dred and Harriet, 22–23
Scraps of African Methodist Episcopal History (Handy), 59
second wave abolitionist movement, 15

secular songs, 5–6
Seeger, Pete, 39, 61
shape-notes, 38, 54, 68
Shapiro, Herbert, *African American History and Radical Historiography*, 50
"Silver Moon," 70
Simpson, Joshua McCarter: "The Band of Thieves," 70, **121**; *The Emancipation Car*, 21–22, 35, 68, 70–71; "No Master, Never," 21; *Original Anti-Slavery Songs*, 21, 35–36, 69; "Song of the 'Aliened American,'" 22, 70, **118**; "To the White People of America," 70, **116–17**; "The True Spirit," 71, **122**; "The Underground Railroad," 70, **114–15**; "The Voice of Six Hundred Thousand Nominally Free," 70, **119–20**
Sinful Tunes and Spirituals (Epstein), 52–54, 63
Sinha, Manisha: on abolition, 5, 37; on slave songs vs. abolitionist songs, 8; *The Slave's Cause*, 34–35, 49–50
slaveholders, 15–16, 20
"Slave Music in the United States before 1860: A Survey of Sources" (Epstein), 53, 59–60
Slave Narrative Collection, 51
slave rebellions, 8–10, 14–15, 20, 23, 25–26, 44
slavery: beginning of, 25; British slave trade, 44; federal government's role in, 22–23; memory of, 73–74; musical legacy of, 3; myths, 32, 35, 72, 76–77; protection of, 42
Slavery Abolition Act (1833), 43
Slave's Cause, The (Sinha), 34–35, 49–50
slave songs: vs. abolitionist songs, 8, 47; coded messages in, 6, 46–47; contemporary relevance of, 72–74; sources and documentation, 56; themes and characteristics of, 33, 43, 46. *See also* abolitionist songs; *and individual songs*
Slave Songs of the United States (Allen, Ware, and Garrison), 29–30, 48–49, 62–63, 191n32

INDEX

Smalls, Robert, 55
Smith, Elias, "Flight of the Bondman," 70, **112**
Smith, James McCune, 22
Social Implications of Early Negro Music in the United States, The (Katz), 32–33, 66
"Social Implications of the Negro Spiritual, The" (Lovell), 33
Society for Effecting the Abolition of the Slave Trade, 18
Society of Friends, 18, 44–45
song discovery and authentication: abolitionist songbooks, 35–38; antislavery literature, 34–35; conclusions from, 40–41; a controversial source, 38–39; evidence of existence, 31–32; first discovery, 25–27; historical records, 27–31; predecessors in research, 32–34; sources of significance, 48–51
"Song for Freedom, A," 18–19, 69, 70, **111**
"Song of the 'Aliened American'" (Simpson), 22, 70, **118**
"Song of the Coffle Gang," 18
songs: Christian themes in, 6–7, 42; freedom songs, 3, 4, 5–6, 8; historical context of, 42–43; hymns, 34, 40, 42, 45, 57–58, 60; influences on, 47, 48, 53; instruments for, 5–6, 31, 53; languages of, 3–4, 43–45; power of, 5, 73; relevance, 72–77; revolutionary, 21, 27, 33, 36, 72, 93; roots, 5–8; secular, 5–6; sorrow songs, 33; spirituals, 17, 29, 33, 49; suppression of, 31, 35–36, 43, 46, 73. *See also* abolitionist songs; slave songs; song discovery and authentication; *and individual songs*
Songs of the Free and Hymns of Christian Freedom (Chapman), 68
Southampton Insurrection (Nat Turner's Rebellion, 1831), 14–15, 42, 60, 72
Southern, Eileen, *African-American Tradition in Song, Sermon, Tale, and Dance, 1600s–1920*, 28, 45–46, 49
Spain/Spanish, 9, 25, 44
Stanton, Elizabeth Cady, 16

"Steal Away," 4, 30
Stewart, Maria, 16
St. Malo, Juan, 9–10, 33, 67
"Stole and Sold from Africa," 71, **128**
Stono Rebellion (1739), 44
Story of American Folksong (Ames), 61, 93
Story of the Jubilee Singers with Their Songs, The (Marsh), 48, 61
"Strike for Liberty," 19

Talley, Thomas, *Negro Folk Rhymes, Wise and Otherwise*, 64–65, 193n17
Tambu (de Jong), 67
Taney, Roger Brooke, 23
Tappan, Arthur, 16
Telemaque. *See* Vesey, Denmark
There Is a River (Harding), 56–57
"This World Almost Done," 7
Thomas, Henry Goddard, 63
thumb piano, 5
"To the White People of America" (Simpson), 70, **116–17**
Treat It Gentle (Bechet), 3, 8
Trotter, James M., *Music and Some Highly Musical People*, 49
Trouble with Music, The (Callahan), 4
"True Spirit, The" (Simpson), 71, **122**
Truth, Sojourner, 16, 22
Tubman, Harriet, 22, 25
Turner, Nat, 14–15. *See also* Nat Turner's Rebellion

Uncle Cox. *See* Cox, Elijah
"Uncle Gabriel, the Negro General," 32, 38, 56, **86–87**
Underground Railroad, 21, 24, 29, 75
"Underground Railroad, The" (Simpson), 70, **114–15**
US Constitution, 16, 19, 23–24

Vashon, George, "Vincent Ogé," 194n1
Vesey, Denmark, 6–7, 11–12
Virginia, 9, 15, 25, 26
"Voice of Six Hundred Thousand Nominally Free, The" (Simpson), 70, **119–20**

"Wade in the Water," 30
Walker, David, *Appeal to the Colored Citizens of the World*, 13–14
Ware, Charles Pickard, *Slave Songs of the United States*, 29–30, 48–49, 62–63, 191n32
War of 1812, 41, 56, 88
Wedgwood, Josiah, 18
"We'll Soon Be Free/My Father, How Long?," 7, 30, 62–63, **94**
"We're Coming! We're Coming!," 18, 69, **110**
"What Mean Ye?," 71, **127**
Wheatley, Phillis, 55
"When I Can Read My Title Clear," 69
Where Have All the Flowers Gone (Seeger), 61
"Where Is Thy Brother?," **127**
White, Newman I., 47

Whittier, John Greenleaf, 17, 55
"Woman's Rights" (Ruggles), 68, 71, **125**
women abolitionists, 16
Work, Henry Clay: "Kingdom Coming," 8, 63–65, **105**; "Marching through Georgia," 64
Work, John Wesley, Jr., *Folk Song of the American Negro*, 48, 61, 62
Wright, Josephine, *African-American Tradition in Song, Sermon, Tale, and Dance, 1600s–1920*, 28, 45–46, 49

xylophones, 5

"Year of Jubalo, The"/"Year of Jubilo," 8, 32, 51–52, 101, **102–4**
Young, Israel, 61

ABOUT THE AUTHOR

Mat Callahan is a musician and author originally from San Francisco. He is author of five books including *The Explosion of Deferred Dreams: Musical Renaissance and Social Revolution in San Francisco, 1965–1975* and *A Critical Guide to Intellectual Property*. His recent projects include the republication of *Songs of Freedom* by Irish revolutionary James Connolly; the recording and publication of *Working-Class Heroes*, and the launch of the multimedia project Songs of Slavery and Emancipation, which includes this book, a CD of song recordings, and a film. For more information, visit http://www.matcallahan.com.

CPSIA information can be obtained
at www.ICGtesting.com
Printed in the USA
BVHW030827240422
635043BV00001B/3